TO CHANGE THE WORLD

TO CHANGE THE WORLD

My Years in Cuba

Margaret Randall

RUTGERS UNIVERSITY PRESS

NEW BRUNSWICK, NEW JERSEY, AND LONDON

Library of Congress Cataloging-in-Publication Data

Randall, Margaret, 1936–
To change the world : my years in Cuba / Margaret Randall.
      p.   cm.
Includes bibliographical references and index.
ISBN 978–0–8135–4431–1 (hardcover : alk. paper)
ISBN 978–0–8135–4432–8 (pbk. : alk. paper)
1. Cuba—Description and travel. 2. Cuba—History—1959–1990. 3. Randall, Margaret,
   1936—Travel—Cuba. I. Title.
F1765.2.F36 2009
917.29104′64092—dc22

                                                2008014123

A British Cataloging-in-Publication record for this book is available from the British
   Library.

Visit our Web site: http://rutgerspress.rutgers.edu

Manufactured in the United States of America
Book design and composition: Jack Donner, BookType

For Haydeé Santamaría,
who took the secrets with her

Roger Clément

CONTENTS

ACKNOWLEDGMENTS

This book began when my son, Gregory, suggested we write about our time in Cuba. Our original intention was to produce a single text in two voices. Because we live thousands of miles apart—he in Montevideo, Uruguay; I in Albuquerque, New Mexico—we each began writing on our own. A year and a half later we had two full-blown manuscripts, his in Spanish, mine in English. We tried to braid them, but reluctantly came to see each as its own entity. *To Change the World* owes a great deal to this joint project, our ongoing discussions, and the emotion and references we share.

Many friends have read parts or all of a number of drafts, and have challenged me on different points or made important contributions that have enriched the final text. Some have contributed photos from their personal archives. Subjective analysis is, of course, my own. I want especially to thank Mark Behr, Kate Hedeen, Jules Lobel, Sarah Mondragón, Jane Norling, Kathleen O'Malley, Gregory Randall, John Randall, Mirta Rodríguez Calderón, Mark Rudd, Susan Sherman, Janet Spector and—always and foremost—my life companion Barbara Byers. I am also very grateful to Cuban photographer Gilda Pérez for her stunning cover image. Unless otherwise indicated, all large format photographs are by the author. Snapshots and press photos are sometimes by the author or from the author's family archives, and sometimes by local photojournalists; photographers' names noted when known.

This is not the first time I have worked with Leslie Mitchner at Rutgers University Press. I brought the book to her because I so deeply respect her editorial skill. I also want to thank all the other good people at Rutgers who helped to make this book what it is.

TO CHANGE THE WORLD

PROLOGUE

SOME REFLECTIONS BEFORE I BEGIN

Fidel Castro came to New York City in the summer of 1960, fresh from his guerrilla triumph. I was a young writer and soon-to-be single mother, enormously pregnant with Gregory—my son who, forty-six years later, would suggest we write about Cuba together—but I longed to see the hero up close, applaud his stance, express my personal appreciation. Carefully, lovingly, I prepared a platter of Spanish paella; not such a tropical staple perhaps, but my signature dish at the time.

I bought choice drumsticks and wings at Mrs. Schiffer's Second Avenue butcher shop, picked over giant langoustine shrimp in the market three blocks uptown, and must have found the peas, black olives, bell peppers and imported saffron in that market as well. I told the food merchants I was cooking for Fidel and all showed their enthusiasm in one way or another. One threw in an extra half pound of sausage, another handed me one gorgeous sweet red pepper. I sang as I cooked. The pungent mix of scents invaded the grim stairwell and shabby hallways of my Lower East Side walk-up. When the paella's colors shone robust and each ingredient had reached its moment of perfection, I covered my platter with aluminum foil and carried it onto an uptown subway train.

Fidel and his retinue had left the Waldorf Astoria unexpectedly. Some said the hotel administration accused them of keeping live chickens in their rooms. Others insisted it had been the Cubans' decision to leave. Whatever the case, halfway through the visit, Fidel and his party moved up to Harlem's more friendly and welcoming Hotel Theresa. Above ground, at 125th Street, I was immediately met by a cordon of New York's Finest; no amount of pleading convinced the police officers to let me through. Nor were they willing to take my aromatic gift and see that it got to its intended recipient.

My body still remembers its disappointment as I headed back downtown with the platter untouched, its metallic covering soiled and torn, its contents beginning to sour.

Many of those who lived the story of that time and place are dying now. Even in Cuba itself, new generations replace those first men and women who dreamed the dream, took the risks, threw out a dictator and began to create a different society, one rooted in justice and equality. Yes, there was a time, in the 1960s and 1970s, when some in my generation believed we could change the world. Many movements waged struggles of varying intensity, achieved degrees of success or longevity. Utopias seemed possible. And the Cuban revolution was the palpable example of a small country leading the way in demonstrating that more equitable relations of production—more equitable human relations—were not simply a worthy goal. With determination and sacrifice, the dream was possible.

Where is Cuba on our map, today, here in the United States in this first decade of the twenty-first century? Public interest quickens as Fidel Castro nears the end of his life, and the revolution's enemies, as well as its friends, wonder what the near future will bring. Still, with attention focused elsewhere (and because we are fickle when it comes to sustained interest in the lives of others), few U.S. Americans think or care about the small island nation ninety miles away. In the United Sates, the Cuban revolution has been vilified, lied about, attacked and isolated by a succession of administrations, and in our mainstream media from shortly after its 1959 victory. Billions have been spent trying to destroy it. Yet it remains, if not as we once knew it, still independent and vibrant.

A small progressive community continues to support the revolution, protests the embargo, and attempts to counter the disinformation. A sizeable Cuban exile bloc, although more diverse in recent years, remains a constituency wooed by Republicans and Democrats alike. "Freedom for Cuba" is always a rallying cry capable of getting votes. Cuban exiles still mostly hope for their country's return to "democracy"—whatever their idea of democracy may be. Meanwhile, almost half a century of embargo and misinformation has kept most of us ignorant about our neighbor to the south.

The George W. Bush administration has greatly intensified this information vacuum. It has done this through bullying rhetoric and by making contact with, and travel to, Cuba much more difficult for U.S. citizens. The growing distance between what we are told about the country and what it is really like, and between how the United States defines its own system and our diminishing quality of life, also conspire to keep us confused and to broaden the knowledge gap. It is nothing short of obscene that we continue to call Cuba a dictatorship when our current president "won" his first term through a judicial coup and stole his second through vote mismanagement and manipulation.

For almost fifty years now, Cuba has suffered continuous attack from the United States and from U.S.-backed terrorist groups. These attacks have ranged from outright invasion and coastal incursions to misinformation, germ warfare, attempts on Fidel's life, and ongoing embargo. To defend itself, the revolution has often taken measures strongly criticized by a succession of U.S. administrations (and also by some of us who love the revolution), such as clamping down on protest, imprisoning dissidents, restricting travel, and controlling internet and other communication with the outside world.

Disturbing as these measures are, they pale when compared with those enacted by the U.S. government in the wake of its own suddenly perceived vulnerability. Following the brutal September 11th, 2001 attack on New York and Washington, the Bush administration's response has been to invade and occupy two sovereign nations, lash out at Muslims everywhere, imprison without trial, torture detainees, and impose a series of domestic measures that have seriously eroded the rights of its own citizens. Under the guise of national security, new abuses come to light almost daily. With his policy of the preemptive strike, President Bush has created a dangerous culture of violence at home and abroad. Ironically, the site of some of the United States's most horrendous human rights violations is its prison camp at Guantánamo Bay, a piece of Cuban territory it controls.

The U.S. government lodges periodic protests against Cuba for the revolution's imprisonment of political dissidents. At the same time, since the 9/11 tragedy the administration has denied established legal process to thousands of its own prisoners, held them for years without trial, and subjected at least some to extraordinary rendition—the illegal practice of sending them to countries where torture is routine. That we also torture here at home is ever more obvious. Much has been made of "Big Brother" in the socialist system, while our own Patriot Act authorizes illegal wiretapping and other surveillance of U.S. citizens, represses political discussion in public schools, and demands that public libraries report on books borrowed.

It is beyond the scope of this book to look at every one of the criticisms leveled at Cuba over the years. Rather, I have written a personal memoir that includes some history and analysis. To set the scene, let's look at quality of life in the United States and Cuba. One way to do this is by comparing statistics. It is easy to get lost in an "apples and oranges" deluge of numbers, or manipulate findings to favor one or another system. I have tried to avoid this by using only United Nations data for the most recent year available,[1] and also by looking at percentages or per capita figures rather than overall numbers. By every criterion one of the wealthiest countries in the world and the besieged Caribbean island draw on vastly contrasting resources but they also have very different priorities.

Medical attention in Cuba, from dentures to open heart surgery, is free to everyone. There are six doctors per thousand inhabitants. Through a comprehensive, family-centered system, Cuban health care providers live in the neighborhoods and rural communities they serve. They get to know their prospective patients in wellness. Emphasis is on prevention. A struggling economy has produced a number of new medications (several of which are being imported into the United States as an exception to our no-trade regulations).

Although only $229.80 per person is spent on health care in Cuba each year, every cent goes to the beneficiary. The country has forty nine hospital beds for every ten thousand inhabitants. Every single Cuban can expect to be visited by a doctor at least once a year in his or her home. U.S. politicians of both major political parties correctly refer to Cuba's medical system as socialized medicine; although on their lips this is a derisive term.

In the United States, some health care is handled through government programs but most people depend on private plans, if they can afford them. These are run by health management organizations and insurance companies. Seventy-five million Americans have no health coverage at all. There are only three doctors per thousand inhabitants, or just about half what there are in Cuba. There are far fewer hospital beds (thirty-three for every ten thousand people), and those without insurance are often denied access to adequate care. The United States spends on average $6,096.20 per person per year on health, but most of this money goes to the insurance and pharmaceutical companies.

A similar picture emerges in education. Cuba spends approximately ten percent of its gross national product (GNP), or under three billion dollars ($246 per capita) annually, educating its population. Through its 1961 year-long literacy campaign and numerous follow up programs, the country has achieved close to total literacy and one of the best educated populations in Latin America. All schools and universities are free, and there is an average one-to-twenty teacher-to-student ratio. One hundred and twelve thousand Cubans are currently enrolled in the tiny country's forty-seven institutions of higher learning.

Among the industrialized nations, the United States is unique in its inability (unwillingness?) to provide good public education. In 2006–2007 the Bush administration cut the federal education budget by $4,379 billion dollars. Increasingly, emphasis is on test-taking, with in depth discussion and analysis discouraged. It would seem we don't want our students to learn to think. With a population of around 300 million, the federal government spends roughly $8,997 per pupil in grades K through 12, and state and local governments augment that expenditure. Yet education continues to get worse. The year 2006 saw a federal education funding decrease of one percent from 2005, with a $56 million reduction for poor students and those with disabilities.

Other areas also offer interesting comparisons. While the United States has moved toward a Christian-faith-based government, with the values of a single religious tradition increasingly affecting both domestic and foreign policy, in Cuba real separation of church and state exists. In the United States, federal funding for scientific exploration may depend upon the scientists's religious convictions, women's reproductive health is severely threatened, and a fundamentalist Christian approach to human relations keeps gay citizens from marrying or enjoying the other rights of straight Americans.

Although the Cuban revolution, too, has struggled with these issues, it is moving resolutely in the opposite, more humanistic, direction. Science is well funded, abortion and other aspects of women's reproductive health have been a part of the national health care system from the beginning, and Cuban law is currently contemplating equalizing all rights for its gay citizens—including same-sex partnership, and gender reassignment surgery under its comprehensive health care service.

Perhaps each country's military expenditure most clearly illustrates its opposing priorities. Although it has never attacked the United States, U.S. Americans are constantly being told that little Cuba poses a threat. Cuba, on the other hand, has suffered continuous assault from the United States, yet only about five percent of its GNP goes to defense. Fifty percent of the U.S. federal budget goes to military expenditure, while health gets roughly six percent, education (including retraining for employment and social services) ten percent, and administration of justice only four percent. The U.S. military budget is more than thirty-seven times greater than the combined spending of the seven nations it labels "rogue states": Cuba, Iran, Iraq, Libya, North Korea, Sudan and Syria.

Despite dramatically hard times, quality of life in Cuba continues to improve. In the United States, for the majority of the population quality of life declines. Now, more than ever, we should be interested in why the Cuban revolution prioritizes as it does, and how its priorities are put into practice.

I tell this story from the very personal perspective of someone who lived in Cuba. This book doesn't pretend to be a scholarly analysis of Cuban politics or economics. Rather, it is my story of eleven years on the island, working, writing, raising four children, and participating in the revolution's dramatic process of social change. I neither exaggerate the positive nor gloss over the negative. I do extrapolate from experience and venture opinions, but they are the opinions of a woman, a mother, a feminist, a poet—rather than those of an economist or social scientist. I hope what emerges is a picture of how it felt to live in Cuba from 1969 to 1980: the energy, hope, pride, generosity of spirit, difficulty, and, sometimes, distress. We believed we were changing the world.

To write in one's seventies about events that took place in one's thirties requires understanding that evoking the meaning and feel of those times trumps absolute accuracy of chronology or even names. For me, finally, it was most important to try to capture the essence. The Cuban revolution remains one of the great social experiments of the twentieth century, and having shared it for even a decade carries responsibility as well as the challenge of portraying how we were back then.

Fortunately, I was aided by having kept a detailed diary. Throughout, I have been forthright about using real or fictitious names, presenting my own memories and also those of my children and/or friends when theirs contradict mine; and noting the shifting textures between how I lived an event and how it lives on in memory. As we get older, memory may contract and expand; but I have learned that this too holds meaning. Here I have wanted to speak about the way things were as well as to reflect upon them from today's perspective.

CHAPTER 1

SCARSDALE TO HAVANA

A Politically Liberal, Somewhat Adventurous Family

My parents were New Yorkers, assimilated Jews of the upper middle class. "Upper" because my father's family had money. "Middle" because Dad sold men's clothing in department stores and later became a public school music teacher. Mother was a sculptor early on, eventually devoting her life to Spanish/English translation; José Martí became a lasting passion. She never worked outside the home. With my younger sister and brother we were five. Gradually, ours would become a politically liberal, somewhat adventurous family, in which the deep tensions woven throughout our parents' marriage produced an unacknowledged but ever-present undercurrent. The oldest, I both appreciated my parents' love and support and fled as soon as I was able.

In 1947 the family moved to New Mexico. Mother and Dad were tired of Scarsdale's constricted social propriety and their own parents' hold on their lives. They piled us into the family Studebaker and we headed west, looking for a place to live. Santa Fe appealed to them but they thought it would be easier for my father to get a job in larger Albuquerque, then a typical southwestern city of about forty thousand.

From the time I was a small child I knew I would one day be a writer. I'd produced my first single-paragraph stories almost as soon as I learned to form letters at the age of six. At nine I bought my first typewriter, with money earned on a paper route and matching funds from my parents.

I can still see myself throwing the papers from my red Mohawk bike, still smell the oily black surface of that old Royal portable. In my teens I co-edited my high school's newspaper and contributed to its literary magazine.

Some time toward the end of 1956, I was recently free of a first, sad marriage. Someone at a party started reading Allen Ginsberg's *Howl* out loud. I didn't live in an urban ghetto or do drugs beyond the occasional toke of marijuana; in New Mexico many of us grew our own. But *Howl's* message hit me in a place I was ready to explore. Sitting alone in a corner of the room, I closed my eyes and listened to the words. The poem mesmerized me, immersed me completely in its images and revelation. Immediately I bought my own copy of that small, square, black and white City Lights edition, which would suffer such a monumental attempt at censorship and go on to become a classic of my generation.

I wrote to Ginsberg care of City Lights. I'll meet you in San Francisco, I said, on such and such a date and at such and such a street corner. All I could think of was being in the presence of the man who had written "I saw the best minds of my generation destroyed by madness, starving hysterical naked." I remember the long drive west, the vain wait at the intersection of streets whose names I can no longer bring to mind. And the return to Albuquerque, foreshadowing my later retreat with that undeliverable paella.

WRITING WAS EVERYTHING TO ME

I decided to go to New York. I was going to be a writer and writers—I reasoned—lived in New York. Writing was everything to me. Everything, even when what emerged on the page wasn't yet all that significant. I was sure one day it would be. I've never completely understood where this bedrock confidence came from, but it may be traceable to my father. Despite his frequent inability to understand what I was trying to say or do, he always made me feel I would be able to say and do it in time. He's been gone for more than a decade now, but his gentle encouragement and pride shine in my experience.

Midway through the twentieth century I returned to the metropolis from the provincial Southwest, arriving with nothing but a few contacts and enormous determination. My friends were artists and writers who survived on odd jobs and spent most of their time in whatever creative pursuit.

Some were just beginning to achieve recognition; others, like me, were beginners. We inhabited Lower East Side cold-water flats and commercial lofts that all too recently had been sweatshops. The more experienced taught the newcomers how to turn back the hands on Con Edison's meters so we wouldn't have to pay so much for electricity. Before dawn we'd go down to the old Fulton fish market where discarded produce from the day before was ours for the taking.

We spent as little time earning a living and as much as possible making art. In the evenings we gathered at the Cedar Tavern on University just off Eighth Street, where a waiter named Johnny carried us from paycheck to paycheck; my nightly dinner was a breaded veal cutlet with a side of spaghetti and a vegetable, accompanied by one or two small glasses of sherry. A phone near the Cedar's entrance sometimes rang. One night the person who answered called out: Someone in Tokyo wants to speak to Franz Kline! Indeed, a Japanese painter was trying to get in touch with his American mentor.

When the weather was warm, around midnight a few of us might wander the couple of blocks to Washington Square Park, sprawl on the grass and read freshly minted poems or stories to one another. Street musicians gathered near the fountain; their drums or guitars provided a soft background to the spoken word. Sometimes one of the artists insisted we come over to see a painting in progress. Our lives transpired below Manhattan's Fourteenth Street; above that line lived the conventional, the wealthy, the uninteresting and unapproachable. Or so we thought.

In New Mexico I'd left college after one lackadaisical year. I was bored by the mid-century's conformist courses, though I knew the gaps in my education were vast and would later sometimes feel the lack of formal scholarship. In New York I cornered older writers at parties or in the street, asked for lists of books they considered important, then made my way uptown to the city's big public library. I entered its great lion-flanked doors and spent hours reading from my eclectic list. Some books I found in the room for reserved literature—titles that couldn't be checked out, like Lawrence Durrell's *Alexandria Quartet*, Henry Miller's *Tropic of Cancer* and *Tropic of Capricorn*, most of Wilhelm Reich's later work. Then I revisited those mentors who had been kind enough to humor the provincial young woman and tried to engage them in discussion. I was fearless and voracious.

I remember an evening with poet Jean Garrigue. She'd heard a poem of mine and invited me to her West Village apartment. I was interested in the work of William Carlos Williams, sent him a selection of my poetry, and was thrilled to receive a reply inviting me to visit him just across the river in Rutherford, New Jersey. Williams was elderly and ill by then; a stroke had left him partially paralyzed. I took an interstate bus and showed up at his modest home with a sprig of pussy willows. I'll never forget his kindness and respect, what it meant to hear him read and critique my incipient work.

A Cold War Mentality Characterized the National Psyche

New York in the late 1950s and early 1960s was a magnet for creativity. The Abstract Expressionist painters and a few writers had the Artists Club, where occasional wild parties spiced up a weekly menu of talks and debates. Painters Willem and Elaine de Kooning, Milton Resnick, and Pat Passlof; critics Harold Rosenberg, Tom Hess, Dore Ashton and Meyer Shapiro; musician John Cage; dancer Erick Hawkins; and theater people Judith Malina and Julian Beck were regulars. Poets—Beats from the San Francisco renaissance, others of the Black Mountain and Deep Image schools—read at the Greenwich Village cafes. Thelonious Monk never removed his hat as he pounded his jazz piano, and Ornette Coleman blew his white plastic sax at The Five Spot. The atmosphere was electric, the community welcoming, and the priorities suited me.

Leading up to this explosive era, the murder of the Rosenbergs[1] had been only the most horrifying in an ongoing series of assaults on a citizenry's freedom and sensibility: a long stifling period of repression and fear. A Cold War mentality characterized the national psyche for many dulling years; conformity was its byproduct. Union membership fell precipitously. Workers were increasingly exploited. Leftist political organizing was largely neutralized. Women were being kept in check by the broad dissemination of a pervasively insidious homemaker image.

Senator Joseph McCarthy's anticommunist witch hunt had murdered and imprisoned, invalidated passports, stolen people's reputations and livelihoods, pummeled their identities. The Red Scare pretty much succeeded in silencing dissent, pushing difference underground. As the Cold War mentality became more entrenched, language changed accordingly. Popular discourse was coopted and words reshaped, often made to signify something very different from their original definitions.

There was talk about the Red Sox changing their name because red could be considered an allusion to communism. With the Second World War, the Japanese maple became the red maple. Then, when the Soviet Union gained strength and appeared to threaten U.S. hegemony, it was suddenly the Japanese maple again. Much like today's political atmosphere when, a few years back, over-zealous patriots refused to call our most popular potatoes French fries because France refused to support President Bush's preemptive strike on Iraq.

The 1950s was a frightening time and, unlike today, it didn't have an accessible model to which we could look for hope. The rebellious thirties had faded beneath the more immediate presence of recent war. Writers and intellectuals suffered from the chill, which was just beginning to lift as the decade came to a close. The country needed a renewal of creative expression, and vanguard poets, artists, and others were at the center of the countercultural movements that rose in opposition to the previous decade's repressive atmosphere. I had come to the great intellectual and artistic center just as those movements were shifting into high gear.

In New York, although I knew some deeply political people, among the artists we were mostly nonconformists, primarily concerned with social hypocrisy, residual McCarthy era threats to freedom of expression and anything smacking of control. The Civil Rights movement was still several years in the future. Feminism wasn't even a blip on the radar; it would be a while before we noticed that the women among us were treated like groupies or had to struggle so much harder than the men to publish or show. Male homosexuality was common and, although not often alluded to publicly, accepted in the art world. Lesbians were more hidden.

The United States had dropped the first atomic bombs on Hiroshima and Nagasaki and we protested nuclear weaponry and the absurd bomb shelters the government was encouraging people to build. Ammon Hennacy, of Dorothy Day's Catholic Worker movement, became a friend; I still remember the single large peach he brought me when I was in the hospital giving birth to my son. I was interested in what the Catholic Workers were doing for the Bowery bums—as we called those seemingly ageless winos begging along lower Broadway. My friend Elaine de Kooning became interested in Caryl Chessman and began working against capital punishment.[2]

WITH GREGORY'S BIRTH WE WERE TWO

On the personal front there were other issues. In October of 1960, at Manhattan General Hospital, I gave birth to my son Gregory. A fellow poet, Joel Oppenheimer, was his father. Since the dissolution of my first marriage, I had been with many men—in Albuquerque and in New York. In New York the field was larger and the artists were free spirits. Men gravitated from woman to woman, and women mostly complied. Romantic relationships might be intense but were usually brief. Women were second-class citizens, whether with conventional small town suitors or the more casual big city men. I had no philosophical framework in which to analyze any of this and simply went with the flow. I had no desire to remarry but wanted a child.

With Gregory's birth we were two. In an era before day care centers I hunted down innovative child care solutions. My artist friends adopted my son as a sort of community mascot. In the evenings there was always someone willing to babysit, or I would carry him in a white wicker basket to gallery openings and readings. Gregory was healthy and inquisitive. I loved being a mother.

In 1959 I got my first meaningful job, at Spanish Refugee Aid (SRA). This small organization was dedicated to helping those Republican refugees from Spain's Civil War who had ended up destitute and hungry in French camps or Moroccan slums. That war had begun in the year of my birth, and my knowledge of its complexities was spotty at best. Many called it "the last just war," a term later also applied to World War II.

My first year in the city I'd worked as a waitress, addressed envelopes, modeled for artists, sat in art galleries, and worked in a Garment District feather factory. Then a man with whom we were both intimate at the time introduced me to Nancy Macdonald; an odd connection if there ever was one. Nancy and I hit it off right away, and I went to work for the Spanish refugees.

DEATH OF ONE ERA, BIRTH OF ANOTHER

The victory of the Cuban revolution was one of those events that marked the death of one era and the birth of another. A line as sharp as any in history, but with subtleties difficult to grasp at the time, at least for someone of my background and experience. I understood that certain values and attitudes would persist; they might take generations to change. But this understanding was intellectual. How the holdover customs might look, how they affected the way people lived, or accepted or resisted change: all that was harder to predict. What I knew was that the people of a small Caribbean island, just ninety miles from U.S. shores, had challenged neocolonialism. They had won freedom from a brutal dictator and his northern boss. Cause enough for celebration.

Like many in my generation—I was born in 1936—the Cuban revolution excited my sense of possibility. So geographically close. So culturally and linguistically familiar, and displaying such sudden and unexpected bravado. The radical shift so close to home immediately elicited insinuations and then outright attacks in my own country's mainstream press. But for the first year, at least, most progressive U.S. Americans applauded Cuba's new government. My immediate and passionate engagement with Cuba was more emotional than political.

At Spanish Refugee Aid, Nancy also shared my enthusiasm for the new revolution but, like many progressive people of her generation, she'd been traumatized by Soviet style communism and soon began to distance herself, fearing what she thought might be a repetition of Stalin's crimes. I was a good deal younger than Nancy. I didn't share her points of reference and remained supportive.

At the corner of Eleventh Street and Broadway, in the same building that housed SRA's one-room office, the New York chapter of the Fair Play for Cuba Committee soon opened its doors. I became friendly with some of its staff, asked questions, continued to feel an emotional attraction to the revolution that had so emphatically claimed control of its territory and was demanding its right to an independent future.

The Kennedy administration began its many-pronged efforts—some overt, others covert—to bring the new revolution to its knees. (I'd voted for Kennedy in 1960, the first time I'd been old enough to cast my ballot. It was a vote against Nixon, whose transparent megalomania and crass anticommunism frightened me. Writing today, I realize how infrequently I've been able to vote *for* a U.S. presidential candidate; in our version of the democratic process, mine has almost always been a vote *against*.)

In June 1961, six other artists and I wrote a Declaration of Conscience in support of Cuba's sovereignty. It was signed by many and published in *Monthly Review*.[3] The New York Fair Play for Cuba Committee organized its first trip to the island. I thought of going but was afraid. To hide my fear I said my son was still too young for that sort of travel and I didn't want to leave him behind.

The poet LeRoi Jones, who would later reinvent himself as Amiri Baraka, went on that initial trip. So did another friend, Marc Schleifer, who in time would rename himself Suleiman Abdullah. LeRoi and Marc were two of those who had written that declaration with me; the others were painter Elaine de Kooning, poet Diane di Prima, writer and publisher Lawrence Ferlinghetti, and novelist and all around cultural figure Norman Mailer. Marc would remain on the island for a number of years and participate in the defense of the increasingly vulnerable revolutionary project. He was in Cuba in April, 1961, when the failed Bay of Pigs invasion took place.

Mexico Seemed a Welcoming Venue

Late in the fall of that year I took my young son and went to Mexico. New York City, once the only place I thought an up-and-coming writer could live, felt spent. By this time I knew I could write anywhere and Mexico seemed a welcoming venue. That country wouldn't break diplomatic relations with Cuba, and in Mexico City the Cold War mentality that still permeated life in the United States was much less pervasive or less palpable.

I soon met young poets and artists heading to Cuba from every direction: North Americans traveling south, Latin Americans traveling north, Europeans making their way west across the Atlantic. During our eight years in Mexico many of them stayed at our home. News about Cuba was much more readily accessible and the revolution acquired a more familiar, though heroic, aura.

In the 1960s Mexico City, with a mere twelve million inhabitants, was still a good place to be. We lived in areas where a jumble of middle class homes and apartments were interspersed with fields where the rural poor, termed *paracaidistas* (parachutists), set up their tin and cardboard shacks. You could find literally anything in the vast markets, La Merced and Lagunilla. A wealth of green graced more parks and public areas than in most other cities of its size. Older neighborhoods were a maze of cobblestone streets bordered by brightly painted colonial houses and exuberant bougainvillea.

The recent explosion of Mexican and international culture personified by Frida Kahlo, Diego Rivera, B. Traven, Leon Trotsky, and Tina Modotti had come to an end, but some of the monumental muralists, like Francisco Orozco, Rufino Tamayo, and David Alfaro Siqueiros, were still alive and working. The country had welcomed Europeans escaping their continent's violence and repression: Victor Serge, Eric Fromm, Agustí Bartra. Refugees like Leonora Carrington were as exciting for their ideas as for their work. Radical writer and translator Cedric Belfrage lived in nearby Cuernavaca. Juan Rulfo was slowly finishing *Pedro Páramo*, Anita Brenner was writing *Idols Behind Altars*, Laurette Séjourné was beginning to dig at Teotihuacán, and many younger artists were taking their first creative steps.

El Corno Emplumado / The Plumed Horn was the bilingual literary journal that Mexican poet Sergio Mondragón and I co-founded and edited throughout the turbulent sixties. A group of us, Latin and North Americans, had been meeting at the home of Beat poet Philip Lamantía, and we recognized the need for a forum in which we could share our work. U.S. poet Harvey Wolin was also involved, but dropped out after the second issue. Sergio and I married and our union gave Gregory two sisters: Sarah in 1963 and Ximena in 1964. The passion with which I'd always approached each new project could be felt in the intertwining of our literary and personal worlds.

A couple of years into the journal's life, Sergio and I began receiving manuscripts from Cuban poets, drawings from Cuban artists, and correspondence about their experiences and concerns. In 1967 we devoted most of an issue to Cuban writing, art work, and letters. Our contributors included figures of such international literary stature as Nicolás Guillén; established writers like Eliseo Diego and José Lezama Lima, and also younger artists such as Roberto Fernández Retamar, Fayad Jamís, Pablo Armando Fernández, Heberto Padilla and Belkis Cuza Malé—those belonging to the generation for which the earth beneath their feet had shifted radically.

For this younger generation, the lives they'd anticipated were changing moment to moment. A few, who were religious, flamboyant in dress or attitude, sexually "different," or otherwise outsiders, would feel their lives becoming unbearably limited. The majority would find new meaning for theirs, and this could be seen in their work as well as in their expectations. Language sought previously unknown expression. What words could convey the totality of such upheaval?

When *El Corno* twenty-three appeared we immediately received a telephone call from Rafael Squirru, the Argentine poet who headed the Organization of American States's cultural branch, the Pan American Union. He was upset we'd provided a forum for Cuban letters and threatened to cancel the five hundred subscriptions the Union had recently purchased. We refused to stop publishing Cuban artists. The Pan American Union canceled its subscriptions.

How to Express an Experience As Subjective As It Was Objective

Progressive political scientists, sociologists and historians began referring to the Cuban experience as "Marxism in Spanish." The reference implied a scientific methodology softened by the nostalgic strains of Sonora matancera[4]

or tropicalized by the beat of the conga drum, the languid image of palms,
Latin humor and a pulsating Caribbean sensuality. The Mexican cartoonist
Riús produced a comic book he called *Cuba para principiantes* (Cuba for
Beginners). C. Wright Mills wrote *Listen, Yankee!* urging readers to think
about the injustice implicit in powerful countries exploiting those that are
smaller, less industrially developed, and thus forced into dependency. Both
books became classics.

In poetry and prose the challenge was of a particular kind: how to fully
express an experience as subjective as it was objective? Meanwhile, the United
States was upping the ante: funding and organizing opposition groups, infil-
trating, invading, launching a diplomatic and trade embargo, and attempting
by every overt and covert means at its disposal the overthrow of this revolution it found so menacing.

Why the irrational fear? What could the most powerful nation on earth
have to worry about from a tiny island of barely eleven million people? The
stated reason focused on the same old national security issue invariably
dredged up in such situations: Cuba had declared itself socialist, was now
beholden to the Soviet Union, and its presence so close to U.S. shores was
perceived as a threat, an unwelcome beachhead upsetting the hemispheric
balance of powers.

And of course, having declared itself socialist, and with a Communist
Party in power, it was also considered godless. The religious card has long
been one of the Right's most insidious political weapons—even more blatant
in recent times. It became increasingly clear to me that the U.S. government didn't want its citizens traveling to the island for fear they might
discover state-proclaimed racial and sexual equality, justice, jobs, education,
pluralistic creative energy, comprehensive health care, and a government
on speaking terms with its people. Perhaps most threatening of all was the
joyous population that loved life and overwhelmingly supported its country's
revolutionary process.

We Aren't Writing about the Revolution; We Are the Revolution

From the beginning, Cuban intellectuals asked what they could do for the
revolution and the revolution asked the same of them. Following what
would be the first of many dramatic clashes and regroupings, the country's
writers and artists came together with passion and determination in 1961
to discuss the issues they faced. Fidel addressed the final session of that
early meeting and pronounced his famous, or infamous, *Palabras a los*

intelectuales (Words to the Intellectuals). Its best-remembered line—often quoted out of context in the years to come—was "dentro de la revolución todo, contra la revolución nada" (within the revolution everything, against the revolution nothing).

Artists and writers everywhere argued about that pronouncement. Did it mean that Cuban poets had to write about the tractor on the collective farm, the lonely militia woman patrolling Havana's nighttime sea wall, or the young people who were putting their own studies off in order to go out into the countryside to teach reading and writing to the hundreds of thousands of adults who had never been to school? Did it mean unquestioning allegiance, in work as well as in life? Did it mean reducing art to pamphlet?

No, our Cuban poet friends told us, we write about anything and everything: life, death, love, loss, a horizon of royal palms. It's our point of view and sense of possibility that have changed. We aren't writing about the revolution; we are the revolution. In truth, Fidel's words meant different things to different people, even within the revolutionary leadership. Some would interpret them rigidly; to others they meant that as long as one did not conspire against the revolutionary project one could expect to enjoy freedom of expression.

As I write now, forty years later, those words and their implications are being revisited—by Cuban artists and writers on the island and in exile. In January 2007, Cuban television ran tributes to several of the most dogmatic cultural hatchet men of the restrictive 1970s, provoking a rapidly growing exchange of telephone calls and emails. This exchange has been fascinating, not least because it displays the courage, intelligence and creativity of Cuba's cultural figures. In a later chapter I will examine this discussion in depth, and quote from some of its more profound and revealing statements.[5] For now, let me say that such cyclical struggle has always defined the Cuban revolution, demonstrating the dialectical nature of change.

Visiting Cuba Was a Statement

In January 1967 I visited Cuba for the first time. The revolution was seven years old. As editors of *El Corno Emplumado*, Sergio and I were invited to *El encuentro con Rubén Darío*, a gathering of poets meeting to commemorate the 100th anniversary of the birth of the great Nicaraguan modernist.

I don't know what I expected on that initial visit. Despite my distrust of U.S. foreign policy, my fervent support for the revolution's right to exist, my epistolary contact with its poets, and deep curiosity about everyday life, I didn't know all that much about the country's pre-revolutionary history, its two years of armed struggle or even the much more complex social change that commenced once the war was won.

Our plane touched down at Havana's José Martí International airport. Everyone on board clapped. We disembarked to the rhythm of Afro-Cuban drumming and greetings of "Bienvenida, compañera." Cuba libres, a blend of fine Cuban rum with the country's postrevolutionary rip-off of Coca-Cola, were offered all around. From that moment my eyes and ears were wide open, taking it all in; and my head and heart struggled to make sense of this place where drab look-alikes and a grim rigidity were nowhere in evidence. Yes, despite my own best intentions, I too had absorbed the stereotypes disseminated by the revolution's growing number of critics.

Before boarding that plane in Mexico City's airport, we travelers had been lined up in groups of three so a businesslike but slightly menacing official in plain clothes could take our pictures. In those years this was routine for anyone traveling to Cuba; and Mexico, despite its loudly proclaimed political independence, made servile room for the Interpol operation. Some travelers bragged they'd flashed an obscene gesture or deliberately made a mocking face for the camera. I stared straight ahead. Visiting Cuba was serious. One proclaimed rebellion by the very act.

We didn't know where those mug shots ended up. Perhaps in some cavernous warehouse; or in the personal file we assumed the CIA, FBI, and other U.S. security agencies were keeping on each of us. Maybe the camera was meant to intimidate and the pictures weren't kept at all. I once dreamed there was no film in those cameras, only attitude. Years later, under a watered-down Freedom of Information Act I would obtain seven hundred and fifty pages of my own personal files. Only a few prepositions had escaped the censor's thick black magic marker. There were no uncensored photos and few uncensored words. Despite charging us ten cents a page, almost everything was blacked out.

On that first visit we were met by enthusiastic young guides—some called them handlers—and driven from Rancho Boyeros into Havana. The salt sea air was intense, and a patina of peeling paint assaulted the eye. Faded blues and greens and mauves and creams and tans and pinks. Lots of palm trees, their gesturing trunks topped by the familiar green pleated fan. Occasionally the rococo curves of a stone façade or fountain, a media luna of richly colored glass above a door. I could imagine what this magnificent city had once been, its colonial smugness and seaport hustle. Shortages were already making themselves felt. People seemed easygoing, plainly dressed yet vibrant. And those amazing billboards were everywhere.

I think the billboards got to us all. Whatever our home country, we were accustomed to living with large-writ messages like "La rubia de categoría"— The High-Class Blonde or "Sin Kleenex no puedo vivir"—I Can't Live Without Kleenex (Mexico), General Motors and IBM (the U.S.), or "Drink Coca-Cola" and The Marlboro Man (worldwide). Cuba's billboards, in contrast, displayed compelling art. They proclaimed "If You Don't Know, Learn—If You Know, Teach"; "One Step Back, Two Forward"; "Commander in Chief, I Await Your Orders!" Or simply "Wash Your Hands: It Prevents the Spread of Disease." All the messages were ideological or educational. None advertised consumer products.

The Hotel Nacional, a stately and beautiful colonial-style building on a promontory of Havana's sea-washed *malecón*, welcomed the visiting poets. Dark wood, rich patterns of inlaid tile, and hundred-year-old canons in the garden. I knew that during the early post-insurrection years several whole floors of the Nacional had been used as a school for domestic servants. Here women with no previous option but to clean the houses of the rich had been retrained as bank clerks, taxi drivers, secretaries, even translators.

The Encuentro attracted some of the era's most important writers. Mario Benedetti arrived from Uruguay. His collection of short stories, *Montevideanos*, had recently situated him among the preeminent voices of Latin America, preceding the famous "boom" by several years. Brazil's Thiago de Mello brought his country's celebratory exuberance; he was the perennial organizer of humorous skits. Jorge Enrique Adoum from Ecuador read his poems in sonorous tones. Alejandro Romualdo from Peru seemed sorrowful, shaken. Gianni Toti, the Communist writer from Italy, had visited us previously in Mexico; something about his intellect and manner particularly appealed to me.

After arriving in Havana, we were taken for a few days to Varadero Beach, to a small promontory where the Dupont family had had one of its many vacation homes. The Argentinean poet and revolutionary Paco Urondo and I took a walk one evening on the Dupont grounds. There are images that remain linked to certain moments and I remember, as we talked, gazing at a brilliant white egret motionless against dark green grass. I would replay that image in grief when, several years later, Paco died in a burst of urban gunfire while fighting his country's dictatorship.

The Salvadoran Roque Dalton arrived from Prague, where he was editing a Communist theoretical journal. An earthquake had split the walls of the small CIA prison in which he'd been held, and he escaped and showed up at our poetry festival in Mexico City. In the coming years Roque would become a close friend. In less than a decade he too would be gone, victim of a militaristic splinter group in his own organization. His death affected me as few before or since.

Among the Cuban participants at that 1967 meeting I remember Cintio Vitier and his wife Fina García Marruz, both fine poets and devout Catholics who stayed in Cuba when others followed their faith into exile. Their loyalty then and later would be rewarded when the Cuban Communist Party softened its antireligious stance in the 1980s. Roberto Fernández Retamar, Pablo Armando Fernández and Miguel Barnet were important poets with major works to their credit; all had published in *El Corno*.

A very young Nancy Morejón gripped everyone with a vibrant reading from her first book, *Ricardo trajo su flauta*. This, too, was when we gathered at the old Dupont mansion for nights of poetic exchange. I still remember a conversation with the aging black bartender who had worked for the Duponts for years and now served the revolution in the same capacity. His dramatic story was punctuated by his own personal anecdotes of class and race.

Cuban poet Nancy Morejón, in the 1970s and 1990s.

Justice Was a Logical Choice

Tania Díaz Castro, a poet with whom we'd been in contact through *El Corno*, took us to La moderna poesía, a famous old bookstore in the city's colonial center. The stock was dusty and depleted but I remember finding several copies of an astonishing collection of poems and drawings by the children at Czechoslovakia's Terezin concentration camp, few of whom had survived their art.[6] The young revolution published and imported literature of many different types, from all over the world.

Leaving La moderna poesía by one of the narrow arteries that webbed the dilapidated but active city center, we started to cross the street just as a jeep full of soldiers rounded the corner, fast. Tania shouted out a vehement reprimand: "You call yourselves revolutionaries?" Her eyes flashed. "You could have killed us!" The jeep stopped. The soldiers got out and apologized. We conversed. I couldn't help but think of the Mexican cop or soldier, hand always out for that folded ten peso note. The following year those Mexican enforcers of law and order would become terrible pawns in a struggle in which thousands would die. And it would be my struggle.

Could this change be real?

The Encuentro featured scholarly papers on Darío, who had been an avowed anti-imperialist in his day and who, our hosts contended, would have supported the Cuban revolution enthusiastically. In this year of his centennial, conferences and gatherings of different sorts took place in a number of countries. In Cuba the event was a serious examination of Darío's life and work as well as a way for the revolution to show itself off to intellectuals and artists from abroad. In the evenings we gathered to read our own poetry. Cuba, cruelly blockaded by the United States, not only broke through its isolation at cultural gatherings like this one; it provided a meeting place for artists and writers who would not otherwise have had an opportunity to know one another.

One day we headed west, to the province of Pinar del Río. There, against a backdrop of dramatic natural beauty and preceded by an impressive outdoor performance by the country's prima ballerina Alicia Alonso, I attended my first of Fidel's speeches. He was inaugurating a whole town: housing, schools, parks, a clinic. Fidel spoke for an hour and a half. I found every word compelling.

I Decided to Stay On for Another Couple of Weeks

When the official gathering ended, Sergio returned to Mexico where his teaching semester was about to begin. I decided to stay on for another couple of weeks to take advantage of a trip being offered to the easternmost tip of the island. We want to show you where the revolution started, our hosts told us. Haydeé Santamaría's younger sister Ada accompanied four or five of us on this journey. We visited Santiago de Cuba and the Sierra Maestra from where Fidel, Abel and Haydeé Santamaría, Frank País and others had initiated their war against Fulgencio Batista.

We went to Moncada, the ex-military camp where Fidel and his comrades had engaged the dictator's army for the first time in the early morning hours of July 26, 1953. Now it was a large school, a place of violence having given birth to one of learning. Students in their clean uniforms and red neckerchiefs, denoting membership in the Pioneros—youngest contingent of communist youth—greeted us enthusiastically. A modest museum told the dramatic story of that initial battle.

Children in Old Havana.

Leaving the school I remember gazing from the car window as we traced the retreat of those young revolutionaries who had survived the attack. As we drove back along the country road toward Santiago, I noticed the simple roadside markers or small monuments where many of them had been gunned down. Our hosts had themselves participated in Cuba's recent war of liberation and they gifted us with personal and collective memory.

We struggled to Minas de Frío, the spot on Turquino Peak where Ernesto "Che" Guevara's command post had been. The last eight miles took us several hours by slow truck. Another day we climbed yet another hill, this time on the Cuban side of Guantánamo Bay, from where we looked across at the military posts surrounding the U.S. owned base. We shared Cuba's outrage at this piece of its territory occupied by another state but would have been hard put to imagine the sinister way in which Guantánamo's history would unfold some forty years into the future.

Argentine writer Rodolfo Walsh and Margaret. Less than a decade later—March 25, 1977—Walsh would be gunned down in Buenos Aires. Days before, his daughter had been disappeared and murdered, moving him to write a public letter denouncing the Triple-A (Argentina's death squad linked to the country's military). During the 1970s and early 1980s some 30,000 Argentines suffered this fate. January 1968.

*U.S. writer and editor Susan Sherman and Margaret, Cultural
Congress of Havana. January 1968.*

We traveled a narrow mountain road through the steep Sierra de Cristal
to Baracoa where we visited a chocolate factory, talked with its workers, and
savored the rich dark sweet. We listened to the music of elderly *trovadores*
and enjoyed folkloric dance performances by the descendants of Haitian
immigrants who had come to cut Cuban sugarcane a century before. Everywhere people greeted us warmly. Many, like our hosts, had personal stories
to share.

I returned to Mexico shaken. My overwhelming feeling was that this was
all so simple: justice was a logical choice and if people wanted it badly enough
they would find a way to achieve it. Over the years, of course, I learned just
how complicated social change can be. But I have never completely lost my
conviction that if people really want to design a system that lifts people up
rather than keeps them down, the task is much more straightforward than
our experts and elected officials would have us believe.

CHAPTER 2

TRANSITION

Doors Opened and Tens of Thousands of Cuban Children Burst Forth

In January of 1968 I went to Cuba again to attend the Cultural Congress of Havana. This time I was alone. Central to my desire to revisit the island was my need to know if the new society I had discovered, and which had made such a profound impression on me the year before, was really all it had appeared. Ever a product of my class and culture, I found it hard to completely trust my instincts. Perhaps, after all, we really had been shown only what the Cubans wanted us to see. This time I was determined to leave the official venue as often as possible, walk by myself in marginal neighborhoods, speak with anyone and everyone willing to talk.

None of which proved difficult. There were no restrictions and I could roam at will. The Cultural Congress with its hundreds of well-known intellectuals and artists was fascinating on all sorts of levels: the discussion groups, the ideas, and those who generated them. French philosophers, English psychiatrists, guerrilla leaders from a number of the so-called Third World countries, Vietnamese political cadre, Latin American indigenous activists, and several of the century's most important writers and artists mingled in the lobby of the Havana Libre, the ex-Hilton that nine years earlier had been taken over by triumphant young revolutionaries even before it could formally open to the public.

Susan Sherman came from New York with the same journalist status as my own; she represented her exquisite cultural magazine *Ikon,* while I was invited as one of *El Corno's* editors. Just as the Congress was getting underway my friend and publisher Arnaldo Orfila introduced Susan and me to Cuba's Secretary of State, the writer and historian Raul Roa. Roa was a statesman of impressive intellect: a mind reminiscent of a dying breed—at least among western politicians. Over a drink he said he thought Susan and I should be delegates rather than journalists and, following a telephone call from him, we were quickly moved from the Hotel Nacional, where the journalists were housed, to the Havana Libre with the rest of the Congress participants.

Susan and I shared a room, and would get to know one another well on that trip—the beginning of an important lifelong friendship. For the past forty years we have shared poems, political satisfactions and disappointments, disbelief, and the knowledge that comes from aging in a time of cataclysm while nurturing a literature that remains committed to change. She is one of the few non-Cubans I still know who remembers the country as it was back then, with all its astonishing promise.

I would also get to know Che's sister, Celia Guevara, visiting Cuba for the first time just months after her brother's murder. Celia and I took long evening walks along the city's malecón or sea wall. Once she emerged from the restroom located just off the Havana Libre's lobby with squares of newsprint in her hand and a wry hurt in her eyes. Try as I will, she muttered, I cannot get used to wiping my ass with my brother's face. By this time toilet paper had become a luxury, even in the hotels.

Tom Hayden, Barbara Dane, and Irwin Silber were among the other U.S. delegates. One afternoon I came upon a group of Vietnamese offering Barbara a ring made from the metal of a downed B-52. She tried on several, hoping to find one that fit. The Vietnamese told those of us from the United States how proud they were of our anti-war work. We cringed in discomfort, in awe of their much greater sacrifice. As fascinated as I was by the personalities and debates going on inside the hotel, I had another agenda: to explore the everyday reality of life in Cuba. For this I had to leave the Congress venue.

One experience I won't forget from those days at the beginning of 1968 was being driven by Cuban poet Pablo Armando Fernández out Miramar's tree-lined Fifth Avenue, past the aging mansions that had belonged to wealthy Cubans when the revolution took power in January of 1959. The vast majority of these people fled, for Miami or other foreign cities. They believed that with help from the United States the revolution would soon be defeated and it wouldn't be long before they'd have their mansions back.

In anticipation of that return, some hid whole dinner services behind false walls. They expected to retrieve them when Castro was ousted from power. Several years later, when my own children attended those schools that had once been the homes of Cuba's elite, kids tapping on their dorm room walls still occasionally found the hidden treasures. Each such find conjured tales of mystery and romance.

It was five thirty or six in the afternoon as Pablo Armando drove me along those transformed streets. Suddenly, as if by magic, doors opened and tens of thousands of Cuban children burst forth. They ran and shouted as they raced from the houses now converted into dorms or classrooms toward those serving as dining halls. It was a great sea of young people, all wearing dark pants or skirts, starched white shirts and their Pionero neckerchiefs. We have reclaimed these houses for our children, Pablo Armando beamed, half of whom couldn't even attend school before the revolution.

I Sensed an Authentic and Growing Democracy

As we slowly drove through Miramar's manicured neighborhoods—hundreds of square blocks where before the revolution black Cubans would have been maids or gardeners—wave after wave of Cuban children flowed from classroom to dinner before my astonished eyes. They were black and brown and white and every shade in between. Theirs were the voices of ownership: raucous, gleeful, free. This was hardly a show being put on to impress me.

Walking alone through different Havana neighborhoods it was easy to engage people in conversation. Everyone had a story. Familiarity with and love for Fidel was palpable. Men and women, young and old, professionals and factory workers and those from the countryside all referred to him as brilliant and courageous. They were proud of his refusal to cede to pressure from the United States. The connection seemed deeply personal, as if they were speaking of a loving father or friend. Often I sensed the same sort of fervor with which many Christians speak of Jesus Christ as their personal savior. But this was a human and practical love. Fidel understood them, they said, he had only their well-being at heart.

Although, at least back then, it was hard to find anyone willing to speak ill of the leader, the praise seemed neither idealistic nor immune to creative Cuban humor. In my mind it was the humor that projected the healthiest take on reality. Cubans called Fidel *El caballo*, The Horse. The deeper one scratched the surface of popular culture the more horse jokes one heard.

At the beginning of 1968, Cubans exuded a sense of participation and well-being. Many spoke of hard lives before the revolution and developing opportunities since. Complaints emerged about a variety of problems—food shortages, an incipient bureaucracy, and the inability to make change as fast as it was needed—but the people with whom I spoke seemed confident that these issues would be dealt with in one way or another. No, not that they would be dealt with, but that they themselves would do the dealing: through participatory forums in schools and workplaces, army units and neighborhood committees. No one seemed afraid to voice criticism.

I sensed an authentic and growing democracy, much more direct than the variety so loudly touted in the United States. The revolution's leadership and grass roots seemed to be engaged in a continuous and respectful conversation. Later, in the mid-seventies, when Peoples' Power was established and elections were held, candidates campaigned with brief biographies and eight by ten inch photos, and sat in neighborhood storefronts on designated afternoons conversing with their constituencies. This seemed much more reasonable to me than the political campaigns back home which, even then, required obscene amounts of money, false advertising and devious lies. In Cuba young people guarded the ballot boxes, assuring a transparency beyond reproach.

In January of 1968, when I left the Cultural Congress and wandered the city, I invariably got into long, in depth conversations with all sorts of Cubans. Many assured me they differentiated between the U.S. government and its people. They told me they appreciated the risk I was taking in visiting, and made me feel welcome. Twice I was invited into strangers' homes and offered a demitasse of strong, sweet, coffee; I was startled and touched by the generosity implicit in sharing this highly rationed commodity. We hope more of you come, these people said, we will set your misconceptions straight.

Although people I met in the street admired many aspects of U.S. culture— ties between the two countries had, after all, been very close before 1959—many had a rather romanticized notion of life in my country of origin. While we believed the socialist state to be somber and steeped in sameness, they were sure that every young person in the country to the north was high on drugs, consumerism was a religion and every adult lived at the expense of others. In the United States the stereotypical views were a result of anti-communist propaganda. In Cuba they reflected another sort of propaganda, repeated daily in an inadequate and extremely poor quality mass media that never missed an opportunity to portray the U.S. as a cesspool of drugs and crime.

During that 1968 visit some people asked for articles of clothing or other consumer items. One poet called my hotel room late the night before I was due to return home, to ask if I would leave a pair of stockings he'd admired. He said he wanted them for his wife. This obsession with foreign goods would grow more intense in the years to come, as more and more things disappeared from the shops.

Later, when we lived in Cuba, I, too, sometimes asked visiting friends to leave what they could spare. Levis, if they fit, were always welcome. Maybe an item for one of the children. Once I started doing photography, film and paper were my most frequent requests. I confess, as well, that I once asked for a small can of V-8 for my daughter Sarah, who missed its evocative taste. On another occasion I would describe a cheeseburger slathered in ketchup with such longing that a friend came back from a trip abroad with one for me in her purse.

FIDEL'S SPEECHES WERE NEVER FORMULAIC OR DULL

Cuba's revolutionary press, as I say, was a disaster. *Granma*, the official Communist Party daily, painted the U.S. enemy with exaggerated adjectives. No nuance at all. Dull speeches by Party hacks were reprinted word for dreary word. Statements of other Communist parties around the world were also published in boring detail. When asked what they thought of the paper, most Cubans I spoke with laughed and threw up their hands. No one pretended they found it interesting. At the same time, people seemed to excuse a certain flatness or lack of opposing opinion. Political education was important and few had an idea of how it could be made more interesting.

Fidel's speeches, on the other hand, were never formulaic or dull. Often three to five hours or longer, they held the attention of citizens and visitors alike. The man was a consummate teacher. He moved from the experiential—situations and issues with which every Cuban could identify—to the general and theoretical. Back and forth he went, deftly and conclusively explaining how the larger political struggles were reflected in people's lives, how politics and economics at the international level affected the country, what caused a particular item to be in short supply, why people should be willing to do without or what effort was required to put it back on the market. His most memorable speeches were history or economics lessons, exquisite in their clarity.

On this second trip I discovered that virtually all Cuban children were going to school, and that previously illiterate adults had been taught to read and write and were bringing their educational levels in line with their ages. The immediate goal was for every adult to have completed at least a ninth grade education.

I learned that health care was free and accessible; several Congress delegates had the opportunity of checking this out for themselves. I saw a population putting its collective shoulder to the wheel, and believed that in their workplaces people really did hold decision-making power. (They did up to a certain point; the Party made the important decisions.) Housing remained a problem, but I saw hundreds of thousands of apartments being built—by the people who would inhabit them.

Congress delegates were taken to the vast apartment complex called La Habana del Este, on the coast just east of Havana. People invited us into their homes: modest by middle-class U.S. standards but airy and functional and, most importantly, their own. One foreign intellectual, I can't remember who, wondered out loud if we were being tricked: shown a model housing project or being invited only into those homes whose occupants would sing the revolution's praises. I had seen enough by this time to know that neither was the case.

Arnaldo Orfila Grabbed My Hand and Pulled

The 1968 Cultural Congress of Havana ended with a reception at the National Palace, a large modern building on Revolution Square. Inside, its broad functional lines were broken by exquisite contemporary paintings by some of the great Cuban and Latin American artists of those years, and the exuberance of large-leafed tropical plants. More than a thousand delegates, journalists, and our Cuban hosts milled about the great hall, chatting and savoring island delicacies. Suddenly my friend and publisher Arnaldo Orfila interceded once more on my behalf. He grabbed my hand and pulled as he told me: I want you to meet Fidel. I, in turn, grabbed Susan.

In my memory of that evening the two of us literally floated through the crowd, our feet barely touching the polished marble floor as Arnaldo steered us in one direction and then another. Soon we were standing before the solid presence of several of the Prime Minister's personal security guards. Fidel was discussing French cheeses with a delegate or journalist from that country; it was clear he was a connoisseur. In the first break in the conversation Arnaldo introduced the two of us. Fidel turned and said: "Oh, Margaret Randall. I've read your *Corno Emplumado*, a very fine magazine. The issue devoted to Cuban poetry was wonderful."

That reference to the literary magazine prompted me to mention Susan's *Ikon*. Fidel said he didn't know the publication and would like to read a copy. René Vallejo, Fidel's friend and personal physician entered the conversation then. He offered to come by our hotel and pick up a couple of issues. It never occurred to either Susan or me that this would actually happen. We weren't used to casual conversations with prime ministers. If we had been, we would have assumed they were formal-speak rather than substantive.

Two nights later, Vallejo did come by the Havana Libre. Susan was on her way home by then, but had left an envelope with several *Ikons*, just in case. I was in a deep sleep when the ringing of the bedside phone roused me and I heard Vallejo's voice asking if it would be alright for him to come up. I said of course and hurriedly started getting dressed. I was still kicking scattered pieces of underwear under the bed when he knocked on the door of my room.

Vallejo had been an obstetrician before the war. He still saw expectant mothers a couple of days a week. I had been working as a midwife in Mexico City's misery belt; an activity to which I dedicated myself along with writing, running a bilingual literary journal and taking part in local politics. Our conversation, as we finished off a couple of packs of *negritos*—strong Cuban cigarettes—included midwifery, literature, revolution, the streets of New York City, and other topics I no longer remember.

René Vallejo and I became friends that night, just as Susan and he would become friends the following year, when he invited her to the island to heal from a problem that poverty, the stress of struggle, and inaccessibility of health care had saddled her with at the time. Neither of us was able to keep

René Vallejo, 1968.

the wonderful letters he wrote. Hers were stolen and I destroyed mine. In later years the danger in possessing such mementos made keeping them inadvisable.

Although extremely close to Fidel and his constant companion, Vallejo never joined the Cuban Communist Party. Nor did he ever hold a position beyond that of the prime minister's personal doctor. It was rumored he practiced Santeria, the Afro-Cuban religion with deep roots on the island, which was looked down upon by the Marxist materialists now running the country.

Vallejo's white hair and beard belied his forty-some-odd years. Much too young, he would suffer a massive stroke and die halfway through 1969, while I was in hiding in Mexico. A friend lost almost before he was found, at least by me. Years later, living in Cuba, I attended a performance of the National Ballet at one of Havana's classic theaters. At intermission a slim young woman approached me: "René Vallejo was my father," she said, "he always spoke so highly of you."

I am trying to return to Cuba, to my family. I need to make the airport's Cubana de Aviación desk in time to check in for the Havana flight. As is true of so many Cubana desks, this one is modest, half-hidden at the far end of a row of more prominent airline counters. I am sure, once I reach it, the Cuban on duty will solve my problem. There is a strong sense—memory?—of that familiar brand of revolutionary creativity, competence, kindness and reassurance. The solution to so many problems, personal as well as collective or social.

In some dreams I make it to the airport, which is invariably almost empty, its cavernous terminals echoing my voice as I beg a cleaning woman or lone security guard to point me towards Cubana. If I can just get there I know that Cuban efficiency, often dressed in disarmingly informal magical realism, will save the day. Even as the minutes tick relentlessly—a large, unseen clock echoes my heartbeat—I believe that if I can make it to the desk I can get them to hold the flight.

That Morning I Dressed Ana in a Tiny Pink One-Piece Cotton Suit

My two visits to Cuba made me want to live there, at least for a year or two. I thought it would be a great learning experience for all of us, perhaps especially the children. By this time Sergio and I had divorced and I was living with U.S. American poet Robert Cohen. In March 1969 we added baby Ana to our family. My new partner had never been to Cuba but was game. And so in late spring of that year we had plans to move to the island. Both of us had jobs waiting. Our departure date was still a few months off. Then, without warning, political events in Mexico spun our lives inside out. Our plans were dramatically altered.

The 1968 Mexican student movement had ended tragically, with the brutal massacre at Tlatelolco.[1] I'd participated in the movement through the pages of *El Corno Emplumado* and more directly: joining the information brigades, translating movement materials for dissemination in other countries, hiding and feeding the hunted, distributing flyers on city buses, and attempting to get into the athletes' village at the Mexico City Olympics to make its occupants aware of our struggle. My home, always filled with political guests, also must have rendered me suspect. The Mexican government, and probably the U.S. government as well, did not take to a foreigner—perhaps particularly not to a foreign woman—who made Mexico's struggles her own. In the late summer of 1969 I was hit by a political repression that forced me underground.

As the one-year anniversary of the movement approached, those of us who'd survived were making plans to commemorate it by honoring our dead. Movement people not in prison or exile began to suffer harassment or worse. We heard about children kidnapped as warnings to their rebel parents, and several suspicious deaths. It was in this context that paramilitary operatives appeared one morning at our home and made off with my passport.

It was a tense moment: I had recently given birth to my fourth child, Ana, and was in bed, sick with some sort of infection. The doorbell rang and Robert answered to find himself face to face with someone claiming to represent Mexico's Social Security Administration. He said they had information that I, a foreigner, was operating a sewing shop out of the house and that I wasn't paying social security for my employees.

Robert told him there was no such sewing shop—he invited him in to see for himself—and that I was a Mexican citizen. The man asked for proof. Robert got my passport and the intruder smiled and said he would correct the problem. All he needed was to enter my data on some forms he had in his car. Then he drew a gun, made for the vehicle where someone else was sitting at the wheel with the motor running, and they took off with my passport in hand. I'll never forget the sound of my partner's rapid ascent to our bedroom as he screamed: "They've got your passport! They're gone!"

I denounced the theft but could get no redress. Soon our neighborhood was staked out with uniformed and plainclothes cops. It was obvious that life in Mexico had become untenable, probably dangerous. Robert quit his job and we took the children out of school. For several weeks we hid in different parts of the vast city: in the homes of friends and in remote and nondescript hotels.

When it became clear that I would not be issued another passport and my leaving the country would be more difficult and take longer than we'd imagined, we asked my parents to take Gregory, Sarah, Ximena, and Ana until we could land somewhere safe. They refused. The alternative open to us was to send them to Cuba. It was a wrenching decision, one made with their safety and well-being in mind. Quickly I weaned Ana, only three and a half months old at the time. On July 25, 1969, Robert took the children to the airport where Cuban officials received them on a plane bound for Havana.

Even now, writing about that day causes physical pain, invading muscle, sinew, bone. I remember dressing my baby in a tiny pink one-piece cotton suit; the white undersides of its booties and white color somehow defining her vulnerability. Six-year-old Sarah was unusually quiet. With five-year-old Ximena I sent a detailed letter, explaining the ear infections that had plagued her almost from birth and begging whoever cared for her to try to keep her right ear dry.[2] Only Gregory understood what was happening. Not yet nine, he assumed his big brother role with confidence, giving himself the job of caring for his sisters, an assignment they later came to feel he carried beyond what was necessary. I always wanted to see wisdom and maturity in my son. He did possess these qualities in abundance, but I know he felt the responsibility acutely.

Underground, we were advised to stay on the move. Dear friends Maru Uhthoff, Laurette Séjourné, and Arnaldo Orfila took us into their homes. After we said goodbye to the children, Carlos and Cristina Payan also offered us the hospitality of a small cupola in their house on the outskirts of the city. Cristina was a big woman, blonde and blue-eyed and with a generous, rapid-fire diction. She had been Gregory's first and second grade teacher. Carlos was a progressive lawyer, founder and for many years editor-in-chief of the progressive Mexican weekly *Uno mas uno*. From a high window in the Payan's attic I could see across an open field to a small country graveyard. One morning a silent line of mourners followed a child's coffin to its freshly dug grave. I watched until the service ended and the people dispersed. My heart ached.

The women who had worked as maids in our home endured visits from paramilitary operatives who tried to get them to reveal our whereabouts. We had disappeared with only hurried goodbyes and meager explanation. These women's livelihoods and lodging ended abruptly. We managed to get some money to them; it was all we could do. Forced to abandon our home and everything in it, we'd overlooked an old wooden card file with the names of contributors and subscribers to the magazine. That card file escaped the notice of the first of those who rifled through our things and our friend Maru courageously went to the house to retrieve it.

Maru also rescued our valuable collection of paintings. Throughout my years in New York and Mexico I had acquired many as gifts or trades, and owned more than a hundred, including the works of many well-known U.S. and Mexican artists. Maru arranged for them to be taken to the Cuban Embassy in Mexico City. There the comrades crated each painting and sent the lot to Havana's Museum of Modern Art.[3]

Days passed, and then weeks. The movement was in shambles, and getting false papers from its broken structures proved impossible. Months unfolded, shadowed by our yearning for the children and punctuated by occasional contact with them, my more and more frequent attacks of what would turn out to be a severe kidney ailment, some writing and translation, a very few carefully chosen goodbyes, and our continuing efforts to find an exit route that might work.

Direct contact with the children was almost impossible, although I remember one, very brief, phone conversation. More often we'd hear from people who would assure us they were well. I still have a letter from Gregory, dated August 1, 1969. This would have been written a week after our separation:

Dear Mommy and Robert: I hope you are well and Goyo fell from a bicycle and hurt my arm and tummy. Don't be sad, it wasn't serious. And nothing happened to Sara. I haven't seen Anna because she is in a crèche with our friends. Saris and Ximena are in House 18 and I am in House 9 here at the summer camp that you told me about before we came. We are well, there are a lot of flying ants, they even get into your nose, they are very annoying, my sisters and I every morning we go to the beach and swim out about ten meters from the shore. I Goyo have been looking for a pen for three days but I haven't found one so I had to write this with crayons. So you can see with how much love I'm writing this letter. Please come soon, every night I ask it of the stars. I have two friends, one from Guinea and the other from Cuba. I am writing to you with so much love and almost with tears in my eyes. Goyo, Saris, Ximena and Anna.[4]

Although barely five at the time, Ximena also remembers the sudden and painful uprooting. Several years ago, in a piece for the Mexican magazine *Generación*, she wrote: "Goyo would sit Sarah and me down beside him at night, right next to a window, and say: 'See that star? That's Mama and Papa up there; let's send them kisses.'"[5]

I ached for the children. They ached for me and for Robert. How deeply they were scarred by this necessary separation, how profound were the feelings of abandonment that would continue to plague at least several of them for years, are issues I have periodically had to revisit.

An Emptiness That Numbed Me to the Core

One month passed, and then two. A third began, with an emptiness that numbed me to the core. My longing for the children, uncertainty around when we would be reunited, periodic kidney attacks, and a nicotine withdrawal that still caused my hands to shake and tears to spill from my eyes were the outward signs of inner anguish.

Finally an acquaintance introduced us to someone with contacts in the Mexican mafia, and he arranged my escape. I left my hideout and went to a beauty parlor in a part of vast Mexico City where I wasn't likely to run into anyone I knew. I think my husband is seeing another woman, I told the attendant as she placed the plastic sheet over my shoulders; I want a complete makeover. When, several hours later I emerged from the salon, my long brown braid was shiny black and cut and teased into a fashionable bob. My unruly eyebrows were tweezed pencil thin. Lip color and nail polish completed the disguise.

Ximena is four, Gregory eight, Sarah five, and Ana one month old, just before leaving for Cuba. Mexico City, 1969.

I believed my own mother would have been hard put to recognize me on the street had she run into me that day. Wearing a striped knit dress unlike the indigenous huipiles that were my trademark, I opened my eyes as wide as possible and had half a dozen passport size pictures taken in one of those little shopping mall photo stalls. Then, purchasing our tickets under false names, Robert and I flew north to Chihuahua.

Our Cuban comrades in Mexico had said that once I was outside Mexico they could help me get to the island via Czechoslovakia. This was one of the only viable routes at the time, and the safest given my situation. In Chihuahua City we were met by one Señor García. We'd been told we would recognize him because he was missing a part of the little finger on his left hand, but when the plane rolled to a stop at the small provincial airport he was waiting at the foot of the ladder.

García was expansive and hospitable. He took us to dinner, put us in a good hotel, and picked us up the following morning to take us to the man we'd been told could fix my document problem—for a price. It was then that the operation began to unravel. García's friend, who worked in local government, couldn't provide me with a real Mexican passport, only a laughable pale blue cardboard booklet good for border residents who routinely crossed from one side to another. To be legal, it had to be registered at the U.S. Consul on the other side, something I would not have dared to attempt.

Hope diminished. Robert and I looked at each other, trying to decide what to do. On a whim, or perhaps because I saw no alternative, I said: "I'll take it." We paid the $200 we'd been quoted in Mexico City and the apologetic official promised to wait until the following month to note my name on the list he sent to his home office.

Thus began a blur of days, nights, different modes of transportation, and anxious waits. Because I had not been able to obtain the normal passport, García smuggled me past the twenty-eight mile checkpoint in the back of a refrigerated meat truck. I rode with him in the cab until just a few miles before we had to stop and he released me, shivering, a few miles past the danger point. Robert took a bus to Juárez, where we met him for dinner at a prearranged Chinese restaurant. As in Chihuahua, García seemed to know everyone on the premises. Once again he insisted on paying for our meal—the last supper, we called it—and directed us to a nearby thoroughfare that led to the international bridge. A half hour later we walked across, answering the routine "Nationality?" with an equally routine "U.S.A."

Once in the United States, Robert, who had a U.S. passport, flew to New York for a visit with his parents, and then on to Madrid and finally Havana.

I had become a Mexican citizen but without a passport my travel plans were more complicated. I flew to Chicago, transferred to a Greyhound bus and crossed the Canadian border at Windsor, using my old U.S. birth certificate as identification. I remember flashes of that journey: fragments of my conversation with a thin Bible-reading young man sitting next to me on the long ride, brief naps and jolts to recovered consciousness. I still suffered from the kidney problem that had plagued me since before Ana's birth, and spiked a high fever on and off.

These were the days before credit cards. I was carrying several thousand dollars in cash. At the Toronto airport I purchased a ticket to Paris. Now I close my eyes and can once again see that sky over the Atlantic, darkening almost as soon as we took off. Brilliant oranges and pinks soon announced a sudden sunrise. In Paris I stayed outside the immigration barrier and bought a ticket to Prague. No one ever asked to see my useless travel document. Just as my Cuban contacts had promised, passports weren't examined on departure, only on arrival.

I Would Spend Nineteen Days in Prague

All of which marked my arrival in Prague as the moment of truth. I very much hoped the Cubans there had been notified of my coming. When I got to the head of the immigration line and handed over the document, the official receiving it shook his head, looked at me, and then called over a fellow officer. Neither had ever seen a passport like mine, and I didn't have a visa for Czechoslovakia. I asked to see someone from the Cuban embassy.

After a few minutes I was ushered into a small room. Although the official doing the ushering spoke no English, I understood I was to wait. I remember having to urinate and being afraid to move. Finally a young woman appeared with a small medical kit in hand. It appeared the Czechs were more concerned about the fact that I had no health card than about my other papers. She asked if I was pregnant and I said no. Later that night I would have recurrent nightmares in which I dreamed I was pregnant and by allowing them to vaccinate me against smallpox had killed my unborn child.

Eventually the Cuban comrade arrived. A man of few words, he barely inquired about my trip. The drive from the airport took about half an hour, often over narrow cobblestone streets through neat neighborhoods of small rowhouses. My savior deposited me in a hotel on the outskirts of the city, where I stayed—accompanied only by bouts of kidney attacks—for several days.

Even in Prague my ordeal dragged on. A single flight a week connected that city with Havana and I would be bumped from one plane and then another in deference to travelers with higher political status. In all I would spend nineteen days in Prague, the last thirteen of them at the Hotel International. There I would meet Cubans and other Latin Americans, passing through for one reason or another. I would learn patience from them.

Some Cuban guests were returning from courses of study in the Soviet Union. A well-known composer had just finished a concert tour in Eastern Europe. Some of the Latin Americans were making their circuitous ways from Cuba back to distant home country battlefronts. A Cuban pilot was waiting for a part from a Russian aircraft factory to arrive for his Ilushyn 18. With him I would experience one of the great magical realist episodes of my life.

The story about the pilot is as good a prelude to our years in Cuba as any. We had introduced ourselves a few days before. Francisco was as frustrated as I; his replacement part had been promised for several weeks and the waiting game was getting old. One night at dinner I mentioned my children and the fact that they had preceded me to Havana. Francisco stared at me. Do you have photographs, he asked, motivated by what seemed an unusual interest. I pulled out the worn images I'd kept with me those hard months and pushed them across the table.

Francisco looked at the pictures and began to laugh. "I can't believe this," he exclaimed. "Your youngest peed on my trousers when the stewardess brought them into the cockpit. The boy wanted a look at the controls." It took me a moment to realize that the man sitting across from me had seen my children more recently than I. He had flown them from Mexico City to Havana. Immediately our exchange became excited, overflowing with exchanges of information, images, rapid fire back and forth. Others at the table stopped talking.

I knew they were traveling alone, Francisco said. The four of them were being taken care of by the plane's stewardess, and a government official met the flight. He looked at my pictures again. "I'll bet you miss them," he said, his tone gentle now.

CHAPTER 3

SETTLING IN

The Door to Room 506 Stood Open

We'd left Mexico in stages: the children first and, when we were able to organize my exit, Robert and I. Hoping more than knowing, when we had to send the kids off I'd promised Gregory I'd catch up with them before his ninth birthday. I got lucky and made it by a day, touching down at Havana's José Martí International Airport early on the morning of October 13.

Aboard the old World War Two Britannia, the twenty-seven hour flight from Prague, via Shannon, Ireland, and Greenland's largely military airport, passed in a daze. Because we didn't really know who was behind my problems in Mexico, my Cuban contact warned me not to deplane. There was no food service on board, but at one of our stops a flight attendant brought me a meal. In Havana I entered the airport building wondering who might be there to meet me. Had anyone in Prague sent word of my arrival? If they had, the news hadn't gotten through. I walked alone into the quiet of an almost empty terminal.

An on-duty immigration official was charged with notifying the appropriate authorities. I felt relieved to be in familiar surroundings where I could speak the language and knew my children couldn't be far. Half an hour later an elderly government official showed up. He had instructions to drive me to the Hotel Capri where he said my family was waiting.

As I peered through the window of the wine red Alfa Romeo at small groups of people waiting for busses to take them to work, catching sight of those familiar billboards and signature palms, I could feel the tension drain from my body. The realization I was finally home free almost succeeded in relaxing my anxious anticipation at reuniting with Robert and the children. I was especially concerned about Ana. Two and a half months is a lifetime to an infant. Even with the older children I had no idea what this time had been like for them, what fears they'd battled, what form their relief would take.

Someone in the lobby must have called up to my family because when I stepped from the elevator into the fifth floor foyer the door to room 506 stood open and my three older children rushed to greet me. Gregory's eyes beamed pure joy. Sarah threw her arms around my legs. I was wearing the navy blue and yellow knit dress in which I'd embarked upon my journey almost four weeks before, was still shod in the nylon stockings and navy blue pumps, still carried the matching bag. My teased hair had gone limp and I'd finally succeeded in scratching the last of the chipped varnish from my fingernails.

Although it had taken me three weeks to get from Prague to Havana, it had been more than two and a half months since that morning in Mexico when Robert drove the children to the airport and they'd been taken onto the plane. Images of their faces receding through a car window moving out of sight superimposed themselves upon our reunion. Ximena held herself slightly apart as if trying to reconcile this woman with the mother she knew. After a few moments she edged forward, touched my dress and then buried her face in it.

Robert watched and smiled. Tears welled in his eyes. He had arrived a week earlier—via Paris and Madrid—expecting to find me at trip's end. The Cubans assured him I was on my way and quickly put him in touch with the children. Summer camp was over and Gregory, Sarah and Ximena were already attending school; in *becas*—those boarding schools in Miramar from which they came home on weekends. Their weekends thus far had been spent with Tania Díaz Castro and her husband Ricardo. They'd also been taken regularly to visit their baby sister, who remained in the wellness center where they'd all spent an initial few days being checked out for possible health problems and other needs. The converted mansion which housed the wellness center had once belonged to the Bacardi family, who'd long since cut their losses and started over in Puerto Rico.

Now Robert explained that Ana had stayed on at that facility because Hortensia, its assistant director, had fallen in love with the little girl so dramatically separated from her parents. Rather than allow her to be placed in a live-in day care environment, Hortensia had asked permission to keep her where she'd receive much more individualized care. She was unmarried and a woman with impeccable credentials. The Foreign Ministry had agreed to this arrangement. Robert said he'd visited Ana every day since he'd arrived the week before; I wouldn't believe how she'd grown.

Soon they pulled me into the room that, along with the one next door, would be our home for the next several months. Despite my exhaustion and unfamiliar look, my credibility was being restored. We gazed at one another. We laughed. We cried. We touched one another, lay tangled on the beds, interrupted each other and ourselves, talked until presence overcame absence and we were together again.

We went down to the hotel cafeteria for breakfast and I ate the first of many ham and cheese sandwiches served on triangular, heavily buttered slices of crustless white bread. Notwithstanding the revolution's considerable nutritional education campaigns, crusts, like *nata*—the film that forms on boiled milk—was distasteful to the sensibility of many Cubans. At the Capri Cafeteria, despite the menu's ample list of evocatively named dishes, this sandwich was frequently the only thing available.

Our Bodies Remembered One Another, Ana's and Mine

It was Sunday. The hours before the children would have to return to school were fast approaching their final countdown. I remember a visit to Tania's and Ricardo's apartment where, despite having a new baby of their own, these friends had so often taken our children during the months of waiting for their parents to arrive. I remember being joined by my old friend from Mexico, Eduardo Canudas, and his Cuban wife Bertica on a visit to the city's aquarium. I remember longing for sleep but not wanting to renege on the promised outings.

And of course I remember that first visit to see Ana. I no longer recall whether Hortensia and her coworkers had been warned of our coming, but as we made our way up the broad steps leading into the elegant foyer–turned–reception I heard someone say: "Es la madre de la niña," it's the little girl's mother.

Hortensia stood perfectly erect and still beside a curved banister bordering stairs leading to the second floor. Her dyed black hair and slightly weathered skin made her age hard to determine. She greeted me warmly, pulling me toward the statue-like straightness of her body. I suddenly knew how deeply she'd dreaded this moment and how determined she was to relinquish with dignity the only child upon whom she had ever been able to shower her great store of love.

Together we climbed the stairs to a second floor nursery. Ana was sitting up in her crib, dressed in a spotless outfit of soft pastel yellow cotton. She was huge, almost unrecognizable. I remembered the wisp of a newborn, barely five pounds at birth and not much larger three and a half months later when I'd been forced to let her go. Now I gazed upon a hearty seven-month-old, freshly bathed and smelling of lavender. Although she had cried through most of Robert's daily visits, she stared at me and broke into a smile. It was a haunting smile, filled with sensory recognition.

I picked my daughter up and held her close to my breast, held her against her confusion, heard and returned her nestling sounds. I felt her soft cheek against my own. I breathed in her scent, her essence. Almost four decades later I can still feel her infant skin, still suffer the spliced connection in the deepest folds of cellular memory.

Ana still in my arms, I sank into one of those big Cuban rocking chairs. We swayed slowly. The room emptied of people, or so it seemed. Hortensia and Robert were still there, I'm sure, but I don't remember their faces. Gregory, Sarah, and Ximena were playing on the broad lawn; from time to time their distant voices floated up through an open window, piercing my consciousness.

Our bodies remembered one another, Ana's and mine. Reconnection was primal. But I also sensed her uncertainty, unraveled seams along which the pain of separation trembled. Some time that afternoon Robert and I decided to leave her with Hortensia until she became more comfortable with us. We would visit, stay a bit longer each day, gradually pull her back into the circle of our healing family. By the time we were assigned an apartment we hoped she would be ready to come home to us full time.

When we left, Hortensia told us which bus to take back to Vedado. You want the ninety-one, she instructed, not the forty. The forty will not work. "La cuarenta no les ser-vi-rá." She emphasized the no and spoke the sentence with an inflection I'd never heard before. Nor would I hear it again. She spaced each syllable with precision, successfully holding back the tears.

So began our new life, different for each of us. For Gregory, Sarah, and Ximena that uncertain time without their parents had ended better than it had for so many of the children with whom they'd shared summer camp at

Santa María Beach: children from Guinea Bissau, the Dominican Republic, Guatemala. Children whose parents had been massacred, died in battle, or were enduring long prison sentences. Gregory spoke of a boy about his age, badly burned by napalm, and of another who had stepped on a land mine and was missing a leg. For him, getting to know these children from struggles around the world put another perspective on the months we'd been apart.

A Socialist Process Was Flourishing
in the U.S. Sphere of Influence

We were living in two rooms at the Capri, one of Havana's upscale hotels a block from Vedado's busy Calle veinte tres. The building, with its squared lines, stainless steel trim and tones of beige and rose, was reminiscent of 1940s-era modernity. It stood tall among shorter versions of similar vintage and style. An era, in my stateside memory as well, burdened with touches of interior decoration that included such blights as gold-accented black and chartreuse comedy and tragedy masks, one invariably arranged beside and slightly above its counterpart.

Occasionally a busier structure broke the sameness—an erstwhile private home with its broad verandah and soiled columns. Some of these were faux Greek or Roman, with graceful arches and cool black and white marble tile floors. There was nothing of the beautiful Cuban colonial here, the *media lunas* of colored glass or the old wooden doors with their ornate knockers I would later photograph in Old Habana, La Víbora, Lawton or Santos Suárez. Vedado was built to mimic Miami opulence. It had once been Havana's wealthiest neighborhood. Like every other part of the city its grandeur had faded.

From the Hotel Capri it was a short downhill walk to the malecón, that sweeping semi-circle of weathered stone washed by its pulse of sea. Meyer Lansky held court at this hotel in the 1940s and 1950s, when the U.S. mafia owned many of the city's lavish nightspots. Through doors leading off the lobby I could still glimpse an inner sanctum of plush red velvet and gilt tassels. In another era showgirls and casinos attracted jetsetters to the Caribbean island. Anything went.

Then on January 1, 1959 it all went: the nightspots, mafia bosses, underworld pimps and the prostitutes caught in their sad webs of exploitation. Vegas-style excess erased in a brush stroke of revolutionary morality—except for the Tropicana, now locally owned and kept as an awkward trophy: It caters to a different clientele, was the oft repeated explanation. Workers with the highest production levels earned a night on the town. Few seemed concerned that these model workers were being treated to the same old exhibition of scantily clad women moving seductively behind oversized ostrich feather fans. Maybe it was enough that the entertainers now had broader options and weren't expected to prostitute themselves. During the revolution's early years, women in hip-hugging attire were more likely to be considered positive examples of tropical allure than sexual objects; at least by most Cubans.

Certainly Cuba was no longer a massive playground where women's bodies were shaped and decked out for foreign lust. Gone were the airstrips where private planes brought U.S. CEOs in for a night of fun. Gone were the gambling and exploitation and anything goes exuberance. Yet images of the chorus girl or the curvaceous mulata woman remained attractive to the Cuban sensibility, and the revolution was slow to educate against such objectification. Years into the process, one could still see these images. And sadly, with the more recent push for international tourism they have once again become commonplace.

When Fidel Castro and his rebel army marched victorious into Havana, hotels like the Capri temporarily housed the exhausted troops. Just up the hill the Havana Hilton, only days before its gala opening, became the Havana Libre. Young men in mismatched uniforms, with uncut hair and strings of santería beads tangled in their beards, slept between freshly laundered sheets and thronged the plant-filled atrium lobbies.

For years I have looked at the print given me by the great Cuban photographer Raúl Corrales. In it a young rebel soldier sleeps on a foldout rollaway beneath an elaborately framed portrait of a Rubenesque diva wearing only a strand of pearls. Just behind the cot, on an antique chest, sits an ornate Chinese vase and the soldier's semi-automatic weapon. It is January 1959 and Fidel's troops have just arrived in the capital.

The mansions of the fleeing bourgeoisie became clinics and boarding schools, like those I had driven past two years before to witness thousands of children running and playing in their once exclusive gardens. The old regime's military barracks became educational centers.

In October of 1969 the Cuban revolution was almost eleven years old. A settling in had taken place, an identity shaped. And the United States, Cuba's angry neighbor to the north, had become increasingly frustrated by its inability to bring the tiny island to its knees. A socialist process was flourishing in the U.S. sphere of influence and no scheme to undo it was working.

Frustration didn't stop the bully, so accustomed to getting his way, from continuing to try. Diplomatic isolation, economic embargo, a powerful radio broadcast aimed directly at the Cuban people, rumor and other lies, one failed military invasion and unending coastal infiltrations: all had been tried and failed. Later, during the years we lived on the island, there were biological attacks on the country's swine and sugarcane and a series of James Bond-type attempts on Fidel's life. Today, almost half a century later, neither the embargo nor any of the other plans to defeat the revolution have proved successful. If anything, they have made a proud people more defiant and resistant.

Patriotism Is Always Double-Edged

Fidel and his men—and some women—had several things in their favor: most important, history. A succession of Cuban administrations, up to and including the Batista dictatorship, had exploited and oppressed the island's people while profits accrued to foreign interests and a small domestic bourgeoisie. Cuba's natural resources—sugarcane, tobacco, citrus fruits, fishing, cattle, and as yet unrefined nickel—were worked by the country's poor but did nothing to improve their hard lives. Basically a one-crop economy before the revolutionary takeover, there'd been no attempt at diversification, or long or mid-range planning aimed at raising quality of life.

Before the revolution a good half of Cuba's children didn't attend school. A high percentage of its population was illiterate or semiliterate. Health care didn't reach the rural areas and in the cities was only available to those who could afford to pay. People routinely died of curable diseases. Above and beyond these and other indicators, though, was a commodity international capital couldn't quantify, and still tends to ignore. That commodity was pride. As small and relatively insignificant an island playground as Cuba seemed to the U.S., its people believed they had a right to their lives. They were fiercely proud and tired of being abused.

An oft-repeated story features a U.S. Marine, drunk after a night on the town, climbing up on the downtown monument to Cuba's nineteenth-century hero, José Martí, and urinating on the statue. More than any other event this one symbolized the assault upon a people's dignity that could only be met with decolonization and ferocious self-reliance. A small country with a modest population showed the world that it could, when mobilized by intelligence, courage and charisma, channel a pride that translates to fierce patriotism.

That patriotism gave birth to a David capable of holding off Goliath. The image was often used to encourage people, get them to make that extra bit of effort. Patriotism is double-edged, though. Fed by nationalism, it develops along a steep curve. It can be a force for independence and creativity but also promotes an insular and defensive disconnection, smug sense of superiority, energetic controls, withering of openness, and unwillingness to allow access to a free-flowing exchange of ideas. Cuba's nationalism showed itself capable of standing up to every kind of attack, and for decades. The jury was still out on how it would shape the country's future.

We wasted no time in embracing its vibrant present. Our arrival in Cuba coincided with the end of the Cuban revolution's first brave decade. We lived there through the end of the second, and one of my daughters, Sarah, remained even longer. I went to work in publishing and culture, Robert in radio. We experienced life in a nation constantly besieged by U.S. aggression, an experience that signaled a one hundred eighty degree change from our earlier conditioning.

We took part in the people's militia, participated in the activities of our neighborhood block committee, did all kinds of voluntary work and were involved in many of the revolution's early campaigns to prevent disease, discuss collective problems and write new law. Participation in the establishment of a revitalized union movement and genuinely democratic forms of governance were among my most satisfying learning experiences.

I remember one project I came up with that initially brought great glory to our local Committee for the Defense of the Revolution. Blood was always needed, and the CDRs were charged with encouraging people to donate when they could. With our continual flood of foreign visitors I had a ready-made source; most people were delighted to be able to contribute in this way and our block always had more donations than any other. I can still see little Ana, aged six or seven, trotting a large group of friends and acquaintances to the blood bank on Twenty-third Street. Over a period of years our family must have been responsible for hundreds of such donations. Eventually, though, some higher up realized that taking foreigners' blood might be misconstrued and we were asked to stop.

We also lived through painful setbacks, such as the failure of the ten million ton goal for the 1969–1970 sugarcane harvest. And embarrassing errors in judgment, among them the resistance to a gender analysis of society, a crackdown on small independent producers and repair people, the excesses of the Heberto Padilla affair, periodic repression against gay and lesbian citizens, and the unchecked frustration and anger unleashed against those who chose to avail themselves of the Mariel boatlift.[1] Sometimes, to my shame, I bore silent witness to these disasters or too readily supported the official position when a more critical stance would have been truer to my sense of things. Sometimes I spoke out against them—never a welcome contribution from a foreign woman.

Writing today, almost forty years later, there is always the risk of imprinting current analysis on the ways in which we saw things then. I want to resist this as much as possible. It is important to remember that we were part of something collective and all-embracing, something huge. We followed our leaders but also contributed to the values, thought processes, and choices that shaped their decisions. We were motivated by the sense that we were making revolution; changing our world for the better.

Cuba was at a disadvantage when faced with the power and reach of the United States. We were forever cautioned against playing into the enemy's hands, or providing it with information it could use against the revolution. I often felt I was walking an extremely narrow road between unquestioning support and a more complex reading of events. I generally came down on the side of what the revolutionary leadership proposed although this did not prevent me, several years later, from becoming suspect in the eyes of some.

It Was Important That All Children Have Access to Education

My children completed a great deal of their schooling in Cuba: Gregory from fourth grade through his degree in electrical engineering, Sarah from second grade through her chemical engineering degree, Ximena from first grade through high school, and Ana from her initial experience in one of the revolution's day care centers through the beginning of fifth grade, when she and I moved on to Nicaragua.

Their education was always free and when it involved boarding school it included lodging, meals, health and dental care, sports, cultural activities, and entertainment. At the university level I remember that textbooks and a monthly stipend were also part of the package; the figure of sixty Cuban pesos comes to mind. My son Gregory remembers it being ninety. My daughter Sarah says there was no stipend but that university students had the opportunity of working on campus. She had several jobs teaching students in lower grades, eventually earning ninety pesos a month.

Stipend or earned, and whatever the amount, it was considerable when compared with the 198 pesos per month recent college graduates made, or even the 230 to 300 which was the average salary after a few years in a professional field. Gregory says he remembers spending twenty-five pesos a month on food back then, a meal at a good restaurant could be had for five, a movie cost one, and a bus ride five centavos. Since commodities were scarce, there wasn't much else on which to spend. In those days Cuba set the value of its peso by the U.S. dollar, but the equivalency was fictitious because Cuban currency was not recognized outside the Socialist bloc. Rent, eventually leading to home ownership, was ten percent of the combined salaries of the adults living in an apartment or house. Health care, education, and recreation were all free.

When I arrived in Cuba the school year had started, and Gregory, Sarah, and Ximena had entered fourth grade, first grade, and kindergarten, respectively. None of them liked being at the beca. They would have preferred attending what the Cubans called *escuelas nacionales*, more like their school in Mexico where students studied each day but lived at home. As yet we had no real home, only those two hotel rooms. Besides, Robert and I were eager to throw ourselves into revolutionary work and wondered if the beca wasn't where our children would get the best, or most radicalizing, education.

Looking back, and with the wisdom of experience, I believe we should have sent them to day school at least through their primary years. The middle and high school becas combined factory or field work with the academic subjects and were more successful models of working class education. The teachers were trained in the new revolutionary values. The buildings had excellent pedagogical resources, at least in Latin America and for the times. The experiences kids, including ours, had at those middle and high schools were very good.

At the grade school level the becas left a lot to be desired. The converted mansions of Miramar had makeshift and often poorly lit classrooms. In an effort to enable all Cuban children to go to school, teachers were sometimes recruited from an early age and given only rudimentary training before being put in charge of children not much younger than themselves. Real pedagogy was scarce.

I have a memory in which Gregory's first teacher was fourteen and responsible for twenty-five or thirty fourth graders. Frustrated at their lack of discipline, he got them up one morning at the crack of dawn and forced them to march up and down as he harangued them: "You're nothing but a

bunch of ... of ... of *crepúsculos!*" That crepúsculo means sunset or dusk
was not yet something he knew. Now Gregory tells me this wasn't a teacher
at all, and that it didn't happen in grade school but much later when he was
at the Lenin (high school); and the person involved was another student, a
kid like himself who for some reason had been charged with marching his
fellow students around.

From those early days on, Gregory brought home other stories: some just
as funny but more problematic. In one a teacher had caught one of his charges
masturbating and told him in all seriousness that each time he engaged in
the practice it would destroy a certain number of his brain cells. Fortunately
for my son, he could compensate with what he learned at home. "I'm going
to see if the library has a book about masturbation," he told us, "so I can
show my teacher he's wrong." Gregory did find such a book and brought it
to school. His teacher was genuinely relieved to stand corrected. But it wasn't
a matter of a few offbeat or humorous incidents. The nationwide effort to
extend education to all Cuban children necessarily brought with it moments
that were surprising and occasionally unnerving. Sarah and Ximena also had
their stories, rife with incidents we could hardly have imagined.

On the one hand we were in the tropics, in a country known for its
sensuality. On the other, Cuban parents had entrusted their children to the
revolution's schools and demanded they not be allowed to get in trouble.
Although there were separate dormitories for girls and boys, curious and
inventive kids found ways of getting together. Looking back, my sense is that
sex education wasn't very advanced, but compared with other countries at
the time it probably wasn't that bad.

For a number of years the Cuban revolution consciously sacrificed quality
for quantity; it was important that all children have access to education.
When that goal was met they would work on the details. And they did just
that. During our years in the country we saw a comprehensive but rough
educational system develop into one of true excellence. Teacher training
schools at all levels prepared the educators who were needed. A generation
or so suffered the improvisations leading up to this accomplishment. Our
children's education improved considerably as they moved up through the
system.

Eventually Ximena rebelled against the beca—today she describes some
of the punishments she endured as having been unnecessarily cruel—and
insisted on transferring to a day school. She characterizes her grade school
experience as the worst of her life but her middle and high school years as

among the best. Sarah and Gregory would have liked spending more time with the family but never complained enough to give us pause. Sarah tells me she quickly learned to maneuver in a repressive system. By the time Ximena insisted upon transferring to day school Sarah had her sights on the Lenin, a very special middle and high school. Although four spaces were allotted to her grade school graduates, she was the only student who earned placement.

At the time I thought of the experiments I'd heard about in the Soviet Union and Israel, and I suppose having the children away for the week also freed me up to contribute to building the new society. We often talked about having to sacrifice attention to one's own sons and daughters in the context of our efforts to make a better world for all children. It was a choice I shared with many parents of that time and place. As critical of it as I am today, the decision seemed right back then.

For our son and daughters, early adjustment was also made more difficult by the fact that the school they'd attended in Mexico had been based on the Frenét educational method, with its great emphasis on each child's uniqueness, personal development, and ability to build his or her own capacity for thought and analysis. By comparison the Cuban system was severely regimented. Education was Marxist-oriented and narrowly scientific; other viewpoints were mentioned but not really explored. Even within the Communist ideology, Marx, Engels, Lenin, and others were emphasized while Trotsky and Mao were ignored or presented as traitors to the revolutionary cause.

Still, each of my children got something important from those years of Cuban education. They all learned independence and resilience, collective participation and fairness. Gregory and Sarah won places at the prestigious Lenin, at that time the first of what would be a special middle and high school for outstanding students in each of the country's six provinces.[2] They were accepted purely on the basis of their desire to attend and how well they had done throughout their previous years of schooling.

Sarah, despite bitter feelings of loneliness—a real sense that boarding school meant she had no family—stuck it out until graduation. She was convinced it would make a difference to her future life. Despite her pain she wasn't about to be deterred. My oldest daughter went through long periods of preteen silence. At the time I didn't understand her misery. Had I been more cognizant of her needs I would have insisted she not deny herself as she did.

Gregory adapted well to the Cuban system and managed to create the sort of education he needed. At the beginning of fifth grade, worried that he was a nerd and unhappy that his physical abilities weren't sufficiently developed, he decided to transfer to a sports school for his last two primary grades. I had no idea he was even contemplating such a move. One day I heard from his principal that he'd taken it upon himself to change schools; he'd already made the switch.

Cuban sports schools were privileged. Students attended all the regular classes plus expert training in a sport of their choice. Gregory, knowing he wasn't going to be an athlete, nevertheless correctly believed a couple of years at such a school would make him a more physically competent young man. He majored in swimming the first year, tennis the second. Then, satisfied he'd filled out physically and could compete on a more or less level playing field, he went back to a school that emphasized the academics he loved.

At the Lenin Gregory did well. When the revolution put out the call he signed up for the *destacamento pedagógico,* a training program for future teachers. His decision to study to be a teacher, however, responded to the needs of the revolution rather than what he really wanted to do. He lasted a year and might have gone back to the Lenin. But in his junior year of high school he once again made a choice only he understood. He decided this prestigious all-out educational experience wasn't really for him.

Now It Was Time to Enjoy What Was Left of Our Family

Gregory complained that his time at the Lenin was overly structured; he wanted more time on his own to think and dream. Today I know he also wanted more family time. As my son approached his last two years of high school Robert and I had separated. Gregory knew that I too might soon be gone. Now was the time to enjoy what was left of our family.

The school psychologist tried to talk him out of his decision, arguing that a degree from the Lenin would be his ticket to the higher education of his choice, his key to a successful future. Gregory listened but disagreed. He knew what he wanted. Against everyone's advice he transferred to the high school in our area from which he came home every afternoon to read and think and be with us. He had no trouble going on to college and pursuing the degree he wanted.

Ana began her Cuban schooling at a day care center in the Ministry of Labor, a short walk from where we eventually lived. It was rumored to be one of the city's best crèches. Light and airy, with a low teacher/student ratio, the children were well cared for as they began their education in the incipient preschool skills, social acclimation, justice, fairness, and field to table production. There was an orchard and a vegetable garden where the tots cultivated tomatoes and carrots, watched them grow, then cleaned and served them to one another. A hearty lunch and morning and afternoon snacks were provided. The children changed from their street clothes into colorful, school-supplied outfits. Diapers were on hand for the youngest. Cuban day care accepted infants from the age of six months.

In the years Ana attended the Ministry of Labor day care center, she and her classmates were taken to a number of factories where they could see how the little cups they drank from were made and meet the workers who produced them. Similarly, they learned the process through which their desks and chairs were fashioned. They developed a healthy respect for these objects of everyday use and for the people who worked so hard to make them.

A visit to a Cuban day care center put you in touch with healthy, happy kids, running and shouting and having a great time. The noise and activity level often seemed chaotic but you weren't likely to see them carving up their desks or scribbling on the walls. Respect for community property came from understanding where that property came from, the effort that went into its production.

Although opening and staffing new day care centers was a major goal, and by the time we got to Cuba more than a thousand existed throughout the country, there weren't nearly enough. Long waiting lists existed and the children of working mothers were given priority. To take up the slack, grandmothers and aunts often bore the burden of caring for the youngsters in their families. Without such relatives, and because I worked outside the home, we were able to get Ana into such a center after only a few months.

The idea was that socialist education should start as early as possible. Children who were trained from a young age in emulation rather than competition developed a sense of solidarity foreign to most children in capitalist societies. Emulation—which not only functioned in schools but in factories, offices, and even military units—meant that those involved decided collectively on their goals and then helped one another to achieve them. Thus, in the school setting, collective analysis was encouraged. A child good in math was expected to help one who had trouble in that subject but excelled in history, and she in turn would offer help in her area of expertise. This way everyone succeeded. Competition, it was felt, created individuals who tried to get ahead at the expense of others. Emulation produced mutual encouragement, collectivity, and social harmony.

We were fascinated by this process of emulation. At all the children's schools and in our workplaces as well we saw how it formed good minds and helpful members of the community. At its best, it changed the way people interacted. When competition crept into the equation—and this happened as well, especially with regard to unrealistic goals or overly ambitious individuals—working and learning were less successful.

We even tried this process of emulation at home, organizing weekly family meetings where criticism and self criticism were encouraged. Our daughters especially remember hating those meetings, where they correctly understood that despite an attempt to simulate equality we adults held the power. At the time we believed in the value of pushing socialist educational methods wherever we could.

OLD VALUES SOMETIMES CLASHED WITH THOSE
THE REVOLUTION WAS WORKING TO INSTILL

At Ana's day care center, as in many venues in the Cuba of the late 1960s and early 1970s, old values also sometimes clashed with those the revolution was working so hard to instill. I got a dramatic taste of this one afternoon when I arrived to pick Ana up. As I approached her classroom I saw that her teacher, a young black woman, was urging her charges into two lines: "All the kids with good hair line up over here," she instructed, "all of you with bad hair over there."

The teacher had an afro pick in one hand, a fine toothed comb in the other. Stunned, I looked at her hair. It was short and kinky, clearly what she was calling bad. I couldn't believe she was using such an adjective with the children, reinforcing the idea that one kind of hair was preferable to another. To me this was racism, pure and simple; to say nothing of promoting a body image that would haunt those girls with nappy hair for the rest of their lives. In the United States, black women of my generation had already begun to fight this battle; afros were popular, as dreads and cornrows would be several decades into the future.

Angela Davis was on trial in the United States at the time. Comrades throughout the world were organizing to demand her freedom. No nation had a larger or more active support committee than Cuba. Angela was adored on the island. How was it that her huge afro was featured on posters everywhere while a preschool teacher was being allowed to categorize her little charges' afros as bad hair?

We parents had been told that if we had a problem with a teacher, the school preferred we take it up with the director. I was sure my complaint would be well received. With my usual confidence I went to see the woman who headed the center. She was receptive to my concern and after the last child had been picked up took me to speak with Ana's teacher. "*La compañera* has something she wants to discuss," she began.

I launched into my analysis of race and culture, sure the offending teacher would recognize the harm she was doing both her black and white students. It was as damaging, I argued, for the girls with straight hair to grow up believing it was superior as it was for those with curly hair to be conditioned to believe theirs was bad.

The teacher looked at me, then at the director and back at me. She laughed a short, contemptuous, snort. "You don't understand," she said, "this is what we call our hair: bad. It doesn't mean anything. No. The revolution considers us all the same. Maybe it's different where you come from but in Cuba we say bad hair. It doesn't mean anything."

The school's director tried a couple of angles of her own but the teacher remained adamant. There was no budging her from the position that as a black Cuban woman she knew her culture. I was an outsider. A well-meaning outsider, perhaps, but an outsider nonetheless. Over the next few years I would receive many such lessons in the difficulties of changing long-held values, the delicate nature of outside challenges to those values, and the cultural insensitivity foreigners like myself often exuded.

Racism was deeply rooted in Cuban society, manifest in many mild as well as blatant ways. Sarah remembers walking up M Street one afternoon and hearing someone call out: "Hey there, *blanquita*!" Suddenly she realized she was the voice's target. She turned and saw a young black woman who shouted again: "Hey you, when we take power whiteys like you won't be able to walk in the streets!" Sarah says she turned away and kept on walking.

I never stopped expressing my views, even when they were less than well-received. Once Ana came home from the same school—she was in kindergarten by this time—and told me about another teacher who had crumpled a page of newsprint, stuffed it into a child's mouth and threatened to light it with a match because the child had used "bad" words. I didn't hesitate to complain. From Ana's description this seemed not such an unusual practice. The crumpled paper even had a name: *tarugo*, or plug. I was horrified. Even if the lit match never actually made it to the child's mouth, I argued, the effects of such a threat could be traumatic. This time the teacher was sanctioned and sent for additional psychological training.

These were isolated incidents. Overall, I was impressed with Cuban education, with the efforts to get every child into school, and with the fact that

*Children in the countryside, Las Tunas province, walking to school along an
abandoned railroad track.*

this effort wasn't limited to Havana or the other urban centers but could be
observed as well in remote rural areas. I still have a photograph I took of a
group of clean, well-pressed, healthy Cuban children I encountered walking
to school along a railroad track far from any community. I loved how clearly
the revolution prioritized and treated children. Even under fairly extreme
food rationing, infants, children up to the age of twelve, pregnant women,
nursing mothers and the old and ill received special consideration. The
slogan "Los niños nacen para ser felices" (Children are born to be happy)
reflected a reality that was always palpable.

Ximena Stood Her Ground

"It's not fair!" Ximena cried, as she looked at me beseechingly.

December, 1969. We'd been in Cuba for a few months and were getting to
know *radio bemba*—literally communication via word of mouth, or gossip.
The word bemba was one of those unexamined holdovers from the old
society. It referred, with its clear but unacknowledged quota of racism, to the
stereotypically full lips of Afro-Cuban features. In Cuba, radio bemba spread
the news faster than a sea bird flew.

To make sure that every child from birth to twelve years of age enjoyed equal opportunity Christmas shopping, an elaborate system had been put in place. Families entered a neighborhood lottery for as many tickets as they had young children. Each ticket stipulated a day and time when the child would be welcomed at a local store to choose his or her toys. If you drew a low number you'd have your choice of stock; higher numbers on later days necessarily meant slimmer pickings.

Each child was allowed a major purchase costing more than three pesos and two smaller items costing less. The lottery, with its element of chance, leveled the playing field. If you drew a low number it wasn't because of economic advantage or some special connection to the salesperson. If you drew high, the toy you wanted might be gone but it wouldn't be anyone's fault. If everyone worked hard and production went up, the following Christmas would surely see a better selection and more of each item. This was something we were already beginning to absorb: under socialism working together toward a common goal raised overall production, accruing to everyone's benefit rather than to a particular industry's profit margin.

Like so many of the details of daily life, the family ration book determined where this holiday toy shopping would be done. We hadn't been issued an apartment so we didn't yet have a ration book. Our contact at the Foreign Ministry came by our hotel one Saturday morning to take us to a special store for foreign workers. He assured the kids the toys were the same.

Gregory, as always, stood back, more interested in his sisters getting what they wanted than in choosing a toy for himself. Besides the items on offer didn't really appeal to him. Since our arrival he'd been dropping by the National Puppet Theater and was learning to make simple puppets from found materials and the little outfits Ana was outgrowing. All these years later, one of these—crafted from the delicate wood of a cigar box whose tiny nails he'd removed, straightened, and reused to attach the face—still hangs in the corner of my studio.

I knew Gregory missed the telescope he'd been forced to leave behind in Mexico. Upon hearing a local radio program about astronomy he'd called the station, gotten the number of the small observatory on the outskirts of the city, and wrangled an invitation to visit. Adriana Esquirol, the young woman astronomer who ran the place, sometimes sent a jeep to pick him up, so he could spend the whole night watching the stars. Gregory told me that before the revolution she had peddled Chiclets in the street.

Ana was easy. She delighted in just about anything one waved in front of her, including the playful fingers of the woman at the Miramar wellness center who cared for her until we arrived. Like all seven-month-olds, if Ana could put it in her mouth it held her attention.

Sarah had her eye on a book about butterflies. She was camped out in a far corner of the store reading it avidly through her sister's noisy complaints and trying hard to pretend this wasn't her family.

Ximena stood her ground. I couldn't have been more pleased. I wasn't that keen on guns but in a revolutionary society, in which women patrolled their neighborhoods and stood guard alongside men at their workplaces, how could children's cowboy outfits display this sexist bias? I looked at our contact from the Ministry. She's right: it's not fair, you know. Isn't there something we can do?

Miguel—that may or may not have been his name—much preferred the course of least resistance. Let's see what else she's entitled to, he urged, trying to divert Ximena's attention from her original choice. But my daughter was in for the long haul. She held the suit's skirt, shirt and belt firmly beneath one arm as she continued to eye the hat and gun that came with the outfit's version for boys.

At five, Ximena was confident in opinion and purpose. Just the day before, to an adult who'd asked the proverbial "what do you want to be when you grow up" she'd responded: "I want to be black. I've only been here a few months and, look, already I'm mulato!" Ximena's skin was very white, her eyes and hair dark. In dramatic contrast with Mexico City's dearth of black people, Havana had introduced her to a range of skin tones, from ivory to ebony. She loved it.

Now she kept her eyes on me. Fix it, they said.

I put my arm around her tiny shoulder and together we marched to the counter. The scene had not escaped the attention of store manager or employees. "We're new here," I began, addressing myself to the woman whose badge indicated managerial status. "I've taught my daughter about the revolution, how people work together so everyone can have their fair share. All she wants is the hat and gun the boys who get this toy receive. Wouldn't it be possible to let her have the complete outfit? It would be a shame to disillusion her so early on. . . ."

My question hung for a moment or two, unanswered. The manager and one of her salespeople made rapid eye contact. Several other shoppers also looked our way, some with bemused expressions. Miguel from the Ministry stared at his shoes.

Left: Sarah, Ximena, Ana, Margaret, and Gregory in living room of Havana apartment, 1970. Right: "Souvenir of my School," "To Be Educated is the only way to be free" (inside book). Ana at a second-grade school activity, image of José Martí at right.

"Of course you can have your hat and gun," the manager said, stooping to speak with Ximena eye to eye as she opened a cowboy outfit marked *varón* and handed my daughter the items in question. Ximena's dark eyes sparkled. I felt redeemed. Perhaps the manager had only wanted to avoid a further scene. Perhaps she had decided this child from another country deserved special treatment. Perhaps she'd realized there was indeed an element of unfairness, and wanted to make it right. Whatever prompted her response, she was one of those all too rare middle management people for whom the revolution meant applying creative solutions rather than retreating into pass-the-buck lethargy. We emerged from the store, our revolutionary faith intact.

Not long after this, December 25th ceased to be the day on which Cuban children received their toys. International Children's Day in June took its place. Christmas remained a religious holiday, celebrated by people of faith, but the state-sanctioned children's holiday was brought more in line with the revolution's ideology.

CHAPTER 4

FOOD, FOOD, FOOD

Our First Taste of Revolutionary Bureaucracy

In February 1970, our Ministry contact called to say we had been assigned an apartment and he'd be coming by to take us to see it. By this time we'd been at the Capri for several months. When we'd realized the move to our own place wouldn't be happening as quickly as we hoped, we'd brought Ana to live with us there. This had meant requesting a crib, but that proved a lot easier than cutting through the red tape to an apartment of our own.

We were getting our first taste of revolutionary bureaucracy. Most problems were solved through one's workplace and often it proved easier to obtain what we needed through Robert's than through mine. I quickly discovered that despite the revolution's line on women's equality, many of the old gendered practices remained in place. Issues raised by men were likely to be addressed more promptly and, where heterosexual couples were concerned, most household problems were solved through the man's factory or office. The problems of same-sex couples were not yet on the agenda, in Cuba or anywhere else.

I had accepted Rolando Rodriguez's invitation to work at the Book Institute. Robert had gone to work at Radio Havana Cuba, the short-wave answer to the U.S.-based Radio Martí. The Cubans not only had their own broadcasts but gave airtime to other Latin American revolutionary movements. Programming was in French, Portuguese, English, Spanish, Quechua, Creole, Guaraní, and maybe another language or two I've forgotten. On Radio Havana the Vietnamese also targeted a U.S. American listening audience several times a day.

It was through Radio Havana that we were finally given our apartment. The day we saw it for the first time I could hardly believe how spacious it was. Located down the hill from the Capri, on Línea just a couple of blocks from the malecón, it occupied the whole ninth floor of a ten-story building. Twenty or thirty years earlier this had been luxury living. The floor-throughs had four or five bedrooms, two baths, large living rooms, dining rooms, and kitchens. A long central hall linked the rooms. An ample terrace looked down on Línea with a diagonal view to the sea.

Through the first decades of revolution, education and health care took precedence over building upkeep and repair. Tropical moisture had corroded window casings and iron railings, glass had been broken and couldn't be replaced, paint was in short supply. Hot water heaters stopped working. Shower heads became clogged by hard water lime deposits, and without the cleaning supplies that might have prevented the buildup, fixing them was impossible. Buildings like ours had gotten run-down.

Considering the limitations, those in charge of making our home livable had done an astonishing job. They had furnished it with beds, tables, chairs, and other items taken from a main warehouse where we were told the contents of abandoned homes were stored. Some of these pieces were beautiful, like the large dining room table upon which we would eat, around which we would talk, at which the kids would study, and upon which I would spread my incipient prints when I learned photography during my last few years in the country. Some of the furnishings were eyesores, like a gilt-edged mirror-covered dressing table, a number of its panels cracked or missing. This became my desk. I wrote many poems and articles and at least a dozen books on its gaudy, slightly higher than comfortable, surface.

The mattresses were worn and lumpy. We found pieces of old plywood and placed them on top of broken springs. A large room off the long central hall must have been a studio or library. One of its walls was covered floor to ceiling with built-in wooden cabinets and shelves. This started out as Robert's study, becoming Gregory's bedroom for a while when he got older. Telltale mounds of fine sawdust told us the wood-lined wall was infested with termites. Following local advice I spent hours with a hypodermic needle shooting spurts of kerosene into the miniscule holes.

Our Ministry contact was able to change the ancient cookstove for a simple but newer four-burner apartment range. It even had a working oven. The refrigerator was another story. By current Cuban standards it was considered adequate, even a luxury. In it I became acquainted with the only cockroaches I'd ever known to actually thrive in subzero conditions. Even the small freezer compartment swarmed with them. They were of the little energetic variety I remembered from my years on New York's Lower East Side. Their giant tropical relatives lived elsewhere in the apartment.

We had brought with us a few posters from Mexico, and a few more were on the walls when we moved in. These and anything else that balanced on a nail had to be placed where nails existed. New nails, as well as the plaster required to fill holes if we hoped to move the old ones, were both unavailable. As was window glass. About half the panes on the glassed in front porch were broken, along with one in the girls' bedroom where even the frame was gone. When hurricane-level winds roared in from the sea and swept through our ninth floor apartment we protected ourselves by shutting doors or, eventually, fixing the occasional piece of found cardboard or lumber over a gaping hole to block the gale's force.

As we settled in, grateful for such space (most Cubans still lived crowded in with relatives, divorced couples often continued to share the same quarters, and newborns piled into rooms with older brothers and sisters), we began to learn what Cuban housewives faced. And yes, despite the fact that women were by then working outside the home in impressive numbers, they still did most of the shopping, housecleaning, and childcare. Wash soap, cleanser, disinfectant, mops, brooms, and buckets were all rationed, most of them severely.

Yet Cubans astounded me in their compulsion to cleanliness. This may have been a cultural characteristic or because a tropical climate breeds infection and cleanliness prevents disease. But it went far beyond any rationale I could understand. For women, freshly shaved legs and underarms were a must (and of course razor blades were also in short supply). Deodorant was the number one item foreigners were asked to leave behind. I quickly noticed that even on a bus so crowded that scores hung precariously from its doors, if passengers perceived the slightest body odor a circle would open around the offending passenger.

An Amazing Collection of Creative Recipes

We wanted as much as possible to live like ordinary Cubans. We knew our condition as foreigners privileged us: we could come and go at will and had been assigned a spacious apartment rather than being forced to crowd in with family or in-laws. We understood the policy of not burdening foreign technicians with the hardship of scarcity; their help in the push toward development entailed enough sacrifice and it seemed reasonable to provide them with special ration books offering the greater quantity, quality, and variety obtainable at designated stores.

But we weren't foreign technicians. We insisted on the Cuban quotas. With our apartment came our ration book, the ordinary Cuban version which we used with pride. Among the foreigners we knew, only one other family had opted for the Cuban system. This was Roque Dalton, his wife Aida, and their three sons, José Antonio, Jorge, and Roque, Jr. The Salvadoran revolutionary poet and his family wanted, as we did, to share as much as possible the country's hardships. Several U.S. American friends barely hid their contempt, arguing that we were making it harder on the Cubans by asking to be included in their system. They offer us something better for a reason, they said, and you have to be different.

Shopping was drudgery. There was no other word for it. Radio bemba would spread the word about a shipment of lettuce or an extra allotment of onions. Long lines would immediately form at our neighborhood market. Standing in these lines when you had a full-time job was all but impossible, so grandparents and elderly aunts and uncles did most of the food shopping. Sometimes a neighbor would offer to take our ration book and get our quota as well as her own.

I still remember the amounts available to our family—with occasional modifications—until our last few years on the island when farmers' markets came into existence and food availability increased. During those early years we could purchase two long and fairly tasteless loaves of white bread a day for our family of six, three quarters of a pound of beef per person every nine days (we could take this as steak or ground or any combination thereof), twenty-four eggs a week for the six of us, four ounces of coffee per week (eventually suspiciously diluted with soy from Mexico), thirty-six pounds of sugar (either brown or white or part one part the other) and twenty-four pounds of rice a month, one smallish bag of pasta for the family, and one small can per month of a tomato sauce called Vitanova.

We received three liters of fresh milk per day, one for each of the younger children, and twelve cans a month of sweetened condensed milk for the rest of us. I often boiled the unopened cans, producing a coffee and milk colored treat we called *cajeta*. The rice ration was ample for us but meager for the average Cuban family. Nine liters of cooking oil and four pounds of lard made up our monthly ration. When such items were available we had access to small but adequate amounts of salt, pepper, vinegar, and other basic condiments. Fresh produce was scant, certainly less than we were accustomed to; depending on availability each family would get its share.

My journal from March 1970 lists a particular day's family ration of ten oranges, one large cabbage, ten medium-sized onions, two sweet green peppers and an indeterminate number of tomatoes. From the same journal entry I see that we were getting some fish each week. Ana, who was still eating baby food, was entitled to twenty jars per month. As she had three meals a day at her crèche this was adequate. Robert didn't drink coffee so I enjoyed more than the average adult. Each adult also got two packs of cigarettes and since neither of us smoked these were always good trades for an extra bit of something we preferred.

Over the years the limitations imposed by long-term rationing produced an amazing collection of creative recipes. We women would exchange them with one another as we did our CDR guard duty, patrolling our neighborhood late into the steamy Havana nights. Tomato sauce made without tomatoes, mango marmalade using only the skins from the fruit, a flan that combined fresh pumpkin with the contents of one of those cans of extremely sweet condensed milk. Sometimes we would get to our neighborhood grocer to find we could buy a couple of pounds of a hot dog-like sausage called *butifara*. This was something special and popular served with the rice.

Split peas were plentiful and split pea jokes abundant. One, told in the form of a recipe, instructed the listener to soak the peas in water, then discard

Cuban farmer.

the water, boil the peas in more water and again discard the liquid. The joke
continued for as many boilings as its teller could muster. And finally the
punch line: then throw out the peas—a long pause—and the pot.

Food packaging was nonexistent. A neighbor, who studied such things,
told us Cubans produced about a tenth of the landfill in countries with
similar populations and standards of living. We brought our own bottles to
be refilled, and our own mesh bags in which we carried our groceries home.
This was effective recycling long before the concept became popular elsewhere.
Neighbors showed great solidarity, letting one another know when there was
something new to be purchased. Trading was elevated to an art.

The best cuts of meat definitely went to the butcher's friends. Our butcher
was married to Florinda. They lived in the broken down shack next door to
our building; it was squeezed between two highrises, remnant of another era.
Carlos—I cannot remember his real name—always had a hibiscus flower
stuck behind his left ear. Each morning he replaced the dash of pale orange
pink from the day before with a fresh one. What it meant to him I never
knew; perhaps *flor linda* was a reference to his beloved. On my last visit to
Cuba in the late 1990s I saw Carlos, long retired, sitting on his makeshift
porch, rocking in the sun, that signature hibiscus still behind his ear. I've
heard that Florinda has since died.

Production and Consumption Ran an Unbroken Line from Field to Dinner Table

The most moving food emotion I remember from those early days, and the
most difficult to transmit, was the sense that production and consumption
ran an unbroken line from field to dinner table. Word would go out that extra
hands were needed to harvest potatoes in Havana's green belt. If allowed to rot
in the fields they would be lost. Friday afternoon would come around, we'd get
home from work, change, and head down to our local block committee, where
trucks would be waiting to take us for a few hours of volunteer digging or
weeding. There was no coercion to participate in this work, unless the example
set by peers could be read as coercion. If we felt like it, we joined in.

The following Monday morning, freshly dug potatoes stood in proud
pyramids at our neighborhood market. Potatoes just in, our grocer would
shout, and we knew we had helped bring the crop from earth to shelf. Surely
the fact that Cuba is a small country and that, at least back then, transportation problems kept foodstuffs pretty well localized, added to the immediacy
of this almost magical awareness of cause and effect. Those potatoes tasted

great. The experience of digging and then buying, preparing and eating them, is one I have never forgotten. Like so many successful endeavors it is exquisitely simple and powerfully satisfying.

Sarah remembers her enthusiasm in seventh grade, when the students spent an occasional weekend harvesting seasonal crops. The school's principal was always out there working with them. Later though, during her university years, she says voluntary work wasn't all that voluntary. *Voluntariamente a fuerzas,* she and her schoolmates called it: forced voluntarism.

As soon as I arrived in Cuba I noticed the long lines in front of pizzerias serving the most uninspired pizza I could have imagined: little more than a smear of watery tomato sauce and a sprinkling of sour cheese over baked on a stale piece of tough dough. Those first days and weeks I couldn't fathom standing in line for such a meal.

But when I'd been in the country a year or two, was living in my own apartment and preparing food for a family of six, I suddenly understood. Variety was the enticement. Anything a bit different was a welcome relief. Cuban pizza reinvented itself again and again. *Pizza a caballo* (pizza on horseback) consisted of a slice of dough with a bit of tomato sauce and a fried egg on top. I remember it costing one peso twenty centavos.

Havana had many restaurants, ranging from pizzerias or places that featured simple bowls of fried rice, to the most elegant eateries, some of which were mostly frequented by foreigners. Some restaurants had romantic histories, like La bodeguita del medio or La Floridita, where in the early 1950s Ernest Hemingway and his friends had hung out sipping the famous Cuban mojito—a short glass of rum and tonic with a sprig of fresh mint.

Some restaurants featured a single food and were named accordingly, like the one just up the hill from us. It was called El conejito and everything was made from rabbit. I remember a period in which we would eat there once every couple of weeks. I would arm myself with a plastic-lined purse—the one that had been part of my attire on the long journey from Mexico to Cuba—and take my place at the head of the table. When we finished eating, each member of the family would pass his or her leftovers along and I'd scoop them into my bag. Those bits of rabbit—baked, braised, breaded, steamed, with vegetables, or in pate—added interest to our meals for days.

The better restaurants required reservations. For years these were made beginning one minute after midnight; we would all take turns dialing until we got what we wanted or gave up. For simpler eating, like everyone else we joined the ever-present lines.

Inside an old foundry, Havana.

Living room, Regla,
Havana.

CHAPTER 5

TEN MILLION TONS OF SUGAR AND ELEVEN FISHERMEN

I Wanted a Second Opinion

I'd been ill my last months in Mexico, actually since the final six weeks of my pregnancy with Ana. The major symptom was a high level of albumin in my blood; dangerous if unchecked. I'd been ordered to bed the month before Ana's birth. The delivery itself brought my albumin level back down to normal but I continued to experience pain and attacks of weakness and nausea. Must be a bad stomach flu, I thought.

Then came the repression. Forced into hiding, I couldn't see a doctor or do any of the tests a doctor would have prescribed. Once, while we were hiding at Laurette and Arnaldo's, Laurette's son-in-law Santiago, who was an internist, examined me. He thought it was my kidneys but without tests couldn't be sure. We didn't want to risk my going to a hospital so Santiago prescribed a broad spectrum antibiotic which I ingested on and off throughout the next few months. My time in Prague was punctuated by bouts of high fever, sometimes verging on delirium. When I started passing kidney stones I stopped blaming a stomach flu.

My arrival in Cuba meant, among so much else, that I could see a specialist, have the necessary exams and find out what was wrong. Bouts of debilitating pain, always accompanied by extreme overall discomfort, pushed me to do this sooner rather than later. I still remember my shock when the doctor, a very young black woman named Ana Espinoza who had just graduated from medical school, told me I needed to have my left kidney removed. It was covered with stones, she said, and badly atrophied. In fact, the infection was so severe that even after the operation I would have to continue taking an antibiotic for months.

My first response, understandable for someone who had grown up under capitalism, was that I wanted a second opinion. How could I be sure my doctor knew what she was talking about? Where I came from all sorts of operations were performed to keep the surgeon's kids in expensive schools, even to provide data for studies that would accrue to the doctor's reputation rather than the patient's health. I decided to call my good friend Roberto Fernández Retamar. Roberto, poet and editor of the important *Casa de las Américas literary* magazine, would be able to tell me what to do.

When I mentioned a second opinion Roberto laughed. There was understanding in his voice but he said in a socialist society this wasn't necessary. No one will be making money on this operation, he assured me, and there are probably a number of patients competing for your hospital bed. If it would make you feel better I'll be glad to give your doctor a call but I'm sure a number of experts have already discussed the case. Here these sorts of decisions are made collectively.

Although I no longer see the decision of a doctor in socialism as automatically superior to one made by a doctor in capitalism (there are decent individuals in both systems), Roberto's explanation reassured me. The prestigious surgeon who would perform the operation—Ana was only my *médica de cabecera*, my bedside doctor—called me in to have a talk. Before the end of 1969 I was operated on at Havana's large Calixto García Hospital and then almost immediately moved to the nearby Piti Fajardo where the rooms were nicer, and mine was private. Despite my wanting to avoid special treatment, the Cubans often insisted on giving those from outside what they themselves didn't have.

At the Calixto I had been in a ward. Adjacent to my cubicle an elderly man was dying of stomach cancer. His family visited him every day. One daughter was a Party member, the other disenchanted with the political process; her husband in prison for conspiring against the revolution. I had long conversations with both these young women, the first of many subsequent talks in which I gleaned a sense of the family divisions such dramatic social change can provoke.

The inveterate journalist, I spent much of my hospital time asking nurses, doctors, technicians, and anyone else with whom I came in contact what the revolution had meant to them; if it had changed their lives and how.

Ana Espinoza sat on the edge of my bed for hours as she told me about her childhood growing up in a poor family of subsistence farmers. "We were nine brothers and sisters," she said. "I couldn't have dreamed of becoming a doctor. Never even heard of something called medical school when I was young."

The woman who swept and washed the floor of my hospital room each morning responded to my question differently. "Honey," she said as she paused and leaned on her mop handle, "the revolution meant I could marry for love!" A broad smile accompanied the statement. "I married young and it was terrible. He beat me and it got worse. But I never dared leave. How would I have supported myself? When the revolution came along I knew I could escape. I got out of that prison, was able to get a job and make my own money. Then I married for love."

Everyone had a story.

Except for the VIP unit on the seventh floor of the Fajardo, both hospitals were old and somewhat threadbare. Many doctors and technicians had been lured to the United States with promises of higher salaries and better living conditions. This brain drain was being felt in many fields. The revolution was graduating new health professionals though, and also sending medical students to other countries for specialization.

Soon there would be more than enough well-trained doctors, and Cuba, with its internationalist generosity, would offer many to countries around the world. The revolution would develop the expertise in medicine for which it is known today. A whole new prevention-based system was put in place. Now teams of health professionals live and work in neighborhoods where they get to know their potential patients in wellness and acquire an understanding of individual problems. Excellent medical attention is one of the Cuban revolution's great successes.

In the late 1960s and early 1970s, in hospitals where trained personnel were overworked, family members stepped in. They brought food, sometimes even a replacement light bulb or two. But even then cases were thoroughly explained to patients and options forthrightly discussed. Procedures were sometimes performed without the privacy I had come to expect as a member of the U.S. middle class or in Mexico, but the expertise was clear. These Cubans have their priorities straight, I thought.

I remained at the Fajardo almost a week. Robert was able to bring the children to visit. All three immediately asked to see my incision, still a bit puffy and raw. Sarah cried, not tears of horror or repulsion but those one cries when someone one loves has been hurt. Ximena asked: "Mommy, why did they have to do that to you? Why couldn't they have cured you with medicines?" I told her some problems can be cured with medicines while others require an operation. "Yes, and some can only be cured by death," added Gregory.

After one of the painful tests to make sure my remaining kidney was healthy enough to do the work of two, a very large x-ray technician had literally climbed on top of me to press closed the recently opened artery in my groin. A few weeks later I recognized the man on a crowded city bus. I greeted him cheerfully but he didn't have a clue. Probably hadn't looked at my face, or didn't recognize his patients upright.

I healed quickly from the removal of my kidney. It was a relief to no longer suffer those repeated attacks of excruciating pain and despair. Eager to return to work I ignored instructions to take it easy, to allow my body—a thin red scar now half circling its mid section—to heal.

In Cuba all of 1969 through the middle of 1970 was like a year and a half compressed into one. The country had taken on a great challenge: harvesting ten million tons of sugarcane through a season arbitrarily stretched from twelve to eighteen months. On the busy section of Twenty-third Street people referred to as La Rampa, across from the Hotel Habana Libre, a huge neon display featured a thermometer on which we watched the temperature of the harvest rise. From four million tons to four and a half. Then five, and less than a month later seven. Everyone was involved; we all had a stake in the challenge.

The plan was to dramatically jumpstart Cuba's ailing economy in the only way a one-crop nation could imagine possible. In the country's most productive years harvests had come in at around six or seven million tons. The price of sugar on the world market was high just then. If we could make ten million tons, those who devised the scheme argued, it would be a great boon.

There were dissenters as well, among them agronomists and other experts. They pointed out that the effort required for such a feat would negatively affect all other areas of production. They made their calculations and presented facts and figures but the revolutionary leadership had taken its decision. Following the Party line became a matter of patriotism. Few wanted to be seen as doubters. Those experts who insisted this was not a good idea were demoted and relegated from view.

Cutting cane is among the toughest manual labor there is, but almost everyone took a turn. This mass participation was obviously more about collective contribution than expediency. It was important the goal be met, but it was clear that energizing people's consciousness was also part of the plan. In fact, transporting and feeding all the volunteers must have cost more than what many of the amateurs produced. Cutting cane for the ten million ton harvest was a matter of honor. Unless you were severely disabled you were going to sign up to do your bit, and many who were disabled also signed up.

I was barely out of the hospital, three or four weeks as I remember. But when I learned about a women's contingent going from the Book Institute I eagerly joined. My doctor said if I insisted on going—she understood I wasn't going to be dissuaded—I should make my contribution in the kitchen. Those who cooked for the cutters got up each morning at three, to peel vast numbers of potatoes and wash rice to feed hundreds. But at least they did this work indoors and sitting down.

We were forty-eight women, most laborers from the Institute's print shops and binderies accustomed to long hours of physical work. Those of us from the editorial departments were in the distinct minority. Within this minority two of us were foreigners. I'd met Basilia Papastamatieu on one of my earlier visits to Cuba. Of Greek origin, she had grown up in Argentina and, like so many of us, had come to the country for political reasons. Basilia was a lovely person and terrific poet. We were friends and chose bunks next to one another in the barracks where we were assigned.

A couple of days into our week-long stint Basilia and I got a hefty taste of Cuban women's penchant for modesty—and cleanliness. Without thinking about it we'd violated the customary attitude around the former by casually undressing each night in plain view of our sister cane-cutters. Off with the t-shirt, on with the night shirt; we were all women. One of the print shop workers took us aside and explained that Cuban women preferred to undress under their t-shirts, removing the daytime garment and replacing it with their pajamas, quickly and with their backs to the others. It was clear they preferred we follow their example.

The issue of cleanliness was brought up with a bit more ceremony. With only three showers for forty-eight women, Basilia and I reasoned one bath a day was enough. Not so the Cuban women. They took two, some of them even three. They didn't seem to mind lining up for a half hour or more as long as they could keep themselves completely clean. The camouflaging scent of Evening in Paris, the cheap cologne in stores at the time, served to override residual odors.

It wasn't long before a camp supervisor asked Basilia and me to come with her for a little talk. She sat us down at the end of one of the long cement dining hall benches—everyone else was taking their afternoon siesta (although no doubt some were showering for the second or third time that day)—and kindly explained how body odor was distasteful to the Cuban sensibility. "The women would really like you to shower more often," she told us. It was more a request than a suggestion.

Although I had come to the camp knowing I would be working in the kitchen, I longed for a chance to cut at least a few stalks of cane in this historic harvest. Each night I watched the other women sharpening the steel of their machetes until the worn blades shone. I sat apart. And so one morning when no one was looking I grabbed a spare machete, slipped from the kitchen and mounted the tractor-drawn wagon on its way to the fields. The cutters were singing. A woman next to me started to object. I put my fingers to my lips.

The sun was just beginning to come up. The early morning unpackaged an almost translucent light. Mist still shrouded the rows of cane, which were taller by a couple of feet than I was. We clambered from the cart and, looking to the other women for clues about method and efficiency, I began to swing my machete. "Closer to the ground," the woman next to me said, "you don't want to waste an ounce of sugar." I bent lower, swung harder, tried to slice the thick cane as close to the earth as I could.

Then—how much later I don't know—I came to on the back seat of a jeep. Someone was driving me into Havana to the nearest hospital. I had passed out. I wondered how many stalks I had cut: a handful, a dozen, two, none? I was overcome by a deep feeling of shame. Because of some romantic notion about participating in the ten million ton harvest I was costing the revolution the precious time and resources being used to rescue me from the fields. In my barely postoperative state the effort had been too much. But people seemed to understand that I'd only wanted to help. At least this is what they expressed to my face. No real damage had been done. I was soon out of the hospital again and back at work, although I sat the rest of the harvest out.

Robert had his own health problems during this time. A serious case of hepatitis kept him hospitalized for several weeks. During the next emotional days he was released for a weekend visit but required to keep a low profile. It was clear that our months underground, forced separation from the children, and risky journeys to Cuba—with all the anxiety and uncertainty involved—had taken a physical as well as psychological toll on us both.

Cuba Wanted Her Fishermen Back

The news spread via radio bemba and every other communication medium. Eleven Cuban fishermen had been attacked, their small boats capsized, the men themselves kidnapped. They were being held on a Caribbean atoll. The rightist group Alfa 66 claimed responsibility for the operation, and demanded a number of counterrevolutionary prisoners in exchange for their release.

Cuba wanted her fishermen back. Havana's streets filled with people. Many carried signs proclaiming the country's sovereignty. Short poems were angry and also filled with the culture's unique brand of comedic irony. I was beginning to understand why the Cuban revolution was so often referred to as "Marxism in Spanish." Some placards displayed pictures of donkeys, and a few people led live donkeys with sandwich signs sporting the slogan: "Nixon is My Son." The X in Nixon was a swastika and this was true in the official press as well. Other placards read: "We will not trade the sons of our people for lousy mercenary worms," "Nixon: Out of Cambodia Out of Vietnam," "Give Us Back Our Brothers, We Demand the Release of our Fishermen."

Since the early sixties, when the United States had broken diplomatic relations with Cuba, the Swiss Embassy handled transactions between the two countries. An Interests Section occupied offices in the old U.S. embassy building, a foreshortened glass and steel U.N. lookalike located on the malecón a few blocks from our apartment. From our balcony we saw dozens, then hundreds and finally thousands of people gathering before the building. That first night hundreds camped out. The kids were home from school for the weekend and joined me in bringing the demonstrators coffee and squares of bread—from the two loaves our family received each day.

The next morning the crowds increased. Looking down from our window I could see workers constructing a platform across the street from the Interests Section. Mostly the assemblage milled about sharing thermoses of coffee and conversing. Periodically, as if on cue, everyone shouted: "We demand the return of our fishermen!" Or "Cuba sí, Yankees no!" Although Alpha 66 was made up of anti-Castro Cubans, everyone knew the United States was behind this latest act of aggression, just as it was behind each new assault upon the revolution.

The phone rang. It was Rolando Rodríguez, director of the Book Institute. Despite the fact that I worked at the Institute, I hadn't seen Rolando since the

Orfilas had given us refuge in Mexico and he'd come to visit one night. He wanted to know if I'd be home for a while, said he wanted to bring someone over. The man who arrived with the head of the Institute was a Party official. He said it was important to encourage people to stay in the streets, keep their spirits high. Cuba might be a small country, he said, but we would show the world we won't stand for this attack upon our sovereignty. We'll remain firm until our fishermen are returned.

Of course I agreed. I knew these two men weren't in my apartment to state the obvious. They wanted my help with something. Soon the Party official revealed what it was: "There are at least fifteen thousand people out there right now," he waved his hand in the direction of the malecón, "and we think the crowd will continue to grow." Party members always spoke in the first person plural. It was a way of downplaying the individual and emphasizing the collective and was a custom I myself would adopt for a number of years, although I never thought of joining the Party. "We're inviting a few distinguished personalities to speak to them tonight, the man added, to encourage them to keep their spirits up."

The comrade continued: "We have asked Che's father to address the people. And Camilo Torres' mother. Several representatives from Latin American revolutionary movements will be among the speakers. We would like you to join them if you're willing." I was flattered to hear myself referred to as a distinguished personality. I also felt honored.

I didn't represent any revolutionary movement anywhere, although I was supportive of many. Neither was I the father of the Heroic Guerrilla, as Che was known, or the seventy-year-old mother of the Colombian priest turned revolutionary martyr. Still, I was thrilled to be asked to speak to the crowd that grew larger with each passing hour. I knew I was being recruited in representation of progressive U.S. Americans. I told the men sitting in my living room I'd consider it an honor to participate. "Someone will pick you up at five thirty," one of them said.

I don't remember what I said looking out at the sea of faces that night. I'd already had some experience addressing large crowds; it had always been easy for me to improvise and my five minutes seemed well received. I was introduced as a U.S. American living in Cuba. I'm sure an important part of my appeal was that I was from the country that sheltered Alpha 66.

The great Cuban poet Nicolás Guillén, the beloved prima ballerina Alicia Alonso, Che's father, Camilo's mother, revolutionaries from Brazil, the Dominican Republic, and Guinea also greeted the crowd. One of the fishermen's mothers spoke, and two grade school children. Young people in Cuba seemed well aware of what was going on in the world, especially those parts of the world struggling for independence.

My own children quickly acquired this consciousness. Walking through the energized crowd in the early days of the crisis, a radio reporter asked Sarah if she had anything she wanted to say. With complete self-assurance she took the microphone: "All the world's children honor the eleven fishermen and demand that the Yankee assassins give them back to us in the same condition in which they were captured," she declared, then smiled sweetly as she handed the microphone back.

The next day or two passed in a haze of patriotic fervor. The children reluctantly returned to school and we went back to work, but everyone's mind was on the drama unfolding on some tiny island in the Caribbean. Rumor had it negotiations were underway, with Britain mediating. The atoll was part of the vast British Commonwealth.

The second telephone call came two days later. The fisherman had been released and would arrive that evening at José Martí International Airport. Those who had been good enough to speak to the demonstrators a few days before were invited to go to the airport to meet them and to be present with Fidel when he officially welcomed them home—again on that platform across from the Interests Section, which was now being enlarged and made sturdier. Powerful night lights were also being installed around the area. In time this would become a permanent protest site.

I was thrilled to be going to the airport. I was curious as to what the fishermen would look like. It was said they were from Caibarién, a small village on the island's northern shore. How would their week-long ordeal have affected them? Had they been mistreated or tortured? Would they be hungry, weak, gaunt, sick?

The first man to descend from the plane carried a tattered Cuban flag. Speaking awkwardly but fervently into a ready mike he said they had fought hard but their small boats had been no match for the enemy's speedboats. Their vessels and catches had been lost. Alpha 66 tried to get them to turn their backs on the revolution, promising them money and women. The man speaking was short of stature, rough around the edges, clearly unused to being in the public eye. "None of us gave in," he said finally, raising the torn flag in a gesture of victory.

We rode back to the city in a caravan of official cars past thousands of cheering people standing several deep the length of Ranchos Boyeros

Avenue. Police had cordoned the area surrounding the newly constructed platform and we were ushered through the crowd and onto it. I remember I was wearing my usual outfit of Levis and a brightly striped shell. From somewhere Fidel appeared and walked to the bank of microphones. The first minutes of his speech were given over to congratulating the fishermen on their exemplary conduct, praising the Cuban people who had stood by them so resolutely and warning the enemies of the revolution that future assaults would meet with similar resistance. We never learned whether there had been a prisoner exchange.

THE TEN-MILLION-TON GOAL WOULD NOT BE MET

Suddenly everyone realized the Commander in Chief's tone had turned from triumphant to serious, even somber: "I have something else I need to tell you tonight, something important," Fidel continued. Little by little the crowd fell silent. The night air turned brittle with expectation.

"There are those who have said I shouldn't ruin this victorious assembly by saying what I have to say. But you know me," Fidel went on, "I cannot keep from sharing with you something that affects us all." The ten million ton goal for the sugarcane harvest finally would not be met. It had turned out to be impossible. Furthermore, almost every other area of production had been affected by concentrating the country's resources in the singular effort. The dissenters had been right. All else had been ignored, to the detriment of the overall economy.

"There were those who warned us of this," Fidel admitted, "and we didn't listen. I didn't listen. I am responsible for this error and I must accept the responsibility." He offered to step down, to relinquish his position as Prime Minister if this was what the people wanted. Shouts of "Noooooo" and "Fidel! Fidel!" broke the silence. The larger–than–life leader, who looked tired and drawn, stopped them with a raised hand. He had decided to use this night of celebration to break the painful news and wasn't going to be deterred.

For a while, to an audience stunned into silence, Fidel offered little more in the way of explanation. The harvest's final tally had been eight million, five hundred thousand tons of sugar, more than any previous year in Cuban history. This was a great accomplishment, he insisted, and the Cuban people should be proud. As proud as they should be that their resistance had succeeded in getting their brave fishermen back. He promised to go on television the following day with a detailed analysis of what had gone wrong with the harvest and ended his speech, as he always did, with the words "¡Patria o muerte (Homeland or death)."

"Venceremos! (we will win!)," the numbed crowd called out in automatic but deadened response, more from habit than with its customary energy.

Slowly, the makeshift stage and large surrounding area emptied. People walked away without speaking. Even the following morning, on my way to work, I noticed an unusual silence on the bus; a pall seemed to have settled over the city. Months of fever-pitched energy, aimed at achieving an almost mythical goal, and then the unexpected realization that the goal was in fact unobtainable, had taken their toll.

Act to welcome the eleven liberated fishermen. Fidel announces failure of ten-million-ton sugar cane harvest. Margaret at extreme left. Havana, May 1970. Press photo by René Hedman.

I wasn't sure whether the numbness came from deep disappointment, frustration, anger, distress that their beloved leader had had to shoulder the responsibility of defeat, or the fact that people just didn't know where to go from here. No one I talked to had much to say about where this failure left the country or what steps could be taken to get it back on a positive economic footing. It was as if everyone was waiting for further instructions from above. I clung to the hope that somewhere, in realms to which I had no access, some serious analysis was taking place.

CHAPTER 6

A POETRY CONTEST
AND A BEAUTY PAGEANT

A Phone Call from Casa

Early in 1970 I received a phone call from Casa. A poet and essayist with several books to my credit, and maybe also because of my editorship of *El Corno Emplumado*, I was being invited to participate in the institution's yearly literary contest as a judge in its poetry division. Each year five distinguished writers—four international figures and one Cuban—read the dozens or hundreds of books submitted in each of the literary genres: novel, short story, poetry, essay, drama, and occasionally an additional category. The winners in each area received one thousand U.S. dollars—Cuban pesos were worthless internationally—and the prestigious publication of his or her book.

Judging poetry with me at the beginning of 1970 were the Cuban Cintio Vitier, El Salvador's Roque Dalton, Nicaragua's Ernesto Cardenal, and Washington Delgado from Peru. More than one hundred poetry manuscripts had been submitted and we read for a month. The last week they took us to Isle of Youth—formerly Isle of Pines—where we reread those manuscripts we'd set aside as having possibilities. I already knew most of the other judges. I wasn't excited about anything I'd read so far and no one else seemed to be either.

Then a last minute entry arrived by messenger. I read it first and immediately felt engaged. That familiar visceral response when great poetry leaps from page to consciousness. This is it, I thought. I also knew that as someone from a non-Spanish-speaking country, perhaps also as the only woman on

Cuban poet Cintio Vitier, Cuban Secretary of State Raul Roa, Margaret, and Nicaraguan poet and priest Ernesto Cardenal. Chilean writer Antonio Skármeta is standing at left. Cuban Silvia Gil at back. Havana, January 1970.

Casa de las Américas, Havana. Left to right: Margaret, Argentine writer Rodolfo Walsh, French/Mexican anthropologist Laurette Séourné, Cuban librarian at Casa de las Américas Silvia Gil, Director of Cuban Film Institute Alfredo Guevara, exiled Guatemalan vice president of Casa de las Américas Manuel Galich, Cuban President of Casa de las Américas Haydeé Santamaría, and Cuban Secretary of State Raul Roa. Havana, January 1970.

the panel, my opinion might not be taken seriously. Of the other judges, Roque was the one with whom I had the closest rapport. We had been friends since 1964 in Mexico and had become closer after both our families moved to Cuba.

Now I passed the book to him, eager to hear what he thought. He agreed with my assessment. "But," he cautioned, "we have to move carefully." Already he was designing a strategy: "If we show ourselves to be too enthusiastic, we may lose. Some of these poems appear to take God's name in vain. Don't forget, two of our fellow judges are devout Catholics. Let's get the others to read this without letting on how we feel."

Roque believed he knew who had written the book. Submissions were blind, of course, but the characteristics of language usage gave this one away as being by someone from South America's southern cone: Chile, Argentina, or Uruguay. And the poet was clearly writing from a prison experience. References to God might be references to the dictator, camouflaged in order to make it possible for the poems to make it past prison walls.

Roque and I played our little game well. In subsequent meetings we allowed our fellow judges to discover the book's power. We didn't need to be the ones to argue on its behalf. Slowly other choices were discarded. It might have been Delgado who first suggested the poems' great merits. By the time

Salvadoran revolutionary and poet Roque Dalton, on Havana bus. Photo by Chinolope.

we returned from Isle of Youth we had our winner: *Diario del cuartel* which, as Roque suspected, was by the Uruguayan Carlos María Gutiérrez.

I loved this book. The poems took up permanent residence beneath my skin. Some time after the winners of that year's contest were announced, I met and got to know its author, who had come to Havana after his release from prison. With his help I translated the book into English but had no luck finding a publisher.

There seemed such a deep disconnect between what was coming to life throughout Latin America, the liberation struggles active in fully a third of the continent's countries, and the popular perception of, or interest in, those struggles north of the border. The Cuban revolution fired imaginations and Che t-shirts were being worn by young people in almost every nation on earth. But a real engagement with the deeper whys and wheres and whos and hows was harder to rally.

ANOTHER PHONE CALL FROM CASA

My participation in the Casa contest that year led to a strange and uncomfortable event, one of the most awkward of my life. As the literary galas were winding down, preparations for Havana's yearly Carnival moved into high gear. Cuba is one of those countries in which the end of the annual harvest is rewarded with raucous celebration: outrageous floats, brilliantly choreographed *comparsas*—the traditional groups of dancers from the city's proudest neighborhoods—plenty of food and drink and, historically, a carnival queen and her court. For one extra-long weekend the city's malecón becomes a stage upon which just about anything goes.

Before the revolution the carnival queen and her court were inevitably chosen from among the daughters of the wealthy white elite. No black or mulatto had ever held the honor, certainly no one who was working class or poor. Cubans pointed proudly to the changes a decade of revolution had wrought: Now any young woman who wants to can try out, and the court is open to all, were among the responses I got when I questioned the politics of such a contest, so obviously based on women's physical characteristics.

So, shortly after my return from Isle of Youth, while at home with my children whom I hadn't seen in two weeks, I was completely caught off guard by another phone call from Casa. It was a message from Haydeé Santamaría, transmitted by her secretary: "La compañera asks if you will represent the

Havana's yearly carnival.

literary judges at a different sort of contest," the voice said. "Casa has been asked to provide someone to help select the carnival queen at the sports arena tonight. Some of the other judges will be . . ." and I recognized a name or two from among a short list of radio and television personalities. All men.

La compañera had asked. The phrase didn't translate as a question in my mind, but as a command. If Haydeé was asking me to do something I wasn't about to say no. At the same time, judging what amounted to a beauty contest? Me, an avowed feminist? How could I, with any dignity, participate in such an event? Then again, how could I say no? My head felt as if it would burst even before I heard myself telling the caller that, yes, of course I would be happy to do anything Haydeé asked of me.

Gregory, who was just home from the beca, had been listening to my side of the conversation. "What," he asked, "what do they want you to do?" The look on my face must have betrayed my anguish. When I told Gregory what Haydeé's secretary had requested my son understood the implications. Wise beyond his years and deeply sensitive to complex issues of justice, he knew how difficult this would be for me. He also knew I wouldn't hesitate. He was as committed as I was to taking on the challenge of revolutionary work, however that work might present itself.

I went into the bathroom and closed the door. Already my headache required medication, something in which I rarely indulged. A car would be coming for me at seven. I had to figure out what to wear to such an affair, which I knew would be televised nationwide. I guessed it was time to bring the blue and yellow knit dress out of what I'd hoped was permanent retirement.

As I tried to ignore the pain in my skull—it felt as if the space between my brain and its shell had filled with agitated knives—I wondered if there wasn't some way I might be able to turn setback into victory, as the popular revolutionary slogan urged. Why had Haydeé chosen me, one of just a few women among the more than thirty literary judges, when so many of the men would have been more than happy to participate? Perhaps she had something I was missing in mind.

I was grasping at straws.

I knew the press would be out in full force to cover the carnival's opening salvo. If I could make some sort of statement.... Less than an hour before my ride was due, I sat at my mirror-paneled dressing table turned desk, composing what I wanted to say. The fact that carnival queen contestants are no longer chosen from among the elite is a big leap forward, I began, following this with an acknowledgment of the importance of the contestants' social participation and knowledge of world affairs. Still, I continued, in a truly revolutionary society this type of contest, so intrinsically linked to women's physical characteristics, has to be put behind us.

My words came quickly now. I remembered Rosalia Cruz, a Miss Guatemala who had only a few years before traded her rhinestone tiara for a rifle. She'd joined one of her country's armed struggle organizations and died fighting within months. I ended my short piece with something to the effect that we will be better served when more young women aspire to social change than to contests in which they are judged primarily on their looks.

I no longer have a copy of that little essay. I'm sure it was somewhat didactic, perhaps even embarrassingly so. My sense of self and the way in which I expressed that sense, my ideas and how I put them out there, were still grappling for authentic voice. But I'd said what I'd wanted to say. I pulled the page from my old Olympia portable, folded it in half and slipped it into my purse. Just in time to answer the door and set out for this unwelcome adventure.

The indoor stadium was packed. We judges were seated at a long table, appropriately supplied with little notebooks, pencils, bottles of water, and microphones. I shook hands with the others—all men in their mid to late forties, all clearly delighted to be participating in the task at hand. The young women filed past, each preceded by a loudspeaker announcement of her name, age, and where she was from. Some contestants clearly had their own cheering sections; every so often the stands would erupt in whistles and applause.

We were instructed to ask questions. They included such examples as "How do you think the failure to harvest ten million tons of sugar will effect the Cuban economy?" and "What do you think of the U.S. war of aggression in Vietnam?" Some contestants gave interesting answers. I was willing to concede this parade of female beauty differed somewhat from its counterparts in the capitalist world. But the women still wore bathing suits and spike heels. They were still carefully made up. The questions we asked might be political but this remained a pretty conventional beauty pageant.

The Cuba libre we'd been served—rum and a local rip-off of Coke—was beginning to go to my head. My earlier headache hadn't completely disappeared and I felt a little sick. Without too much discussion the judges had agreed on a tall light-skinned woman as queen and two others as her attendants. One of the latter was mulata. I had argued for her inclusion; I'd been struck by her responses to our questions and actually hoped she would be voted queen. Appearing to take my suggestion seriously the other judges pushed for compromise and I'd talked myself into believing I had wielded some small measure of influence.

Our decision was announced. The queen and her court posed for pictures. Reporters closed in to record comments from those judges wishing to elaborate on the contestants or our choices. The anchorman from Cuba's main nightly newscast was expounding on the beauty of Cuban women. I took out the piece I had written and handed it to the reporter from *Granma*, the Communist Party daily. The next morning it appeared top right on the paper's front page.

I Chose You Because I Knew You Would Hate It

Robert and some of my colleagues at work ribbed me for days about having judged a beauty contest. I found it difficult to explain why I hadn't been able to refuse Haydeé's request and soon stopped trying. Several years would pass before I found myself alone with Haydeé one afternoon and was able to ask her why she'd made me participate in something she must have known went against everything for which I stood. I had no doubt she knew she had made me do it.

"You're right," she said, "I could have chosen any one of the men who were our guests at the time. Any one of them would have loved it. But then, the carnival queen judges were almost always men. Why not send a woman? I chose you precisely because I knew you would hate it, that you'd find a way to move us a bit closer to stopping those terrible contests. You did that, very well as I remember, with your press release. The armed struggle part of revolution is relatively easy," she added. "It is changing society, changing the old values and replacing them with new ones, that's hard."

Blacker women, older women, women from the countryside, women whose beauty was less the conventional sort, made up the carnival courts over the next few years. Then, sooner than I could have predicted, the carnival queen contest was no more. No one seemed to miss it. I came to believe I had done my small part to bring this change about, although I knew it responded most deeply to the new values that had come with new relations of production, new education, and opportunities.

When, during those early years, I'd sat down with Haydeé to formally interview her for the book I was writing about Cuban women, she'd told me about another moment in which she had drawn morality from those who resisted doing what she asked them to do. I'd asked about her role in the struggle against Batista, about her time in the urban underground when I knew she had been in charge of sending young fighters out to plant bombs, blow up bridges, and carry out other acts of armed sabotage against the state.

"What was that like," I'd queried.

She'd looked at me and smiled: "I always made sure I chose those I knew hated what they had to do," she said, "I didn't want to pick someone who might grow to enjoy the job. It was important we take care not to attack when people would be around, during rush hour or on busy streets where children might be killed. I knew if I picked comrades who hated doing what had to be done they would be less likely to kill innocent victims."

Casa Was an Extraordinary Institution

Casa de las Américas was—and is—an extraordinary institution. Almost single-handedly it succeeded in breaking through the cultural embargo levied against the Cuban revolution by the United States and supported by almost every country in its sphere of influence. This embargo not only prevented people on the outside from becoming acquainted with the literature, art, theater, and music of the revolution. It made it hard, if not impossible, for Cuban writers and artists to connect with their counterparts throughout Latin and North America. A creative community, one that shared language, aspirations, and overlapping cultural influences, was rent in two by a mean-spirited political policy.

Casa wasn't the only Cuban cultural institution. There was the Union of Writers and Artists (UNEAC), the National Art School, the national and provincial universities, the world-renowned Alicia Alonso Ballet, the excellent folkloric dance troupe, provincial cultural centers, a wealth of theater groups, orchestras, choruses, music combos, even an opera company.

The New Cuban Song Movement was just getting off the ground—with Silvio Rodríguez, Pablo Milanés, Noel Nicola, and Sara González. Cuban film was making a name for itself and the Cuban Film Institute (ICAIC), under the brilliant direction of Alfredo Guevara, had already produced films that would become classics, like *Lucía, Seventy-nine Springs,* and *Memories of Underdevelopment.* A Cuban Culture Council (more about this nefarious institution later) would soon be replaced by one of the continent's first Ministries of Culture.

But Casa was special for a number of reasons. Its mission went beyond domestic artistic expression. It was specifically charged with breaking the cultural embargo. And it was headed, from its inception, by one of the Cuban revolution's great personalities, Haydeé Santamaría. Haydeé had made Casa de las Américas what it was: an institution of impressive reach, with a stellar journal, one of the most important literary contests in the Spanish language, a publishing program, and departments of music, theater, fine arts, and cultural studies.

Haydeé, as everyone called her, had been one of only two women involved in the 1953 attack on Santiago's Moncada Barracks, the second largest military installation in Latin America. Fidel and his movement had decided to charge the well-fortified barracks during Carnival, when it was assumed a majority of soldiers would be sleeping off a mammoth drunk. In the early morning hours of July 26th clandestine fighters converged on the site from several directions. They believed they would be able to take it and the city of Santiago would rise up in support. A number of things went wrong, and Batista ordered his soldiers to kill ten rebels for every dead soldier. Fidel and a few others managed to escape. An honest sergeant captured him; someone else might have shot the revolutionary leader and Cuba's future would have been quite different.

Fidel's trial is well documented. He defended himself, and his closing statement, published as *History Will Absolve Me,* became a classic of revolutionary literature. After their convictions, Fidel and the others who had survived began long prison sentences. Two years later an amnesty exiled them to Mexico, from where they planned their return. Following a couple of years of guerrilla warfare, the 26th of July Movement took power on January 1, 1959.

The two women at Moncada were Melba Hernández and Haydeé Sant-amaría. Like Fidel, they also survived the attack, were tried, convicted, and imprisoned. Haydeé's brother and lover were both tortured to death, and legend has it her jailors brought her the former's eye and latter's testicle in an effort to get her to talk. "If you did that to them and they didn't talk," she is reported to have said, "much less will I."

A half century later it is immaterial whether or not these things happened exactly as they've been recorded. No one who knew Haydeé doubted she was capable of such heroism. She was a passionately engaged and committed woman, uniquely creative and with a brilliance that seemed entirely intuitive. It's hard to know exactly how she fit—or didn't—into the male-dominated Cuban hierarchy. She became a member of the Cuban Communist Party's Central Committee, served briefly on its Politburo, and presided over the founding conference of the Organization of Latin American Solidarity (OLAS). She was president of Casa de las Américas from its inception.

Deeper and More Complex Layers of Deception

Did Haydeé feel privileged or relegated to this cultural post? Hard to say. She may have hoped for a more overtly political position. There was nothing in her background that had prepared her to work with artists and writers, and I'm sure many in the revolution's leadership would have seen the post as secondary. Haydeé was a disciplined Party member but I suspect she was also sensitive to the ways in which some of the most independent women within the Cuban process were kept in check.

In the interview with her I did for *Cuban Women Now* she said she thought it was absurd that we say mankind when we mean all people, or his when we mean theirs (Spanish is a gendered language). This observation preceded by at least a year the linguistic modifications made by feminists in the United States and Europe.

Haydeé married Armando Hart, who eventually became the first and brilliant Cuban Minister of Culture. Publicly, at least, they seemed to have a harmonious relationship. They had a couple of children of their own and adopted many more: sons and daughters of Latin American revolutionaries who had died on a number of battlefronts.

In the late 1970s Armando left Haydeé for another woman. It must have been a terrible shock. Some were sure she took her life because her husband left her. I thought this may have been a contributing factor but that her heart may also have been broken by deeper and more complex layers of deception.

Perhaps, too, her spirit was depleted beyond its capacity for renewal. Every year, in the weeks leading up to the July 26th anniversary, Haydeé and the dwindling number of other survivors of the attack on Moncada Barracks visited schools and workplaces to bear personal witness to the heroic event that had sparked the revolution. The idea was to keep the history alive for generations born too late to remember. At one such talk, in 1980, someone I knew overheard Haydeé say: "I'm so tired. I don't know how much longer I can do this. I don't know how much longer . . ." Several days later, she shot herself in the head. She was at home with all her children.

In minutes the terrible news invaded every corner of the city. Haydeé was at the funeral home on Paseo and J, people said. It was almost midnight but I walked over to the teeming establishment. This was no ordinary night, no ordinary death, no ordinary loss. Although the woman to whom we were saying goodbye was laid out in one of the larger viewing halls I found it almost impossible to fight my way past the door. People were raw, grief stricken, and also strangely agitated. No one understood why Haydeé's body had not been placed at the foot of the Martí statue in Revolutionary Square: the farewell spot of choice for all high-ranking deceased.

That night I remember bumping into Roque Dalton's son, Jorge. His father, too, was long gone; Haydeé had been particularly sympathetic to Roque. Jorge and I embraced and held one another. Time seemed to stop.

My friend and neighbor Silvia Gil, who worked at Casa, touched my shoulder and asked if I wanted to stand honor guard beside the coffin. I nodded. It was difficult to make our way through the throng of mourners to the smaller inner viewing room where the open casket lay surrounded by

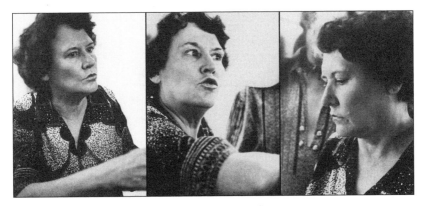

Haydeé Santamaría, photos taken in 1976.

banks of flowers. At the indicated moment I moved into place at Haydeé's head, replacing the honor guard before me who stepped quietly aside. I tried to stare straight ahead, but couldn't help casting a diagonal glance at this woman who had been, above all, my mentor and friend.

Her body seemed so frail in death. Her delicate hands were clasped in the traditional gesture across her breast, her eyes closed. But it was as if I could see through their delicate lids to the piercing blue of those eyes, eyes that had seemed crazed and visionary at one and the same time. She would look at and into the person with whom she was speaking in a way that affected that person long past the moment. I would never be able to think of Haydeé in any way but living, making, doing.

It was too late for a farewell in Revolution Square. But some time before dawn of the following day word came that Fidel had changed his mind. Despite the Party's disapproval of suicide—in the Communist Party, as in the Catholic Church, one is not forgiven for taking one's life; it belongs to a higher power—Haydeé's body would be placed upon a carriage and taken with all pomp and ceremony to the appropriate corner of Colón Cemetery for burial with full revolutionary honors. Fidel hadn't changed his mind, I thought; thousands of grieving people had changed it for him.

CHAPTER 7

WOMEN AND DIFFERENCE

I Asked to Remember

I started writing this chapter wishing I could remember the name of my boss at Ambito. He was a young ex-army officer, or maybe in Cuba you're never ex-army. Sometimes he wore his uniform to work. He'd been charged with publishing books and clearly took it as seriously as any defense task. Younger than me, he challenged my preconceptions about military people. Growing up in the United States and having lived through 1968 and 1969 in Mexico, fear most often attended my contact with people in uniform. Especially men in uniform.

> In the dream I am barefoot and struggling, walking through something . . . what is it or do I want to know? A shudder in sleep can rip me from dream but I manage to stay where I am in this one. I look down at my feet, half covered, slowed, fighting viscosity and fear, the temperature rising . . . The struggle to keep myself moving, the soles of my feet resisting the heat, through pools of rotting matter, a sour ooze, the unmistakably revolting odor of death. Flashes of my own life surface through the stench: Nicaragua just after the Sandinista victory when the dead had to be retrieved from where they had been provisionally buried and moved to proper cemeteries. Sudden winds across a highway, the gagging repulsion. Turn away and breathe. Breathe.

But this dream is about something else. Here there is blood, bits of muscle, an occasional sharp knife of bone. And yet I keep going, eyes fixed on a door that gets farther away as I try to reach it. Disappears as I....

On the threshold of sleep I had asked to be able to remember. Dream would bring the answer as it had so many times before. Now, balanced between sleep and wakefulness, I try to stay on course. For much of my life this has been a method that works. I am always astonished.

Jaime Rivero—the name fills my mouth as I wake—was welcoming, intelligent, and open to creative suggestion. He started me out working on a coffee table compendium of the hundreds of different fish that inhabit the island's coral reefs. The book was for export, an effort to earn the dollars always so much in demand. It had been put together by someone else; I'd arrived in time for the final revision. Jaime kept me busy checking facts and doing a general style correction. We both knew this wouldn't be my job for long.

Jaime was also the person who, when I'd come back from my disastrous experience in the ten million ton harvest, had called me into his office and asked me to sit down. "The revolution needs years," he'd told me then, "not days. If you don't take care of yourself you will die and deny this process the talent and energy only you can give." Advice I've recalled on more than one occasion since.

Another job I was offered in those first weeks was translating a two volume collection by José Martí. Martí was the nineteenth century patriot, writer, and organizer in Cuba's war of independence from Spain. Look-alike plaster busts of the man stood in at least a dozen public squares in every one of the island's cities, towns, and villages. A very funny Cuban film of that era, *La muerte de un burócrata* (Death of a Bureaucrat), portrayed a worker in the plaster bust factory who was mangled to death by his machine, and the drama faced by his family when it was discovered that he had accidentally been buried with his Party card. Cubans have great talent for laughing at their own idiosyncrasies, failings or tendencies to excess.

Martí understood colonialism and was prophetic when he warned that "Estados Unidos caerá, con esa fuerza más, sobre nuestras tierras de América" (The United States will lunge, with its tremendous power, against the countries of America).[1] He had done some of his organizing inside the monster itself, among the immigrant cigar makers in Ybor City, Florida. He'd martyred himself in 1895, shortly after his return to Cuba, by riding into battle at Dos Ríos. Martí's intellectual contribution to his country's independence was enormous; more seasoned military figures, such as generals Máximo Gómez and Antonio Maceo, led the campaign that brought about Cuba's victory. Independence wasn't achieved, though, because the United States intervened before the end of the war.

It was my friend Roberto Fernández Retamar who suggested I translate Martí. He had made the selection for this anthology and contributed its sixty page introduction. I started by working on that. By this time I'd had quite a bit of experience translating from Spanish into English—*El Corno* had given me the opportunity of rendering work by such diverse authors as César Vallejo, Raquel Jodorosky, Ernesto Cardenal, and Javier Heraud. Sergio's and my partnership had its important translating component. During the repression in Mexico Robert and I translated to help make the waiting bearable. I'd translated entire books by Otto-René Castillo and Jorge Masetti, would later do English versions of Roque Dalton, Domingo León, Daisy Zamora, and Fernández Retamar himself. But Martí proved to be more than I could handle.

Martí's sentences were often a page long, his baroque language convoluted by today's standards and extremely complex. It was the language of a particular time and place. And as a hero claimed by revolutionaries and dissenters alike, Martí's voice was closely scrutinized: no place for poetic license. Even the introduction required a greater knowledge of the era and of Martí's cultural and political positions than I possessed at the time—or probably possess today.

I remember the night I went to see Roberto, my first sixty pages in hand. It was a typical Havana evening. The air exuded a kind of semi-liquid tropicality, heavy but strangely energizing. The three of us—Roberto's wife, the art historian Adelaida de Juan, joined us on the veranda of their home—started reading out loud, addressing the problems I'd encountered in every paragraph, almost every sentence. It was a painful reading. Before we'd gotten through the first four or five pages I knew, and they agreed, I was not the one for this job.

I suggested to Roberto that my mother might be able to handle this work. She had been translating Spanish into English for a number of years and was just then between books. He agreed and Mother took the challenge. Translating Martí—this little book and much of the rest of his more than thirty volumes of essay, journalism, poetry, and children's literature—would become her life's work. In the last days before her death at ninety-six she was still revising pieces she'd worked on forty years before.

I'd Start My Workday Eager to Be of Service

After my failure with Martí I went to work each morning at Ambito and tried to get excited about doing style correction on the book about tropical fish. My attitude was that anything the revolution asked of me I would tackle willingly, doing the best job I possibly could.

My workplace was in Old Habana, on Ayestarán, one of the narrow cobblestone streets lined with old buildings that spoke in many registers of prerevolutionary history and postrevolutionary disrepair. It was only blocks from La moderna poesía, near where we'd had the incident with the jeep full of soldiers who had been in such a hurry a couple of years before.

Each morning I'd get to the bus stop early. I'd rather arrive at the office before anyone else than risk being late: a lifetime compulsion. I'd take the first overcrowded bus that stopped, travel from Vedado up and over the hill that borders the University of Havana through vast Revolution Square and into the warren of busy neighborhoods that make up the old city. Today part of this old city center is a UNESCO World Heritage Site, its main plazas and most important structures beautifully restored: a living museum. Back then the neighborhoods looked much like their outer fringes still look: dilapidated, run-down, and sad.

I'd start my workday eager to be of service. The elaborate books the publishing house had been charged with producing—to compete for foreign currency, always badly needed in order to balance the hardships provoked by chronic underdevelopment and the U.S. embargo—were aimed at tourists and an out of country readership. But high quality paper was expensive and high quality reproduction beyond Cuba's technical capabilities at the time. Ambito was already beginning to falter.

A Project I Wanted to Pursue

Jaime was one of those people who took the revolution's centrally planned schemes in cheerful stride; if he suddenly received an order to toss the fish book and launch something else it was all in a day's work. As it turned out, Ambito was a concept before its time and would close within the year.

I had a project I wanted to pursue and as Ambito was my assigned work-place I decided to try to pursue it there. During my last two years in Mexico I'd become aware of a new consciousness energizing women in the United States and parts of Europe: feminism. More than just a consciousness, it was an awakening, a great collective leap in human experience and understanding; at its most profound a new way of looking at power relations. One of those moments history gives us with such force from time to time that we wonder how it is we hadn't made the connections before.

Several events converged to bring this latest wave of feminism to the fore. By this time the United States, France, Italy, Germany, and several other countries had active antiestablishment movements. They ranged from workers' struggles, organizing for racial equality and civil rights, against the United States's war in Vietnam, and around other political issues, to the fringes where establishment hypocrisy and control were encouraging less focused but no less motivated youth rebellions.

As usual the men in all these movements assumed they were there to strategize and lead. Women were expected to make the coffee, type the manifestos and have sex on demand with their male comrades. In the United States, Stokely Carmichael, of the Student Nonviolent Coordinating Committee (SNCC), was reported to have said the only position for movement women was prone.

Gradually U.S. women were dissatisfied with these subservient roles. We had achieved monumental progress with the vote, certain legal victories, awareness of the need for control over our own bodies (if not yet full possession of that control), and progress in a number of other areas. In organization after organization and venue after venue we staged takeovers, locked the men out and claimed our own space in which to come together, share ideas, speak, and act. Women took over some of the movement newspapers, turned our attention to the struggle for legal and reproductive rights, began talking about the business world's glass ceiling or shunned the business world altogether.

Women in the developed countries were ready for change. Wars had thrown us into previously male-dominated trades and professions. During subsequent periods of peace we were encouraged to return to the domestic sphere where, insisted the media message, our husbands and children needed us. With men at war and women required to replace them on assembly lines, we had been told formula made healthy babies. Now we were being regaled with studies showing the advantages of breast milk. This back and forth pattern had repeated itself long enough so that women were tired of being manipulated, our talents recognized only when we had to step in because men were busy wielding power elsewhere.

The sexual revolution and more dependable birth control methods had also freed us considerably. More women had entered public office; in rather insignificant numbers overall but more than enough to be role models.

Women were excelling in science, the arts, and sports. There wasn't a single feminism. Or even one that was theoretically convincing to a mainstream that still reaped the benefits of the double standard, although educated white women with more access to the media were able to speak the loudest; their ideas and experience attracted the most attention. The truth is, women of different races and classes rallied around different feminist issues and, contrary to what the establishment press would have people believe, many individuals and groups were advocating for change.

In Mexico in 1967 I had begun to read the materials that were coming out of the various feminist movements in my country of origin. There were detailed socialist feminist essays like Juliet Mitchell's *The Longest Revolution*. A number of analysts treated women's labor as essential to the overall economy and proclaimed—because they privileged class over gender—that all would be solved if women were paid for keeping men fed, their homes and clothes clean, and raising their children; in other words for being the silent partners who kept the economy running. Some Italian feminists proposed wages for housework.

Others based their theories on Engels, pointing out that the first division of labor had been between men and women. They saw gender as important but clung to the Marxist concept that the greatest social contradiction was class. Some women, like Naomi Weinstein, looked at the problem through a psychologist's lens. Some feminist theoreticians centered their arguments in the domestic sphere; Pat Mainardi was one, and her piece on housework would become a movement classic.

Ellen Willis looked at women and consumerism for clues to understanding our second-class citizenship. Some feminists were so angry they visualized a world without men. Valerie Solanas's *S.C.U.M. Manifesto* reflected one such vision: crazed enough to recommend murder (which she herself later attempted against the artist Andy Warhol). Over the next few years many women who were not at all crazy would find that they needed an all-woman space at least long enough to gain the confidence mixed venues had taken from them.

Roxanne Dunbar's piece on the birth of her daughter and the utter loneliness that mothering in unequal social situations can bestow moved me to tears. Poets Diane di Prima and Marge Piercy were producing scathing feminist commentaries in verse. At the time I agreed with a number of these works, disagreed with others, and was deeply shaken by some. But all changed me. They enabled me to begin to look at my own life in a new way. For the first time I understood that what I had assumed were personal problems—a frustration when men treated me unfairly and I was blamed or suffered the consequences, a repeated tendency to trust men who ended up betraying that trust—weren't personal at all. They were rooted in patriarchy.

I Wanted to Find Out What Life for Cuban Women Was Like

Colonialism and neocolonialism produced a subservient culture that favored skewed power relations between nations and within the colonized structures. Capitalism only sharpened patriarchy's verticality and male control. As a Marxist I still believed that class was the greatest contradiction and it would be a while before I really understood how gender factored into the equation. But feminist theory explained a great deal and feminist practice began, just began, to set me free from a particular set of social and psychological inhibitions. Feminism redirected me. And as was the case each time I discovered a powerful new truth, its influence on my work and the changes it provoked in my personal life were profoundly intertwined.

I wanted my Latin American sisters to have access to these feminist ideas so I read everything I could get my hands on, made a representative selection and wrote an introduction. Siglo XXI Editores, headed by my friend Arnaldo Orfila, had the collection translated and published it under the name *Las mujeres* (The Women).

Arnaldo's was a stroke of genius in that era of Latin American censorship. If the word feminist had appeared in the book's title it never would have made it into Nicaragua, Colombia, Peru, or a host of other countries. A book called *The Women* seemed innocuous. These were the years when Marx's *Holy Family* made it past Nicaragua's censors only because they thought it was religious.

Las mujeres, published for the first time in 1970, has gone into a dozen editions. It remains in print. And occasionally I still hear from someone who tells me that little collection of early feminist writings changed her life. Because I was curious as to how socialism might begin to alter the sexual balance of power I had included, almost as afterthoughts, a piece about women in China and another on Cuban women. Tellingly, both were written by men: William Hinton and Jorge Risquet.

By this time I had lived in Latin America long enough to understand that women there had their own histories and cultures. Informed by indigenous strength, colonial plunder, Catholic punishment, and the array of relationships, customs, and ideas that were their heritage, they would unearth their

own discoveries, wage their own battles and share their own lessons with
women worldwide.

Freshly arrived in Cuba, working at Ambito and with an immediate
superior who seemed amenable to new ideas, I decided I wanted to find
out what life for Cuban women was like. What their participation in the
revolutionary process had been. How their lives had been changed or not
by the victory of 1959. Socialism promised radical change. Was this change
freeing, using, overlooking, or abusing women? Or perhaps some uniquely
Cuban combination?

I knew women had made up the highest percentage of the country's
illiterates and that after 1959 tens of thousands had learned to read. More
young women than young men had worked in the literacy campaign. I
knew there were more girls than boys at almost every educational level, and
more women than before in the labor force. I knew the revolution had given
women control over their bodies and that abortion, like all aspects of public
health, was safe and free. (When I discovered I was pregnant again too soon
after losing my kidney I myself had gotten an abortion in Cuba. When I
awoke from the anesthesia, I went right into journalistic mode, questioning

Three little girls in a Cuban day care center, Havana.

those sharing my ward on how they felt about their procedures, emotionally as well as with regard to the attention received.)

The exploitation of women as prostitutes had been all but eradicated and the women who had once been forced to sell their bodies retrained for more dignified work. In 1967 and 1968 when I'd stayed at the Nacional I had felt the spirits of those ex prostitutes still walking the halls in search of a future they couldn't have dreamed of only a year or two before. Today there are some sex workers who contend their professions empower them, but back then this was not something Cubans could have imagined.

Although there was still a long list of jobs off limits to women workers (the rationale being that these were dangerous to women's reproductive health), they earned the same as their male counterparts in jobs for which both were considered apt. Day care and workers' dining rooms alleviated some of the workload women still shouldered at home although it would be years before a serious effort was made to politicize the home sphere and try to convince men to shoulder their domestic responsibilities.

I found that many Cuban women valued the fashion and beauty products feminists in the United States considered oppressive. In the 1970s I met women making eye shadow from colored chalk and drawing dark lines down the backs of their legs because nylon stockings weren't available. An expert female cane cutter removed her heavy gloves and proudly showed me her elegantly painted nails. Shortages of consumer goods sparked creativity and also prolonged the need for a certain feminine ornamentation. Even with razor blades in short supply, few Cuban women failed to shave their legs or underarms.

The Cuban revolution proclaimed women's equality and seemed to have made enormous strides in its direction. The Federation of Cuban Women (FMC) had been established at the beginning of the revolution in order to organize women around the new social goals and make their needs known to Party leadership. It quickly became a mass organization with a membership of ninety seven percent of all women over the age of fourteen. It mobilized women very effectively to an array of necessary tasks.

But the FMC never embraced a feminist ideology. On the contrary, its upper echelons, like the revolutionary leadership overall, made it clear that decolonization was the priority and they considered feminism an imported bourgeois notion that would ultimately divide the working class. Cuba's condition as a neocolonized state was always the driving force behind the program of social transformation. It has been responsible for such impoverished concepts as *cubanía*, that which emanates from Cuban culture.[2]

Feminists from the developed countries were seen as dangerous, at the very least out of touch with Cuban reality and perhaps intentionally disruptive. Many younger FMC members were feminist in practice even when the theory was alien to them. But the organization's ideology was and continues to be antifeminist.

I Was an Incipient Feminist

Back in 1970 I didn't understand how much we needed an in depth gender analysis of Cuban society. I was impressed with such a mass mobilization of women and didn't know how to ask the hard questions. In fact, looking back I remember thinking that certain European and U.S. American feminists were being too critical of the Cuban process when they warned that a women's organization under the thumb of a male dominated political party would be unable to advocate for women in the deepest sense. I, too, was becoming blindly defensive of poor little David.

The clear changes that had taken place in women's lives by the end of the revolution's first decade, impressive as they were, couldn't tell me everything I wanted to know. I would have to talk to women of all ages, from all parts of the country and many different backgrounds. Fair-skinned Cubans born into aristocracy or members of the middle class. Black Cubans whose prerevolutionary options had marked them for the service sector or as sweatshop workers or the wives of impoverished peasants. Mulatas who, in line with the rigorously stratified Cuban color code, occupied one or another position of subservience or relative privilege. I was curious about how gender and race intersected. I wanted to talk to professionals and factory workers, farmers and students, very old women and young girls just coming up—for whom life before 1959 was barely remembered.

I had a problem but it didn't stop me (although it caused others to try to stop me). I had never completed university and thus had no formal training in history, ethnography, social anthropology, economics, or any of the other disciplines that would have given me the academic credentials to undertake such a project.

I was an incipient feminist, a poet, a writer—and of course a woman myself. I had always been inclined to trust my intuition and my newfound feminism encouraged me to trust it more fully. As an artist I saw patterns, instantly grasped situations and people's feelings about them. I believed in the power of stories and knew that if I could interview Cuban women, listen

Women with their babies, waiting their turn at a neighborhood clinic, Camagüey.

Women cigar factory workers, Havana.

to them talk about their lives and research the larger picture, I would gain
valuable insights into their situation.

By the end of their revolution's first ten years, Cubans placed enormous
importance on formal training. Early on, great projects were launched simply
because they were needed; spontaneous and makeshift as they often were,
many were also extremely successful. By 1970, though, education, college
degrees, postgraduate work, and specialization were becoming more impor-

Mother and son, Havana street.

tant. The first wave of graduates had already returned from their studies in the Soviet Union and other socialist countries.

An example of how this emphasis on education affected one area of women's work in particular was the ban on midwifery. Cuba intended to lower its infant and maternal mortality rates by—among other efforts— discouraging home births. Many of the traditional midwives were forced out. Those who wanted to become medically trained were welcomed into hospital

Women construction workers, La Guinera, Havana.

obstetrics wards. Those who resisted going back to school retired. I learned not to talk a lot about my own midwifery experience in Mexico.

I may have been viewed by some as suspect not only because I was a foreigner—a foreigner from the very country that headed the list of Cuba's enemies—but also because of my lack of academic training. When, several books later a Mexican, oral historian visited Cuba in order to update my entry in a registry of professionals in the field, it was the first time I'd heard the term. I briefly flashed on oral hygiene, then on the fundamentalist preacher Oral Roberts. I learned that I had acquired a reputation in a discipline about which, theoretically, I knew almost nothing.

On the other hand, the fact that I lived in Cuba worked in my favor. I wasn't someone who had come for a few weeks or months, taken notes, and gone home to write a book. I shared Cuba's privations and joys. My children went to Cuban schools. I had chosen as much as possible to live like my neighbors. I'm sure much of the openness and generosity shown me responded to the fact that for many Cubans I was one of them.

Cuban Women Now

I talked to Jaime Rivero about my idea for a book on Cuban women. He told me to write a proposal and model questionnaire. I labored over these for a couple of days and returned, sure that they would be found lacking. I was surprised when my boss told me to get a working group together and go for it. Before I could thank him he was on the phone with someone at the Federation of Cuban Women asking the organization to support my endeavor.

The Federation was less than enthusiastic. I would learn that any women's project that didn't originate with them was suspect in their eyes. Coming from a U.S. feminist, as they surely saw me, mine would be found wanting on any number of counts. But more tolerant heads prevailed and eventually the FMC supported what I was doing.

When one of our early interviewees complained to the women's organization that I'd asked impertinent questions about sex, things got rough. Eventually strings were pulled and feelings smoothed over. Someone sat down with me and explained how questions might be better posed to the Cuban sensibility. Through trial and error I myself discovered the importance of asking open-ended questions rather than those in which the response I sought might be implicit.

The project continued.

Problems developed inside our working group as well. The original configuration—colleagues who'd shown an interest in the project—included a young woman named Mayda who was genuinely interested and had interviewing talent, another young woman called Mayra, a beginning photographer who would produce images for the finished book, and an older man we called by his surname. I'll refer to him as Gómez. Gómez was so unconsciously sexist we had to exclude him after a couple of weeks. This accomplished, we proceeded.

By this time Jaime had been recalled into active military service. His replacement was more intellectual, with a broader knowledge of what we were doing and great people skills. Pablo Pacheco and I remain friends. When, a few years back, we ran into one another at the Guadalajara Book Fair I was as glad to see him as I'd been decades before when he first showed up at Ambito.

Juggling my particular load of advantages and disadvantages, and with the support I received from my workplace and other institutions, the fieldwork on Cuban women moved forward. It was an important learning experience. That first oral history project became a book called *Cuban Women Now*, which was eventually published in several languages and a number of countries.[3] Researching and writing it gave me valuable insights. In subsequent years as I wrote and published more books in the genre the body of work began to speak for itself.

PIROPOS

What I was working on and what was going on in my personal life were always inextricably meshed. I remember my indignation when I walked on Havana sidewalks and men called out their sexualized, sometimes ugly, comments: "Oye, mamacita.... ¡qué nalgas! Dame un poquito...."[4] Or made loud sucking sounds meant to simulate exaggerated kisses. I resented being the target of this sort of sexist vulgarity, especially in a revolutionary society.

I had hoped this would have disappeared or that the Cuban Party might have thought it worth challenging. I began engaging these men, asking what they thought they might feel if someone spoke to their mothers or sisters or wives like they were speaking to me. Once in a while this provoked a conversation, once in a great while one that seemed productive. More often I got a belligerent stare or the offender ratcheted up his aggressive behavior.

A few years later the Cuban film industry would take on the subject of these cat-calls known in the local jargon as *piropos*. The term implies a compliment. While some piropos were complimentary—if one enjoyed being addressed by strange men—and some were robust with the humor so typical of Cuban repartee, many were just gross. Cuban women pretended to ignore the come-ons but many admitted that if they didn't attract a fair number of them on a given day they went to their mirrors to find out what was wrong. The film was meant to bring attention to the phenomenon but I didn't think it went far enough.

My daughters Sarah and Ximena hated going out with me; my verbal challenges embarrassed them as did my less than up to date fashion sense, my insistence on being myself rather than trying to fit in. Such is the shame of preteens everywhere and adolescents growing up in Cuba were no exception. Just as I, as a young woman and to my parents' discomfort had aspired to be my high school's homecoming queen or a member of its cheerleading squad, my daughters would have to travel their own routes to the values they eventually acquired. In Cuba when we walked together in the early seventies—perhaps to the wonderful outdoor ice cream parlor Copelia—they often trailed me by half a block.

As for what the Cuban revolution has meant for women, as I learned by interviewing hundreds, producing several books and many articles, and by living in the country for eleven years, it has meant both immense change and no small amount of frustration. Cuban women outnumber men in the universities, including in those disciplines previously reserved for men. Women hold high percentages of jobs in almost every sector, although they're still not anywhere near being equally represented in Party, government, or administrative positions. This deficiency is often at least partially explained by the fact that women hesitate to run for offices that would double or triple the unequal workloads they already shoulder, because besides holding a job they are still unfairly burdened with most of the childcare and housework.

Cuban women have access to free health care, including family planning and abortion. Universal health care exists for everyone and so women are also relieved of the worry women elsewhere contend with around their children's wellbeing. Many working mothers send their children to day care centers.

Later, with the increase in tourism especially, disrespectful female images have increased in the press and on billboards. Prostitution has returned. Legal protection for women is good (except for lesbians), but many of the traditional gender roles persist. Eventually, a group of Cuban women did take it upon themselves to challenge these stereotypes and the FMC's failure to address them adequately.

Magín

In 1993, long after I left Cuba, a group of brilliant feminists began getting together to talk about gender on the island. They felt it was obscene that four decades after the triumph of the revolution, and especially with the surge in tourism, denigrating stereotypes of women could still be seen in the media. They were outraged by images of seductive mulatas, their full buttocks barely covered by bikini thongs, and full-breasted sex objects beckoning from beneath the ever-present royal palm.

The Magín women were revolutionaries, many of them Party members, and most worked in mass media. Some wrote for newspapers or magazines. Others worked in TV or radio. A few were filmmakers. One was a sociologist. They thought of themselves as communicators and believed they must engage a broad range of other communicators—teachers, doctors and health care workers, librarians, and anyone whose work put them in routine contact with the public—in an effort to change their country's unequal power relations where men and women were concerned.

They had chosen their name with care. *Magín* is an old Castilian word meaning imagination and creativity. At first they tried to interest the FMC in their ideas. They thought the mass women's organization would welcome their input. Not so. FMC leadership felt threatened and did everything possible to discourage those they must have believed were treading on their territory. The FMC never stopped opposing Magín until it managed to put the new group out of business.

Magín did develop workshops which they held successfully in different parts of the country. The group produced some literature. And each of the women, in her particular niche, published studies revealing the ongoing gender bias and wrote articles espousing a more conscious point of view. They made contact with feminists in other countries and became an important part of the regional and international movement for gender equality. During the 1990s I brought seven groups of women from the United States to Cuba; on each of these visits we would visit the Magín women for an evening of valuable discussion.

Magín had plans to send two of its members to the 1995 Fourth World Conference on Women in Beijing, China. The women prepared a workshop on gender and communication which was listed among the event's nongovernmental activities. OXFAM UK gave them 10,000 U.S. dollars to cover travel expenses for a couple of their members. Before they were due to leave, however, the FMC advised them that Cuba's delegation was already complete; if they wanted to donate the money they'd received to cover some of the official organization's expenses they were welcome to do so. They knew they had no alternative but to comply. Throughout its short life Magín consistently took principled positions. But that didn't stop the FMC's long-time president Vilma Espín from accusing it of malfeasance![5]

Magín wanted NGO-status, for which it needed official recognition. This was not forthcoming. In 1996 when the group's core members approached the Party's Central Committee to apply for legal status, they were told they would have to disband. They could no longer meet as a group, could not continue their work, and would have to cease all workshops, publishing, and the like. The reason given was patronizing in the extreme: in light of the ongoing efforts of the U.S. government to destroy the Cuban revolution, Party officials said, they were afraid these women might be duped into making contacts or doing work which inadvertently played into the enemy's hands.

As it has done rather consistently through close to half a century of revolution, the Cuban Communist Party used the ever-present threat from the north to legitimize a lack of support for diverse efforts and justify repressive measures. There is no doubt that the United States had done and continues do everything possible to destabilize the Cuban project. Still, there have been many situations in which trusting the insights and intelligence of its own best citizens rather than relying on such insulting excuses might have pushed true revolution forward. This was one of them.

Although none have emigrated, a few of the Magín women temporarily live and work outside Cuba. Others have remained in their jobs, and through the influence they wield, continue trying to be a force for gender equality. They have been pushed underground, they say, but not defeated. These are women, I am sure, who will be powerful agents for change once Cuban society is no longer so controlled.[6]

The Important Thing Is That We Rectify Our Mistakes

Today there are signs of hope. Mariela Castro Espín, youngest daughter of Raul Castro and FMC founder and first president Vilma Espín, heads Cuba's

Center for Sex Education (Centro de Educación Sexual, CENESEX). She is one of a small group of enlightened officials who are trying to eradicate the country's residual heterosexism and provide its lesbian/gay/bisexual/transgender (LGBT) community with the same rights straight Cubans enjoy. The Center publishes *Sexology and Society*, a journal featuring artwork and poetry with sexual themes and scholarly articles dealing with everything from gay bashing and domestic violence to hormone therapy for transsexuals. In a number of published interviews, Castro Espín's statements, although they don't yet reflect life as it's currently lived, promise better times to come.

When asked if Cuban society is sexist, she replies: "All modern societies are patriarchal, each in its own way ... We've inherited a macho society, and women as well as men hold sexist attitudes. But we're seeing changes in the new generations, especially among those in their forties and younger." When the interviewer points out that Cuba's repression of homosexuals has provoked international criticism, she says:

> In the seventies, like elsewhere in the world, there was an intolerance of homosexuality in Cuba, although there was never torture or anything like that. We did have military units, it's true, and not only in Cuba, because people thought that was how you made men tough. Back then psychiatry judged homosexuality a curable mental illness. Outrageous, but we must admit this error. And this produced some painful episodes. The important thing is that we rectify our mistakes, and that's where my work comes in. . . .
>
> Transsexuals who want it are now able to obtain hormone treatment here. Already a government panel reviews individual cases of those wishing to change their sex and refers some transsexuals to therapy and hormone treatment. Currently, twenty-six transsexuals have been approved for treatment by the committee and another fifty cases are under review. . . . And right now we are studying how we can cover all health issues, including sex change operations, under our Family Code.

In this interview Castro Espín also touches on how the emphasis on tourism has increased prostitution and HIV, and the incidence of Cuban women and men marrying foreigners as a way out of the country. She acknowledges the existence of these problems but sees a gradual return to socialist ideals and feels Cuba has entered a very positive period in terms of discussion, proposals and more inclusive legal protections. She points out that Cuba has one of the lowest rates in the world of people living with HIV/AIDS: 0.09 percent of the population.[7]

Ricardo Alarcón, president of Cuba's National Assembly, has recently spoken of same-sex marriage as something on the country's near future agenda.[8] "We have to abolish any form of discrimination . . ." Alarcón says, "[and] are trying to see how to do that, whether it should be to grant [gay men and lesbians] the right to marry or to enjoy same sex unions." A change in the law has yet to be made but its mention by such a high government official is indicative of an extremely positive direction.

CHAPTER 8

INFORMATION
AND CONSCIOUSNESS

Lines Outside Bookstores Were Longer Than Lines to Buy Bread

By the time I finished *Cuban Women Now*, two years or so after I first went to Jaime Rivero with my idea, Ambito had closed its doors and I was working at another of the Book Institute's publishing houses: Ciencias sociales. Set up according to the type of text each produced, the semiautonomous units under the book manufacturing umbrella published adult or children's literature, medical and other scientific titles, art books and more. Ciencias sociales was responsible for titles in the areas of history, economics, sociology, and philosophy. *Cuban Women Now* appeared under the Ciencias sociales imprint.

Other Cuban institutions had their own publishing programs as well: Casa de las Américas, UNEAC, the universities, and provincial endeavors large and small. At the time they were all official, government or Party funded and run. Much later, long after I left the country, a smattering of independent publishers would open their doors. Promoted by small groups of mostly young poets, these were allowed to flourish—perhaps because their range of influence was considered insignificant. Or perhaps because forces favoring greater freedom in the arts were gaining some degree of agency.

One of the revolution's great early successes had been getting a nation that had previously suffered such a high illiteracy rate interested in reading. During my years on the island Cubans read absolutely everything. Book publishing was largely government-subsidized so what people read wasn't tied to a market economy. Books cost almost nothing and the population devoured them. Lines outside bookstores were often considerably longer than lines to buy bread or other foodstuffs.

After the 1959 victory the first major press run of a single book had been the classic *Don Quixote* by the sixteenth-century Spanish novelist Miguel de Cervantes; a million copies sold in less than a year. Later other titles enjoyed million copy press runs, among them *The Autobiography of Malcolm X*, Che Guevara's *Bolivian Diary*, and *Tania la guerrillera*—about the young German woman who gave her life in the same campaign.

In 1973 my parents came to visit, and they accompanied our family in hours of voluntary work at one of the Book Institute's big old midtown factories. We joined the assembly line to help bind *De mi patio al cielo* (From My Patio to the Sky). This was a collection of poignant poems by a young and badly wounded Vietnamese teenager named Tran Dang Khoa. The paperback was illustrated by Cuban artist René Mederos and the press run was something like four hundred thousand.

Gregory and Sarah were avid readers, Sarah especially. In her teenage years she particularly loved science fiction and detective novels. When my daughter returned each Friday from the beca I'd have a new book waiting on her pillow. She even read as she walked. I remember Sarah alternating with friends to stand in bookstore lines that sometimes assembled before dawn so she could be sure of getting a title she wanted. Gregory's early favorites were Russian novels of youthful morality and action. Later he gravitated to the great Latin American classics.

BAD PRESS

With such emphasis on good literature I was always perplexed by the poor quality of Cuba's press, especially its daily newspapers. *Granma*, the official voice of the Cuban Communist Party, appeared each morning in a format of six to eight or ten pages. It was almost unreadable. Long speeches by Fidel or other government officials were printed in their entirety, as were the formal addresses given by distinguished visitors from the other socialist countries. Opinion wasn't present in these pages unless it mirrored official opinion. There were lots of articles on production goals that had been met, very few on the real problems that often made meeting such goals impossible. Proud coverage of Cuban sports and cultural events pretty much rounded out the day's offering.

It was true that in the Cuban press one could read about countries, peoples and struggles unknown to a U.S. public. But such news always adhered to the

Cuban Communist Party line. Dissent—which existed fairly freely in public discussion, in neighborhoods and workplaces, on buses, among students and citizens from every area of life, rarely found its way into *Granma*, at least not while we lived in Cuba.

The afternoon paper, *Juventud rebelde*, was published by the Young Communists and was only slightly less boring than its morning counterpart. It too represented a poor use of resources. In the mid-seventies a third Havana paper, *Trabajadores*, came out of a revitalized union movement. None of this press approached the standards of a decent European, Latin American, Asian, or African newspaper.

When I asked Cubans what they thought of their newspapers they just laughed—or gave me a look that said: What? You crazy? Some replied that although a bit rough they made acceptable toilet paper. *Granma* especially was a frequent subject of Cuban humor. When I asked people why they thought the dailies were so bad, some used the shortage of paper as an excuse; others simply shrugged. The poor quality of the country's press wasn't high on most people's list of concerns.

I have wondered why Cuban poets and writers have taken such risks, even during periods of censorship, while the press has so little in the way of opposing opinion. Perhaps the press has been seen as a more openly political instrument, to be controlled more tightly. Perhaps it's been easier to hire journalists who adhere to policy than to persuade novelists and poets to do so. The latter work in relative isolation; when they produce a finished work suggesting changes would be seen as imposition. Journalists hand in daily articles which pass through the hands of editors who can more easily suggest direction, cut and paste.

Cuban magazines and journals were better than the newspapers. From those featuring basic news to the cultural, literary, artistic, scientific, or theoretical publications, interesting, well-researched articles held one's attention. Graphic design was often exciting. Every once in a while younger or more radical editorial boards would produce a magazine that entered uncharted waters or challenged an accepted political position. Almost invariably, after the expression of a point of view that differed from the Cuban Party's official line, its editor's curiosity and courage would be rewarded with closure. Despite Fidel's frequent plea that the revolution not talk down to the population but rather work to raise its intellectual level, Party and government alike seemed to fear giving too much alternative information or straying from a position that had been decided upon at the top.

Surely the most interesting theoretical journal to be published in Cuba while I was there (and of interest as well far beyond its borders) was *Pensa-miento crítico*, closely aligned with the University of Havana's Philosophy department. It was launched in the creatively diverse 1960s and its fifty-three issues, of several hundred pages each, remain a compendium of the very best Latin American revolutionary thought in a variety of fields: the social sciences, psychology, economic theory, history, decolonization, sociology and the arts. The journal's brilliant minds belonged to a new generation of Marxists. They attacked sectarianism and engaged in polemics on the relevant topics, theories and practices of the times.

Pensamiento crítico was much more than a journal. Argentine philosopher Néstor Kohan situates the publication in the context of the political culture of an era.[1] He sees the popular and student movements of the 1960s in France and the United States as emblematic of a phenomenon of worldwide rebel-lion and points out that both First World countries were mired in colonialist wars they could not win, France in Algeria and the United States in Vietnam. The Cuban revolution, coming to power as it did at the very beginning of the sixties, became a palpable example of the new winds of social change, vibrant with creative possibility.

Kohan argues that Cuba was the beacon symbolizing a range of efforts, a few successful, many eventually unable to sustain themselves or vulnerable to imperialism's efforts at destabilization. It represented a viable response on the part of the world's oppressed and exploited to that project we would later call neoliberalism. The Cuban revolution influenced the Civil Rights and Black Power movements in the United States as well as many other struggles for justice throughout the so-called Third World.

Politics Is Never Separate from Culture

We cannot understand these political movements, however, if we do not take into account their cultural and artistic manifestations. To name just a few of the most noteworthy Latin American examples: the new literary boom (par-ticularly in the novel), dependency theory (put forth by political economists in more than one country), liberation theology (and its political praxis in dozens of Catholic communities), the new cinema and new song movements (in the arts), oral history, testimonial journalism, and the pedagogy of the oppressed (primarily as espoused by Brazil's Paulo Freire).

Cuba welcomed and contributed to all these movements and the revolu-tion provided a rich context for discussion and debate. Kohan enumerates a few of the most important. In 1963 Alfredo Guevara publicly confronted Blas Roca (leader of the prerevolutionary Communist Party) when the latter tried to ban the exhibition of important films by Fellini, Pasolini, and Buñuel. In 1964 the vanguard critic Ambrosio Fornét and José Antonio Portuondo (another of the old timers) engaged in heated discussions on vanguardism and aesthetics, realism, snobbism, and populism in the arts. The year 1966 saw important discussions pitting the generation of artists and writers who had come into their own with the revolution against the older, more Social Realist generation. That same year, debate went beyond the art world to question the use of the old (mostly Soviet) manuals in the teaching of Marxism.

Politics is never separate from culture. Perhaps it is this that so frightened those ignorant and shortsighted lords of Cuban culture who wielded such unfortunate power at the end of the 1960s and beginning of the 1970s, and succeeded in stifling the revolutionary criticism and ideas for social change rooted in the creative critiques that had characterized the country's intellectual and artistic vanguard during the previous decade.

The Cuban Communist Party shut down *Pensamiento crítico* and closed the University's philosophy department in June 1971. As we will see in a coming chapter, this culminated in a protracted period of cultural repression, privileging presumably safe but often second-rate artistic production. The overall revolutionary project suffered and so did many of its most creative spirits.

Despite this sad history, one of the revolution's most impressive and unassailable accomplishments has been the importance it has placed on learning. "If you know, teach. If you don't know, learn," the Cuban leadership urged; the slogan could be seen on billboards, walls, and in the daily papers. "An educated people is a free people" is also something we heard a lot. Once the great literacy campaign reduced illiteracy from more than thirty to less than four percent, all sorts of follow up courses became available.

The effort didn't stop at teaching people to read. Classes in every imaginable field were offered constantly and all over the island. One could always get time off from work to study and taking classes was broadly encouraged. As a sometime freelance journalist, I was required to take a short course on Marx's *Capital*; grasping its complex concepts proved extremely difficult. I considered myself a Marxist and was sure I understood the basic tenets of Marx's analysis of capitalism. The finer points were harder.

Education wasn't only to be found in books. Cubans are passionate about film, theater, music, ballet, poetry, and the visual arts. When I lived in the country, theatrical and ballet productions, concerts, and museums were always crowded. School children were taken regularly to cultural events. The amount of money and effort spent on artistic ventures never ceased to amaze me. Many artists received government subsidies, and when the U.S. embargo blockade made it difficult to obtain paper, typewriter ribbons, canvas, paints, musical instruments or strings, photographic supplies, and the like, the cultural institutions made them available.

During our time in Cuba, cultural activity of all kinds remained innovative, often stunningly good. Informal performance spaces, or *peñas,* opened. Many younger poets and musicians got their start there. I remember the Sunday morning peña at Lenin Park where poet Francisco Garzón Céspedes and singer and guitarist Teresita Fernández performed in a clearing surrounded by beautiful trees. Large rocks provided seating. Each week there would be a special guest or two.

Eusebio Leal, then curator of the capital's City Museum and later the man behind the exquisite renovation of Old Habana, once brought a pair of dueling pistols which he invited those interested to examine while he explained the history and class nature of the cruel tradition. On another occasion prima ballerina Alicia Alonso—by then almost completely blind—came to the peña to talk about ballet and illustrate some basic positions under a canopy of leaves. Just watching her move from so close was thrilling. I had interviewed Alonso for my book about Cuban women and been fascinated by her loyalty to the revolution, her ideas about making classical ballet more friendly to the typical Cuban body type, and her efforts to convince parents that the art form could be an acceptable activity for their male offspring.

Needless to say, when Cuban boys were urged to explore ballet it was explained to their parents—first thing—that their participation didn't mean they were gay. Needless to say, many of them were. This was just one of many expressive endeavors where exquisite sensibility joins skill and endurance and may involve a sexuality that hasn't always been understood. In the arts and in other arenas as well, the revolution would have to deal with its homophobia.

When I lived there, Havana had museums of fine art, colonial art, decorative art, religious art, armament, ceramics, silverwork, anthropology, archaeology, music, cigar making, natural history, firefighting paraphernalia, pharmaceutical history, science, African culture, Islamic culture, stamps, glass, and cars. Sites were dedicated to the Napoleonic period, José Martí, Simón Bolívar, Benito Juárez, Humboldt, Ernest Hemingway, and Abel Santamaría, among others. Later the homes of the poets Dulce María Loynaz and José Lezama Lima were opened to the public. Festivals and fairs were frequent and almost always worth a visit. The Pabellón Cuba, on the Rampa, was a large venue that changed shows often; its well-planned exhibition space was always free and crowded with people.

Even just strolling along a street, especially in the old city center, one passed dozens of doors showing off their proudly preserved hardware, balconies hanging with potted plants, media lunas of richly colored glass and shutters that still somehow retained a patina of elegance amidst the disrepair that threatened to swallow these architectural gems as the shortages of paint and building materials became ever more critical.

He Asked Me to Go to the Local Precinct

The almost two years I spent working on what would become *Cuban Women Now* provided me with incomparable access. I traveled the country interviewing women who had participated in the armed struggle that brought the revolution to power, women who had taken on a variety of leadership roles, factory workers, educators, cane cutters, doctors, administrators, students, artists and writers, tobacco workers, Party members, dissidents, women who mouthed the official line, and others who went beyond official rhetoric in their extrapolations and questions. Mostly, women whose horizons had been bleak before this great experiment in social change now found themselves with a broad range of opportunities. I also got to see what men were doing, what an entire people was building.

I saw the country as I wouldn't otherwise have had the opportunity to see it, from the rugged mountains of Oriente to the tobacco fields of Pinar del Río. In this westernmost of Cuba's provinces I had an experience that reflected the ambivalence and hesitation Cubans often felt when confronted with the attention of people from somewhere else.

I had come to the area outside of the small town of San Juan y Martínez to interview an elderly tobacco house worker everyone called Grandma. It was a frank and animated conversation. Grandma, the granddaughter of slaves, was now a member of a Party nucleus. She could neither read nor write so I had to return to the province to read our interview to her; my practice always included getting feedback from my informants before I edited their words for publication. In Grandma's case this process led to an enduring friendship.

Walking back into town after the interview I stopped to photograph a young girl on a back street. She was skipping rope by herself, obviously having a great time. Dressed in clean but threadbare clothes she seemed healthy, vitally energized, a picture of the new Cuban youth. And she was happy to pose, proudly showing off her rope jumping skills. As I snapped the last in a series of pictures a policeman approached and asked for my camera.

She was skipping rope by herself, having a great time.

He wasn't pleased that I had chosen to photograph poverty and demanded my film. I explained that I was working on a book and showed him my Book Institute letter of introduction. Unconvinced, he asked me to go to the local precinct. He didn't insist I accompany him, but gave me directions and asked me to meet him there. I walked the half dozen blocks, sure the problem would be amicably resolved.

It was an amicable solution in that no voices were raised and no suggestion that I stop my work was made. But the police were intransient about taking my roll of film. They didn't know, nor did I explain, that I'd changed rolls while shooting the young girl and that only some of my images of her were still in the camera. I had another roll in my pocket that contained, among much else, my first shots of the scene.

I rewound the film and handed over the just-started roll. The officer with whom I was dealing took my name and address and promised that once his superior had a chance to review what was on it he would see that the film was returned. I believed him. For weeks I expected those negatives to arrive in the mail.

I could understand and to some extent accept this Cuban defensiveness. More than one writer had betrayed the generosity of the revolution by bending facts to a preconceived argument or abusing access in some other way. Still, I always felt these foreign intellectuals had a right to their opinions, quite naturally filtered through their own experience and assumptions. It was hard to gauge just when perceptions that differed from the official point of view would be perceived as attacks. Cuban officials, at least during the 1970s, 1980s and 1990s, had a hard time accepting viewpoints different from their own.

During the years I lived in Cuba, the U.S. American social anthropologist Oscar Lewis was asked to leave the country because the Cubans believed he was working for the CIA. "Working for the CIA" became a mantra, an accusation impossible to disprove but which served on more than one occasion to dispense with someone whose analysis might not turn out to be what the Cuban CP hoped. The Frenchman René Dumont and Poland's K. S. Karol similarly became personae non grata. At the time I accepted the accusations against these men. Today I wonder if they weren't victims of fear, hysteria, and also perhaps opportunism in the context of unequal war.

I felt grateful for the Cuban revolution's confidence. It enabled me to learn a great deal and transmit much of what I learned in books, articles, poems and thousands of pages of personal journal. It changed my life and made possible what I am today.

CHAPTER 9

CHANGING HEARTS,
MINDS, AND LAW

WHAT IS HUMANISM?

May 1972. My journal draws me back to events that layer themselves in memory. So much has shifted. What once seemed so clear now asks to be revisited from a different direction, a more complex understanding.

GREGORY: Mommy, what is humanism?

ME: Well, a humanist is someone who loves people, wants the world to be a happy place, without misery, someone who hates war, who hates killing, a good person. But if she is only against misery and killing, but doesn't understand the reasons why some people have everything and others nothing, she is a humanist but not a Marxist or a revolutionary. A Marxist understands the reasons. A revolutionary tries to do something about the situation. A humanist just says she wishes it were different, wouldn't it be nice if it were different. . . .

GREGORY: That's what I thought. My grandparents are humanists. But I also have a teacher who is a humanist. . . .

ME: What do you mean?

GREGORY: Yeah, my tennis teacher. He's a good guy, and he plays with us and we like him. But he's a humanist. Remember Nixon's Saturday night speech? Lies, all lies! This teacher agreed with parts of it. He said that North Vietnam invaded the South and that's why the retaliation.

ME: What did you tell him?

GREGORY: I said how could the North invade the South if it was all one country. Vietnam is one country, the division was imposed. I explained the Geneva Accords. . . .

ME: Is this the same teacher you were telling me about a couple of weeks ago who laughed when he heard you were studying Vietnamese and said that wasn't any good for anything, that Vietnamese is just a dialect, not a language?

GREGORY: Uh-huh.

ME: But how is it possible that you have a teacher like that?

GREGORY: Braulio and I just walked away finally, and when the teacher left we talked about what we could do. We decided what that teacher needs is some political education. So we're going to talk to him and try to raise his consciousness. He's all mixed up about the war and everything.

ME: I don't know . . . maybe we should talk to the principal about a teacher like that . . . .

GREGORY: No, we can handle it. There are a bunch of younger kids who don't yet have political concerns. They sit around and play marbles. Little kids like César and Marcos, kids like that. They're not interested in reading the paper every day like we are. They never talk about the war. For us that's our everyday conversation. And we don't want them to be influenced by someone like this teacher. Because we—Braulio, Lázaro, and I—we aren't surprised when he talks like that. But we want to do some political work with him so the little kids won't be affected. And to raise his own consciousness. We always argue about something. And we always come to a conclusion. I can't remember now what the last argument was but we always discuss things with him. And he kids around, he's always kidding around with me, saying things like: "Hey, Cohen, you CIA agent, you!"[1] Or telling us: "Sure I'm a *gusano (worm)*."[2] He's kidding, but he does it so much you know there's something to it. . . .

ME: So you're sure you don't want me to talk to the principal?

GREGORY: No, we can handle it. We're doing political work with him, don't worry. He talks about U.S. interests. He says everything the United States does it does to protect its interests. Like in Vietnam, and invading Cuba and all. . . .

ME: Well he's right. It is protecting its interests but. . . .

GREGORY: Well yeah, but what interests? That's the point.

Gregory was eleven when we had this conversation. At forty-seven he says the dialogue frightens him. It isn't only the dogmatism that makes him uncomfortable but the fact that a student, from his position of youthful inexperience, would attempt to control a teacher in this way. I wonder about my own inclination to want to talk to the principal about this teacher. The teacher was doing nothing more than challenging his students, from his own political position. My response reflected an extremely narrow view of teaching and learning, as well as the idea that it was okay to turn a teacher in for expressing opinions contrary to the Party line. I look back on both attitudes with embarrassment.

I Am Excited about This Meeting

The Committees for the Defense of the Revolution, or CDRs, were established on September 28, 1960. Inside Cuba they represented the broadest possible grassroots organizing. Outside, they were like light bulbs for the critics, giving them their most useful material for attack, their straightest arrow to an I Told You So exposé. Big Brother, those critics claimed triumphantly, you have neighbors watching neighbors, children judging their parents. No one is safe.

Top-down structures do run the risk of power abuse and the Cuban organizations were no exception. Just as not everyone in Cuba considered Party membership a privilege and responsibility rather than a stepping-stone to personal advancement, some also used the block committees opportunistically. But the Committee for the Defense of the Revolution on my block, far from making me feel watched or controlled, offered protection, aid, and opportunity. Our CDR president, Masa, was a large, middle-aged black man from Camagüey. In his youth he had worked in a sugar mill; no higher education, no opportunity for a better life—until the revolution came along.

Under Masa's enthusiastic leadership our CDR established neighborhood patrols to keep our streets safe, absolved Robert of having to give a blood donation when I had my kidney removed,[3] and organized voluntary work brigades, blood drives, yearly pap smears, and other preventative health measures. Through our Comité we kept our neighborhood's public areas clean, and joined others in helping to build a new wing on a cancer hospital and rehabilitated the country's largest baseball stadium.

Early February 1973. At the far end of our block, neighbors begin to straggle from their apartments. Some carry folding chairs. Others sit on the

Our CDR president Masa, his daughter Krushkaya, and wife Helena.

low wall fronting the building next to Masa's. Masa himself—corpulent, with shortly cropped graying hair and an embracing grin—emerges from the lobby of his corner building hauling a long wooden bench. His booming voice asks some of the younger men to fetch the two he left behind.

It's 8:30 P.M. The meeting of the CDR will begin in half an hour. Having finished dinner, the last members take their places along the sidewalk. Fidel, in a recent speech, emphasized the need for punctuality and people seem to be taking that to heart. Even the parent-teacher meetings at Ana's school have suddenly begun starting on time. I'd been surprised and momentarily distressed at the last one when—after years of being the only parent to show up at the stipulated hour and deciding to get with the Cuban tempo and amble in along with everyone else a couple hours late—I'd interrupted a meeting that had begun almost two hours before.

This is being described as a transitional period. Prompted by the revolutionary leadership, people seem more conscious of the need to engage in better planning, eliminate unproductive work habits, and increase efficiency. Tonight's meeting is unusual in that it is obligatory for all neighbors, not just those who belong to the CDR. We will discuss the draft proposal of a new law covering casual or criminal abuse of public property, hunting and fishing, the misuse of uniforms, and protection of the family. This last category contains decidedly gendered implications.

I am excited about this meeting. Participating in making new law is like going out into the fields to dig potatoes and then seeing them on the grocery store shelves a couple days later—only better. When new law is needed a committee of experts under the auspices of the National Assembly is charged with researching the subject and drawing up a draft proposal.

This proposal is then published and studied throughout the country: in work places, schools, military units, CDRs and other mass organizations, as well as Party and Young Communist structures. People suggest additions or modifications to particular clauses or show their displeasure over some piece of the whole. All this input is then recorded, tabulated, and sent up through each organization to a committee that feeds its findings back to the Assembly. Where there is consensus for change that change is reflected in the final draft, which is then voted into law by the legislative body.

If this isn't democracy I don't know what is.

Tonight's meeting starts slowly. Nereida, our block committee's ideological secretary, reads each article and Masa illustrates what it covers with anecdotes from his own experience or the experience of fellow workers or friends, sometimes from his past in the sugar mills of the 1930s and 1940s.

Sometimes someone else chimes in. In this era of scarcity people have no trouble recognizing that community or public property must be protected, that misusing or destroying it will be to everyone's disadvantage. A woman from our building, whose comments seem intended to show participation rather than real concern, periodically raises her hand: "It's not going to be a crime to trade evaporated milk for clothing all of a sudden, is it?" And: "My son's been wearing his army jacket to go to voluntary work. I hope that's not against the law."

Masa and Nereida respond patiently to every comment and question. Participation, whatever attitude it may reflect, is encouraged. The articles having to do with care of public property, proper use of military uniforms, hunting, fishing, and the like are all pretty straightforward. No one raises a major objection. If I am surprised by anything it is the relative leniency of punishment proposed in cases where infractions are established.

Then we come to a discussion of those laws regulating family life: sexual offense and misconduct. I've read the draft proposal, taken part in a similar discussion at my workplace, in fact, and have been looking forward to contributing my thoughts on this section of the draft. I raise my hand and Masa calls on me.

"Since the law is concerned with parents who prevent their children from studying or going to voluntary work," I begin, "I wonder if we could suggest that men who prevent their wives from working—in cases where the wife wants to—shouldn't also be seen as committing a punishable offense?"

Nereida snorts: "Any woman whose husband won't let her work can always get a divorce!" She looks around. A smattering of those present nod. There is a ripple of laughter.

"But many women don't yet have that level of consciousness," I insist. "Plus this wouldn't be the only consideration in a relationship going bad . . ."

No one seems to second my idea. Although Masa's wife Helena works, it is clear he doesn't like what I've said.

I fall silent for a while. I know the protocol for this type of meeting. If a suggestion is made, even if it's not seconded by anyone else it's supposed to be entered onto the form provided for that purpose. There's always the possibility it will reflect a concern voiced somewhere else. My comments are not recorded but I decide to let it go. As an outsider, even one who has shared Cuban life for several years now, I don't want to press my opinion.

The articles continue to be read, the questions and commentary remain lackluster, most aimed at small points of clarification.

Then we are discussing another part of the family law proposal and I can't continue to restrain myself. I've been troubled about its implications ever since first reading it in preparation for my workplace meeting. The article in question states that if a man gets a young woman between the ages of twelve and sixteen to sleep with him based on a promise of marriage, the woman denounces him, and he is convicted, he will be given a sentence of three to eighteen months.

So far so good. Or at least not so bad. But the clause goes on to stipulate that if he does in fact marry her, he will be exonerated.

I find it shocking that this be considered revolutionary law. I raise my hand again: "I certainly think that kind of act should be punished," I say, "but I don't believe encouraging marriage based on coercion is good for anyone."

There's absolutely no enthusiasm for what I'm saying. Again Masa tries to dismiss me. With uncharacteristic paternalism he tells me we have to be realistic, that the main thing is that this new law discourages the crime. Then he throws in a comment about the girl's honor. I am stunned. And also angry because I feel he should be supporting my right to make my point and be writing it down whether or not he agrees.

From the deepening evening shadows Mercy raises her hand. Mercy and her husband live in our building, on the second floor. They are currently detailed to the Cuban Embassy in Chile but happen to be home on leave. I know Mercy as a brilliant and forward-looking woman. To this point she has been sitting quietly to my left. I hadn't expected her to intervene but she does so now, speaking slowly at first:

"We're in a transitional period and in general I think the spirit of these proposals for new law is good," she begins. "In a transitional period some people inevitably retain the old ways of thinking and some move on. The challenge is to push a majority to the most advanced positions possible. We've got to remember that our job is always to reach for the higher level, the most progressive ideas not the least progressive. I agree with Margaret's argument and I'll tell you why."

Mercy is speaking to people who respect her status and ideological depth. They perk up, listen, weigh her words.

"A lot of the new law is okay," she continues. "But this whole part that has to do with family law seems badly phrased, badly written, even defective. I can't see much difference between some of these proposals and the old Cuban Constitution of 1940 with its bourgeois notions of justice. Except then it wasn't enforced, or it was only enforced against the poor. This new law will be enforced for everyone so we've got to make sure it's what we want.

"What do we really mean by some of the words or descriptive phrases used in this proposal? Terms like honest woman or good habits? What is an honest woman today? Is she your idea of an honest woman or my idea or that fellow over there's idea of what honest means? More to the point, what do we mean when we talk about honesty and womanhood in the same sentence?

"And consider what marriage means today? Certainly not the same as it meant in the old bourgeois order. That is, it means the same to some of us but not to everyone. To many of us marriage is no longer a ritual through which we can try to save a girl's honor—whatever that means. In the new society, where unmarried mothers have the same rights as married mothers, where children are recognized equally without regard to who their father is—the old bourgeois concept of illegitimacy is no longer valid—where women can work, where children are educated and cared for by the state, marriage can't possibly have the same meaning it once did.

"Marriage in the socialist state should be an equal partnership, entered into equally. Even if a young woman becomes pregnant she should be able to decide—based on what she believes is good for her child and for her own future—if she wants to marry her child's father. To begin with she should be able to decide if she wants to have the child or not."

By now a few heads nod. Murmurs of agreement swell along the block. Even Masa seems to soften, less invested in his earlier statements. But he still doesn't look too happy. I realize most if not everyone present understand what Mercy has said. When the vote is taken, it's unanimous. Even Masa has come around.

Mercy knows how to speak to this crowd.

I have a lot to learn.

The meeting, which had gotten underway before nine P.M., comes to an end just before midnight. Some of us have neighborhood guard duty on the midnight to 2:30 A.M. shift.

Mercy and her first husband, Juan Carretero,[4] eventually separate, then divorce. Later she marries Roberto González, a tall, quiet man as gentle as he is analytical. Sometimes we visit in the evenings, talk about the struggles going on throughout Latin America and the more complicated struggles in Cuba itself.

Ana, Robert, Ximena, Sarah, Margaret, and Gregory, on the balcony of our Havana apartment. Havana, 1974.

Ten years later, no longer living in Cuba, I hear that Mercy committed suicide. Jumped from a high balcony at the University's School of Economics where she taught. Besides Roberto she leaves two daughters, Alicia and Tania. As I write this I learn that Roberto recently died from a sudden, fast-growing cancer.

Tania had been one of Ana's dearest childhood friends. The same age, I remember them spending hours together. When many years later on a journalist's trip to the island, Ana seeks Tania out, she cannot find her.

Big Changes

June 26, 1974. My dear friend Arnaldo Orfila is visiting from Mexico and we spend the evening sitting in on People's Court. A friend of Arnaldo's who participated in the organization of these courts, and now travels throughout the country in an advisory capacity, has offered to show him how they work. And just as so many years before, when he dragged me and I dragged Susan through that cocktail party crowd to meet Fidel, my friend has asked if I'd like to accompany him tonight. I jump at the chance.

We're in the modest courtroom at the Seccional Habana Vieja, on O'Reilly next to the Banco Nacional building. This is near the old Ambito office where I worked when I first came to the country. I know the neighborhood. It's rundown, impoverished, just blocks from the city's port area. Living conditions here are pretty miserable: inadequate housing, men and women with low cultural and educational levels. Although everyone now has greater access to education, work, and health care, problems as serious as overcrowded living conditions are a long way from being solved.

Before the revolution prostitution flourished here and men—many of them dockworkers—hung out at the corner bar on Friday nights drinking half their paychecks away. Even if they didn't, what they brought home hardly made ends meet. Families often lived in a single room. Many still do. It's not uncommon for a man and woman, joined in free union or legally married, to separate or divorce and continue to have to live with their children in a couple of small rooms because a decade and a half after taking power the revolution still hasn't been able to provide them with adequate housing.

There have been big changes for these people, important changes like universal health care and education, college for anyone wanting to attend— not just the wealthiest strata of society—the same subsidized basic food basket everyone gets, and many other advantages. But when you live in substandard housing and in neighborhoods where many of the same old social ills persist, such changes can seem very partial.

Havana's City Planning Department intends to remodel this whole area: dotted with examples of priceless colonial architecture but plagued by overcrowding, shaky and dilapidated structures, patched electricity, lack of water. What will happen to these people then? What are their lives like now?

This court reviews a compendium of their problems and takes decisions designed to bring modest change, a whisper of justice, and promise of better times ahead in the midst of overcrowding, alcoholism, domestic violence, and the ongoing frustration generated by so much misery.

The People's Court began in 1963. Like so many other ambitious projects, it was Fidel's idea. Until 1970 it operated in every neighborhood and throughout the entire country in a more or less experimental fashion. Judges were elected by neighbors through their Defense Committees. Once elected, they were given crash courses in basic civil law. They labored voluntarily after working hours.

Those first years produced a wealth of experience. Some things worked while others didn't. Innovations were introduced and gradually the whole system was revamped and unified so that as of January 1, 1974, what had been a trial and error way of dealing with non-criminal cases became the well-respected bottom rung of the country's entire civil court system.

Judges are still elected by the people, in their neighborhood CDRs, from among Party cadre, the Federation of Cuban Women, Young Communists, and members of the National Association of Small Farmers in the countryside. The president of each court and all judges receive an intensive forty-five day course and systematic supervision from trained legal personnel. Instead of having to work nights and carry out detailed investigations in their almost nonexistent free time, People's Court judges are now relieved of their normal workplace obligations for four-month periods. They continue to draw their regular salaries and can devote themselves full-time to this demanding work. Each court's president serves for a year, providing the necessary continuity. The president as well as the lower judges can be recalled by the electorate at any time.

Arnaldo and I take seats at the back of a room filled with interested parties in various stages of delivering documents, making motions, and waiting for their cases to be heard. The atmosphere is charged, but serious and strangely orderly. I have the sense that these are people who know their job is important. They don't seem to be cutting corners, taking unwarranted breaks, indulging in cronyism, or letting anyone off the hook.

I notice a number of men and women with whom one or another of those present consult from time to time. I'm told these are retired judges who have come to help out. This court is extremely busy, hearing an average of four hundred cases a month. Court personnel work all day every day and almost all night long on Tuesdays. They are required to keep up with their ongoing legal studies on Wednesday nights.

I ask what sorts of cases are generally heard. Anything civil, I'm told, including incidents of domestic violence, child support when no legal marriage is involved, traffic violations, and the like. When we arrive three male judges—the president and his two assistants—are in the process of hearing a traffic violation case. A man riding a motorcycle was caught speeding with a young child sitting between his body and the handlebars. He was strongly cautioned that had he, the child, or anyone else been hurt, no public admonishment, monetary fine, or revocation of license would have made a difference. He was fined ten pesos. Education is clearly the goal.

The next case was to be handled in private and the judges retired to a side office accompanied by the accuser and accused. Arnaldo and I were permitted to sit in on the arguments. The story was dramatic. A young woman accused her ex-husband (in free union) of having come home drunk, insulting and attacking her with a machete. Her sister got between them, trying to intervene. So did the couple's nine-year-old daughter, who was hit by a chair in the fray.

This couple has been separated for almost two years but the lack of housing has forced them to continue living in the same one bedroom dwelling. The man, a swaggering macho type, clearly considers himself a Don Juan. His story is: okay, he did come home with a few drinks in him and she'd noticed love marks on his body made by one of his current girlfriends. This, he said, enraged her and she started the fight. When she hit him with a pressure cooker cover he had no alternative but to put her in her place. He also claims that the sister tried to knife him in the back.

During this initial telling of events the child is kept outside in the main courtroom area. The woman's story is one of continual harassment by this man. She says he comes home drunk every night and almost always tries to force her to sleep with him. When she won't, he insults and attacks her. In an earlier case a year before she had brought him up on charges of attacking and hitting her in the street while she was taking their youngest two children to school.

The man works. He is a barber and earns 190 pesos a month. The woman, who only has a first grade education, has no job. The man therefore, for better or for worse, supports the family. The sister has completed sixth grade but is looking for work and currently has no income. One of the man's accusations is that his ex-wife often keeps the children out until one or two in the morning.

In its pretrial investigation, the court ascertained that, in fact, this man drinks heavily. Several women judges, off duty at the moment but clearly interested in the case, have come to testify that living in the neighborhood they themselves have been targets of his catcalls and sexual innuendos. They also admit that the woman does keep the children out late and in general leads a disorderly life. The main problem is obvious in every accusation and counteraccusation: low educational levels and overcrowded living conditions in which people who no longer get along are forced to share cramped quarters.

The judges in this case go into the main courtroom to interview the child. When they return they say they are convinced that the sister did in fact try to knife the man—in defense of her sibling. The case is filled with contradictions; in general both plaintiff and defendant say what they imagine best supports their arguments.

After deliberating, with the three adults and the child out of the room but Arnaldo and me permitted to stay, the Court comes to the conclusion that the man bears the brunt of responsibility for what's happened. Because he'd been drinking, because of his sexism, because of his aggressive behavior. And because he attacked, even just verbally, someone weaker than himself. However, the judges have checked with the Urban Reform Office, which is currently considering giving separate living space to one of the parties. If they rule against only one of these people it will jeopardize that person in terms of his or her receiving the much needed separate space. This, of course, will be bad for everyone involved. The crux of this problem, as of so many, is the issue of shared quarters.

The Court condemns them both although the man's condemnation is considerably stronger than the woman's. The sister is absolved since it is decided she had a right to try to defend someone being attacked. With everyone but the child assembled once more the president of the court begins to talk to them all about the important aspects of the case. More than anything he points out the effects of their behavior on their children. He uses the term sexual damage when describing a child being forced to witness her parents' fights. He says the girl is doing well in school—she is nine years old and in third grade—and acquiring the education that will enable her to make something of herself. It is a shame, he says, to hurt her in this way, when the revolution is giving her the opportunity her parents never had.

The man is severely admonished for his drinking, and enjoined never to come home drunk again. He is told that if he does and is brought to court he will definitely be deprived of his freedom. This is his last chance at a moderate sentence. He is fined sixty pesos, close to a month's minimum wage, with the prerogative of paying it off in cash or jail time. The woman is urged to take better care of her children, not keep them out so late. But the bulk of the sentence is aimed at the man. The woman is fined five pesos for insults and aggressive behavior. A simple, clear explanation of what sexism can do to human beings, what tradition it comes out of and how it should have no place in the new society, is a centerpiece of the decision.

The judges in these cases, coming as they do from the same neighborhood as the defendants, know who they're dealing with. When imposing fines they always take into account the accused person's financial situation. They also consider the effects curtailment of freedom may have on production. In this particular case the judges are a chauffeur for the National Culture Council, an office worker, and a civilian working for the Armed Forces.

People have seventy-two hours from the time a sentence is imposed to comply with its terms or appeal to a higher judgment, in this case the Regional Court. After the hearing I speak with the man. He says he thinks the sentence is too stiff but doesn't seem inclined to appeal.

Out in the open courtroom once more, three women judges are hearing a case of alleged coercion. After the death of their mother, a young woman accuses her brother of making her life in the house they share impossible. She married a student of veterinary medicine and they have a small child. The husband is *becado*, meaning he lives at school and only comes home on weekends. He claims that his brother-in-law refuses to allow him into the house; he must visit with his wife and daughter in a nearby park. The young woman says her brother removed the door to her room and put it up in another part of the dwelling.

This young woman is a member of the Young Communists and her husband is also actively involved with the revolution. Not so the brother. These people were in this same court a few months back in a case in which the woman accused her brother of using her ration book to steal her daughter's food. The house is in the brother's name and this seems a clear case of the brother doing everything possible to get his sister and her husband and child to move so he will have the place to himself.

Under Cuban law, when parents die their house becomes the property of all their children equally, regardless of age or sex. This is really a problem for Urban Reform rather than People's Court. In the earlier case this woman had been instructed to take the issue to the Urban Reform Office so it could make an official decision on her right to part of the house, including her right to have her husband live with her there. For whatever reason, she has yet to do this.

After some deliberation the three women judges decide to put the case on hold, pending a people's inspection of the premises. They want to determine if the door in question really has been moved (the woman says it has, the brother says no). "He better put that door back where he found it this very night," exclaims the president of the court, laughing but with an edge that says she means business. The woman is once again urged to take her problem to the proper authority. When the brother understands that the judges themselves are going to come to his house to inspect the situation he becomes considerably less belligerent.

I find the women judges in general stronger and more articulate than the men. They seem to run a tougher court. These three judges all work, two of them in factories and one in an office. They're all also married with children.

Case by case the night unfolds. By one in the morning both sets of judges still have full dockets and are going strong. We leave. I could have stayed a while longer but Arnaldo is tired—and also concerned about his driver. He'd invited him to come to the sessions with us but the man had preferred to catch a few hours of sleep in his car.

Another night. Another glimpse at how lives are being changed under the most difficult circumstances. And yet a tragedy within my own circle of friends will soon remind me that developing ways to deal with domestic violence and prevent crimes of passion before they occur is a complicated matter, one the People's Court is only beginning to address.

Within the small community of foreigners, a Canadian woman named Mary Todd left her abusive husband, a Cuban, taking her five-year-old son with her. She had repeatedly denounced the man's threats, both while they were married and after their divorce. She was frightened for herself and for her child, and her friends were frightened for them. As continues to be true today throughout much of the world, the Cuban authorities told her they couldn't arrest the offender unless and until they caught him in an abusive act. We who knew the situation were afraid that by then it would be too late.

As it turned out to be. Mary began a new relationship and one night her ex-husband showed up where she, her new partner, and son were living. He tried to kill them all. The tragic crime ended with him murdering the son, the man who had replaced him in Mary's affections, and himself. His rampage left Mary herself with horrific knife wounds, one of which almost severed her tongue. She was left without her son, without her new partner, and literally mute: voiceless before a system that had failed her in every way.

I do not single out Cuba for this tragedy. Throughout the world legal systems continue to fail abused women and children. Change requires generations—and a profound revision of values. All the more important that it be rooted in the most solid concepts of equality and justice.

REFERENDUM ON THE NEW SOCIALIST CONSTITUTION

February 15, 1976, from my journal:

Extraordinary enthusiasm today. Discussed by people for months, changed, amended, brought to the Party Congress and discussed further, today was finally the referendum on the new Socialist Constitution. Polls opened at eight but people began lining up at four and five in the morning. Especially older people who remember what elections used to be like. Throughout the country hundreds of thousands of Pioneers (children from six to fourteen) guarded the urns and generally helped out at the polls.

The results have yet to be certified (mainly because of the mountainous regions of Oriente and Las Villas) but by ten A.M. eighty percent of those eligible had voted. The evening news reported that ninety-six percent of the more than five million people above the age of sixteen did their civic duty, with only a bit more than one percent voting against the referendum. Around noon someone from our CDR came to the door to tell us the word had just come down that foreign residents could vote if they desired. Antonio,[5] Gregory and I hastened to our polling place; (Gregory just to watch as he won't be sixteen for a few months). I called Robert and he came over later. . . .

THE MEAT PROBLEM

November 1976. Lidia, who lives on the third floor of our building, rings our back bell to tell us about a hastily pulled together meeting of our local CDR. The meat problem . . . the meat problem, she calls out, as she dashes off to inform our upstairs neighbors. Through the iron grate I can hear her elaborating in response to Silvia's questions: "They're going to take all the meat away from the boarding school students, and half their food quota as well!"

This doesn't sound right. We go to the day's *Granma* to consult the communiqué we know must contain an explanation. The revolutionary government has indeed published something on the paper's front page, explaining the decision in the clearest possible terms and asking for people's support.

Due to several years of drought, an increase in the price of imported animal feed, last year's African swine fever that required sacrificing so many pigs, and the need to continue raising the country's milk production, supplying people with their usual quota of meat has lately become more difficult. It's important not to have to slaughter cows, the communiqué explains, to keep milk production high. Because of all this the following measures are being adopted:

> From now on the individual beef ration will be distributed every nine instead of seven days—we've all noticed this has been the case for a while. As of next school term, all new boarding school students will receive only half their home-based meat ration, since they get three good meals—including meat—the five days they are in school. And due to recent increases in fowl and pork production, in a few months consumers will be able to choose beef, pork or fowl at least once in a while, instead of the beef only allotment.

This is the series of new measures. Nothing about taking away all the boarding school students' meat. Despite the fact that Lidia is calling the neighbors to a meeting at which they will quickly discover she has exaggerated the measure, she continues to stop the service elevator on each floor and call out her alarmist message.

Radio bemba at its finest.

Up Against the Hard Wall of Convention

How can I judge these efforts at dealing with the toughest problems people face? Poverty, substance abuse, violence, out of control anger, and lack of job training are endemic social problems that cannot be easily turned around. Generations must be educated into different values. Material solutions such as the all-important availability of adequate housing and equitable food distribution depend upon a palpable increase in production, and this too takes time. Much depends upon the economic model.

In the years I lived in Cuba the revolution initiated hundreds of ambitious programs: in literacy, education, industry, manufacturing, job retraining, nutrition, medicine, the sciences, housing, civil defense at times of natural disasters, recreation, sports, and the arts. Many of these programs were successful. Impressive statistics were published every day: in the newspapers, on television and radio, in Fidel's speeches. The emphasis was still necessarily on the overall picture. So many hundreds of new doctors. So many thousands of new apartments. Vegetable production rising in Matanzas. Crime going down in Camagüey. Such and such a minimum number of daily calories achieved per citizen.

Another parallel story was being written in areas where certain people or groups of people fell between the cracks. Young people who were reluctant to give up a personal dream in order to answer the call for new teachers. Women who worked outside the home, shouldered all housework and childcare and yet were judged unenthusiastic, uncooperative or, worse, marginal to the revolution if they didn't show up for weekend voluntary work. In time there was an increase in prostitution that few have wanted to admit was anything but an anomaly: "no one today has to sell sex" was the phrase that too often passed for explanation.

During my years on the island I was always acutely aware of the distance still to be traveled to true gender equality. It wasn't long after the initial victory that women began studying to become scientists, doctors, engineers, architects and other previously male-dominated professions; and it wasn't long before women outnumbered men in the requisite courses of study. Equal pay for equal work, as I've said, came rather quickly; even when a fairly lengthy list of jobs remained off limits to women. The most difficult change had to do with attitudes, customs, tradition.

"It's just the way it is" was something I often heard when I wondered out loud how a woman who carried one or two full-time jobs could be expected to take on the extras—the political tasks or voluntary work—that would win her revolutionary distinction. In my own family these issues came up again and again.

When we arrived in Cuba Robert and I had been together for little more than a year. He'd been surprised I had maids in my Mexican home and highly critical of the unequal relationship this sort of domestic service involves. I had come into the situation almost without thinking about it; babysitters weren't available and I needed someone to care for my children when I went out. Almost imperceptibly, household employees took on more and more chores until it seemed normal to have someone living in who cleaned, washed, cooked and helped care for the children.

I assuaged my guilt—and eventually also my feminism—by arguing that I treated my household help well. I paid them considerably more than the going wage. I considered them friends. I encouraged them to study, they sat at the table with us when we ate, and traveled with us on occasion. I'd lived in Mexico for the better part of a decade and had assimilated the country's lifestyle—even among the very poor domestic help was the norm; there was always someone poorer who needed the job. Robert had recently come from the United States. His discovery of the revolution was also recent. Extremely principled and articulate when making a point, he knocked one after another of my arguments to the ground.

When we got to Cuba it was suddenly just us. There was no one we could pay to handle the drudgery running a house entails. In many ways this was a relief. And it won't be so hard, I thought, we'll share the workload. Sharing to me meant Robert and I would each do half and the children, when they were home, would also be responsible for certain age-appropriate tasks. My kids point out that they did much more than other children their ages. After his acerbic critique of my Mexican living situation I believed Robert would do his part.

He didn't. If it doesn't bother me that it's dirty why should I clean it up, was typical of the reasoning he and so many men of his generation used. We argued. We did battle. I resorted to a variety of tactics by which I thought he might be induced to see my point. Once I left a sink full of dishes unwashed for a day, several days, a week. The stench was unbearable. In the tropics such filth can be dangerous. And it was. When Ana was taken to the hospital with a bad case of gastroenteritis one of us broke down and cleaned the kitchen. I no longer remember whether it was Robert or me.

Society made it easier for Robert to retreat from his household obligations. At both our workplaces emulation would set goals that could only be satisfied if everyone did his or her share. If Ana was sick and had to stay home from her day care center, I as the mother was expected to stay home to care for her. It was not nearly so acceptable for Robert to do the same.

Robert and I might struggle to accommodation and try to live by our own rules in this regard. We might try to figure out who had a less important workload on a particular day and be less likely to be missed at the office. To us it seemed reasonable that that person be the one to take off from work. But our individual solutions frequently came up against the hard wall of convention. If I stayed home everyone in my workplace understood. If Robert did, his boss and coworkers had a hard time accepting the decision or blamed me for being so feminist.

I knew the solution lay in broader collective answers. Early on I had written and published an article in the Cuban press urging the creation of neighborhood work brigades that might clean people's houses so the burden of housework wouldn't fall exclusively on women. My suggestion was met with derision, even outrage. "You can bet I'm not letting anyone come into my house and clean," a woman on our block sneered, "now that would be an invasion of privacy!"

A Few of the Lenin Girls

In Cuba during the 1970s most people agreed on the need for a change in attitude. How to bring this about was the question. Obviously, the schools provided the most fertile ground for such change. When my daughter Sarah was at the Lenin she came home one weekend with an interesting story. It seemed the male students had long expected their female counterparts to wash and iron their uniforms. This was the way it had always been. Many of the girls, educated in the age-old tradition of female service, went along with the expectation. Some even reveled in the all too familiar "I can do more than anyone and do it better" justification.

But one day a few of the Lenin girls asked themselves why this situation persisted. Why no one had challenged it, particularly when the official rhetoric affirmed gender equality. These girls decided to make a change. They refused to go on washing and ironing their boyfriends' uniforms and defended their decision quite publicly. These were strong young women, articulate about what they were doing and why. They managed to convince a few and then many others. It became a matter of human dignity and those young women who still might have wanted to please their boyfriends in this way dared not try. It wasn't long before the majority of the Lenin's female students were refusing to wash the young men's clothes.

At first the male students complained. They used all manner of coercive measures to try to keep things the way they'd been. But then a few of them broke ranks with the majority. They could see that the girls were right. The balance of power shifted and soon few could remember a time when the boys expected the girls to do their washing and ironing. A battle had been won.

On these issues, as I've said, our household was always somewhat at odds with Cuban society. Sometimes it was me alone moving against Robert's entrenched sense of male privilege. Sometimes, usually as a result of bitter struggle, Robert too would embrace a particular area of change. But then it was still us against the neighbors, the community, society as a whole. Again and again I would be confronted with a situation in which, despite the rhetoric of equality, it was simply understood that I would make the multitask sacrifice while Robert won some vanguard status for his work above and beyond.

During our years on the island certain moments stand out as exemplary in the struggle for gender equity. One was certainly the 1974 passage of the Family Code: legislation stipulating that men take on half a family's housework and childcare, encourage their wives to work or study, actively support their doing so, and in other very specific ways try to level the playing field with regard to the division of domestic labor. The new Family Code went so far as to rewrite the civil marriage vows so they included references to the more equitable division of household work. A decade later my son and his wife Laura would be married by a judge who recited clauses twenty-four, twenty-five, twenty-six, twenty-seven and twenty-eight of Cuba's Family Code as a standard part of the civil ceremony. Three and a half decades later, the Family Code is being rewritten to include same-sex couples.

Although many progressive initiatives were introduced, change would take time. A big problem remained the revolution's refusal to look systematically at the issue of male/female power. The FMC's continued disparagement of feminism and its inability or unwillingness to allow a gender analysis of Cuban society has proved all too successful in resisting hardcore change.

CHAPTER 10

"POETRY, LIKE BREAD, IS FOR EVERYONE"

Potato Dirt under My Fingernails

I wanted my poems to reach those poets with whom I shared the everyday astonishments: potato dirt under my fingernails, pumpkin pudding made from sweetened condensed milk and a rare allotment of squash, tropical heat plastering shirt to skin, the ticket taker at Copelia who remembered I always ordered chocolate, even when I'd been away in Vietnam for three long months, my woman's yearnings, disappointments, and joys. Royal palms: so familiar yet so eternally other. My life and community: so familiar, yet so eternally other.

Those close to me took the brunt and balm. My children. My partner. This latter, after Robert and I separated in 1975, and during my last five years on the island, was Antonio Castro. Antonio was a Colombian whose family had walked across to Venezuela in 1947, part of a desperate migration. His youngest brother died of hunger on that trek. Antonio was a poet and singer. He played the *cuatro*, a four-stringed instrument he used to accompany his passionate song. His fingers flew across the strings and sounding board, faster, faster; his rich voice soared.

Antonio had come to Cuba to care for Domingo León, a Venezuelan guerrilla commander who had been paralyzed in a gun battle some years before. I felt deeply loved by this small, intense man, but eventually found that although he tried harder than most he didn't really understand my creative need. My poems were often beyond him.

Certain neighbors became friends, though others remained unknowable and uninterested in knowing me except perhaps as the foreign oddity. On the fourth floor Alicia and Tomás were to be counted on: in the know, friendly, generous, and practical. Mercy on the second floor and Silvia and Ambrosio on the tenth were those with whom I felt the greatest political and intellectual kinship.

Carmen on the eighth floor was warm and neighborly. The family that lived next door, in the wooden shack stuck between two highrises—Florinda and her husband and twin daughters—were people with whom I had a relationship. And of course Masa, our Defense Committee president who lived down the street. Only a few of these people read poetry, none that I knew of in English.

That's Where the Poets Came In

And that's where the poets came in. There was Alex Fleites, whose quick humor and fragmentary knowledge of English prompted him to say, each time he left our apartment, "Te quiero y me quedo short" (I love you and I remain short—his particular word play around the idiomatic *me quedo corto*, Spanish for "and that's not the half of it"). There was Arturo Arango, who would later become an important novelist and short story writer. Víctor Rodríguez Núñez, at twenty, was the youngest of the group. Poetry spilled from him like rain germinating all manner of growing things. He and Gregory once shouted each other down over Gregory claiming Mao was a revolutionary and Víctor clinging to the Soviet line which disparaged Mao, Cuba's position at the time.

Bladimir Zamora smiled a lot. He was from a peasant community near the eastern city of Bayamo where, years later, his father would die drunk beneath the wheels of an ox-drawn cart. On an infrequent visit to Havana his mother once opened up to me about her hard life with a drinking man. Bladimir's parents had named him after Lenin but their Cuban pronunciation had rendered the "V" a "B."

Reina María Rodríguez was elf-like and ethereal. Her poetry even then was highly original, evocative, sometimes magical. Later she and Víctor would have a son, Eduardo, and much later she would retreat to a couple of rooms atop an old building, where today she nurtures a salon that continues to attract new generations of poets and artists.

Soleida Ríos' work resonated with me but I only saw her at national events or on a rare visit to Santiago de Cuba. She had been involved in the revolution's nationwide literacy campaign. When we met this was a recent enough experience that it was engendering some very powerful poems.

Alex Pausides was another good poet from the provinces. Shy and deferential, I cannot remember him ever using the familiar form of speech when we spoke. His goodness was palpable, his verse surprising. Milagros González lived on Isle of Youth. Her poetry was stunningly feminist, especially for the times. A signature poem called "First Dialogue" asks: "Where are you: manspirit of my time, / every afternoon coming home from work / exuding your fountain of rude stares / reproaching me . . ."[1]

In a corner of huge Lenin Park, Francisco Garzón Céspedes and Teresita Fernández organized their peña every Sunday morning. Sometimes we would take the children there to sit on rocks beneath the trees and listen to poetry or song. Garzón, as people called him, had a peculiar affect I would only understand years later when I realized he had lived in a painful closet. Back then, when he confided in me about a current romance, he referred to his love interest as female. It wasn't until many years later, outside the country, that he revealed they'd been men. I was shocked at this subterfuge, not yet understanding how dangerous coming out in Cuba would have been during those early years.

Bladimir, too, was gay, but he never spoke of his intimate life and I wouldn't have guessed at the time. In him the identity presented, at least publicly, as a kind of asexuality. He inhabited a tiny room in a decrepit building in Old Havana which he referred to as his *gaveta*, literally, drawer. Sometimes we would hang out there and he'd ceremoniously serve us steaming cups of rich Cuban coffee. It would be years before he accepted and revealed his desire for men. When he did, he shed a great deal of weight and began the long journey back from self-hate.

Norberto Codina lived across the street from us on Línea. His Venezuelan mother had brought him to Cuba and left him there as an adolescent when she went on to the United States. Norberto didn't possess a ration book (a necessity if one wanted to eat, and for many other things as well) and he'd lived without one for so long he didn't know how to remedy the situation. His apartment was filthy. Antonio once took it upon himself to clean everything in it; I remember the buckets filled with once shiny sheets soaking in soapy water on our back wash porch for a week. Today Norberto has a ration book. He is married, has a daughter, and lives in a different apartment, presumably kept clean by his wife, who is an urban planner.

Arturo was once fired from his position as managing editor of the *Casa de las Américas* magazine because—his version of the story—he had been critical of a writer with more political clout. His novels and short stories have been published throughout the Spanish-speaking world. He is the recipient of many literary prizes and is one of Cuba's most respected writers and intellectuals.

Victor, his U.S. American wife, Kate, their little girl, Miah, and his son Luis by a previous marriage now live in Ohio, where both adults teach at Kenyon College. After obtaining his Masters and Ph.D. in the United States, my old friend has made a life for himself here. He is part of the growing community of Cuban intellectuals who move freely between their native and adoptive countries; almost every summer finds him on the island.

Bladimir divides his time between Cuba and Spain; he has become an authority on, and well known producer of, Cuban music. When he's in Havana the gaveta is still home. Reina María continues to live and write in her rooftop salon; she has become a mentor to younger generations of poets. Garzón spends most of his time outside Cuba; in Mexico and Spain last I heard. He has developed a reputation as a *cuenta cuentos*, a teller of stories to audiences around the world who are gripped by his magic. Milagros died of heart trouble in her forties.

Alex, Arturo, Reina María, Soleida, Norberto, and Pausides all remain in Cuba. All are successful in their chosen fields; all travel widely.

There were others but these were the closest. None spoke or read English, not really, and try as I would I had never been able to write a successful poem in Spanish. Prose, yes. Essays, if someone was willing to do a style correction. But never poetry. My poetic voice was too personal, too intimate, too much a part of whom I was before leaving my early New Mexico landscape, before Spain or New York or Mexico. I communicated with my children, my lover of those years, and my community of friends in Spanish. The English waited, still but impatient, in some hidden recess of my psyche. It claimed its place in the poetry.

One afternoon, at a meeting of UNEAC's young writers' brigade, members' upcoming readings were being scheduled. I was there as a guest. It so often seemed as if I were a guest: half belonging, half not. As current brigade president, Bladimir was running the session. I caught his eye. In that single glance he understood how much I wanted to share my work. As he continued to talk he passed me a brief note: "¿Le gustaría a Ud. leer su poesía aquí?" Would you like to read your poetry here? Of peasant origin, he always addressed me formally.

I wrote an emphatic ¡Sí! on the same scrap of paper and passed it back. My heartrate accelerated. Without missing a beat Bladimir announced my forthcoming reading, date and all. I knew I would have to get busy and get some of my work translated. This didn't prove as difficult as I feared. Since my years in Mexico with *El Corno Emplumado* I'd routinely rendered into English the work of poets who moved me. Now several good Cuban poets offered to translate some of my work into Spanish. A feeling of belonging washed over me.

Varadero Celebrated Its Ninetieth Anniversary

This from my journal of December 9–15, 1977. I have elaborated here and there, to fill in gaps that seem to grow wider and deeper as the years go by:

Early on the morning of the ninth a car from Varadero came to pick me up. Already in the vehicle was Grandal, the *Revolución y Cultura* photographer who would accompany me to the big Culture Week at the town flanking Varadero Beach, Cuba's best known seaside resort. Others who would participate included Víctor Rodríguez Núñez, Alex Fleites, Arturo Arango, Francisco Garzón Céspedes, Alberto Molina, Margot de Armas, Angel Antonio Moreno, Eliseo Diego, and El Indio Naborí. Víctor, Alex, and Arturo are close friends. Garzón is also a friend, the poet and storyteller who—with Teresita Fernández—has sustained the wonderful peña every Sunday morning in Lenin Park.

Eliseo, in his late fifties, is of an older generation; one of Cuba's finest poets. To my astonishment and deep gratitude he once offered to translate three of my poems so I could read them in Spanish. I've yet to meet Margot. Angel Antonio Moreno lives in Matanzas.[In less than a year, he and I would collaborate on a book about José Manuel "Che" Carballo, a peasant decimista[2] known as El guajiricantor.[3]] And El Indio, as he calls himself, is also older; one of those people's poets who has recited for years at factories and farms. A pretty diverse group despite its not unusual paucity of women.

A week packed with activities of all sorts, some extremely moving. I participated as a performer—reading my poems—and also as a journalist; Grandal and I were assigned to come back with an article and photos for *Revolución y cultura*. These articles come easily to me so I just made sure I talked to the other performers, pumped them for special moments, got an overview and took a lot of notes. As always I gave my best energy to the cultural work itself.

Antonio had also been invited to this week of nonstop cultural activity. But he'd just returned from Granma Province at the extreme easternmost tip of the island. There he'd done a week's worth of events—poetry and song—on his own. He said he was too tired to head right out again. In my journal I note: Since Antonio didn't come I had a luxurious room to myself at the Internacional—sort of like a honeymoon minus the husband. At the time, the Internacional was the most upscale of the hotels on Varadero Beach.

Varadero's claim to fame was its pristine expanse of white sand and turquoise blue Caribbean sea. The town of the same name was best known as home to those who served the visitors. They drove the buses and taxis, worked in the dive and snorkel shops, staffed the hotels, cooked, or waited tables at the variety of local restaurants.

Many of the tourists were foreigners: Europeans, Latin Americans, and a small number of U.S. Americans, most of the latter political tourists. There was a smattering of Cubans who were spending a week there on honeymoon or as recipients of some special workplace reward. As with most such towns, a certain amount of wheeling and dealing went on. But Cuba during the decade of the 1970s hadn't yet seen the sort of internationally connected subculture of prostitution and drugs that would return—though never to its former extent—in later years.

Varadero had that look of newness so many small Cuban towns had acquired since the revolution came to power in 1959: a certain uniformity of style in storefront and signage. Primary colors repeating their reds, yellows, and greens in graphic design that seemed to have come from a single hand. Communities hidden in what was once an impoverished backwater might still display the accidental browns and grays of worn palm thatch and weathered wood; these towns closer to the tourist centers displayed brighter colors. The Copelia ice cream parlor replicated in miniature Havana's much larger version.

Still, Varadero had nurtured little in the way of genuine culture. The lavish shows at a series of beachfront resorts were what passed for entertainment for tourists and locals alike. The town's cultural authorities, supported by the Communist Party and People's Power, hoped this week would begin to give the inhabitants of Varadero a sense of their authentic roots. The idea was to bring in performers from the capital but showcase homegrown talent as well.

This week Varadero, the town, celebrated its ninetieth anniversary. For eight days and with the help of a number of civic groups, the authorities would simulate a series of historical reenactments. An old Spanish fort at what is now Forty-third Street had been restored; and on one particular night students dressed as Mambí rebels[4] would storm its walls. The following morning a group of pioneros—the youngest contingent of Cuban youth—were to have staged a landing commemorative of the one that took place on March 17, 1896. The sea was too rough for these plans to be carried out without risk to the children so they simply gathered on the beach and pretended they'd just arrived by sea.

Armed with Cuban flags, wooden swords and great bouquets of flowers, the children ran toward a group of mothers of local men and women who had given their lives in the more recent war of liberation. Amidst hugs and kisses they handed the flowers to the tearful recipients who hugged and kissed them back, visibly moved.

Promoting the Arts Has Been a Priority

We soon learned that Varadero has a great many native performers. As in every other part of the country promoting the arts has been a priority here. We visited one large show of paintings by local artists; it was well displayed in a spacious gallery next to the mini Copelia. The Matanzas Symphony Orchestra performed for what surely must have been the first time in the Hotel Internacional's grandiose nightclub. The town's single movie house provided a venue for the province's Hermanos Saíz string ensemble and for Nuestra América, a combo specializing in Latin American music.

A middle school put on an exhibit of student writing and drawing. This was accompanied by a contest, and I was asked to be one of the judges in the poetry and décima genres. Dozens of professional poetry readings took place throughout the week; I participated in six of these.

Eliseo Diego, El Indio Naborí, and Alberto Molina had recently published books; the local bookstore ordered great quantities and their authors held a number of outdoor signings and informal sessions at which they discussed their work with a highly motivated public. People lined up; some bought a single copy but others purchased four or five. Molina's was a very interesting police novel, a successful example of the up and coming genre of socialist mystery adventure.

Considering Varadero's tourism-heavy atmosphere, the week was a rousing success. Traditionally the town's inhabitants were either getting drunk at a local bar or in bed by ten or eleven each night. This week they filled the central square, crowded the different performance venues and engaged in heated discussions about the various events. At any hour of the night or day and on every street one could find groups of people offering their opinions about one or another of the activities.

Most encouraging to me weren't the activities in and of themselves but the seeds they planted for future work, the clear interest in the arts this endeavor awakened. This could be felt in the interest in those performers who'd come from the big city as well as in the enthusiasm for and pride in local talent.

Who's Going to Tell Me I Didn't Understand That Poem!

In Varadero I had some moving experiences, especially at the workplaces.

The first afternoon I was scheduled to read at the Pioneer Camp where Sarah, Ximena and Ana spent two weeks of vacation that past season. I read for some forty workers, men and women selected from the camp's various departments. There was also a smattering of representation from the town's mass and political organizations. I chose poems by Chilean political prisoners, then one of my own: "De la prima a la completa." When I tried to get my audience to respond, at first all I got were a few timid comments like: "very nice."

Then a guy who clearly had a higher educational level than most of those in the audience raised his hand. He explained that most of the comrades didn't have much education . . . they're not used to attending poetry readings. I heard his tone as condescending; now, looking back, I imagine he felt a sort of misplaced shame that, particularly in front of a foreign guest, none of his coworkers seemed willing to engage. That was enough to get people started. Whatever the guy's motives, others in the audience were no longer willing to let him speak for them.

A woman immediately raised her hand: "Listen, I've worked all my life. Every morning I get up and go to my job. Before the revolution I suffered a situation very much like the one described in that last poem. Who's going to tell me I didn't understand that poem! I may not have much education, but. . . ." And she went on, incensed. Others concurred. It was a terrific activity, showing that poetry can reach anyone when the poetic experience taps into shared experience or emotion.

They wanted more and I decided to read "Carlota," my long poem about the African slave trade and Cuba's return to Africa. Much of the country's population traces its ancestry to kidnapped Africans who survived the Middle Passage. In 1827 on a plantation near Trinity a slave named Carlota urged others to rise up with her. She was the first Cuban slave to rebel, and even though the uprising she led was put down after only three days it entered Cuban history as a symbol of resistance. Cuba's 1975 operation in Angola was named after the heroic woman:

> Hundreds of miles inland
> you still find the little shell,
> the cowry still burns the earth in Congo,
> Guinea, Mozambique, Angola . . .
> . . . Here they dug hollows in the earth
> and placed the pregnant women face down
> bellies protected by that space
> so they could whip them backside
> blood to bone to earth . . .

Several stanzas in I knew I had everyone's attention. I projected my voice into absolute silence. "Carlota" is a long poem but the audience stayed with me. When I stopped reading the applause was prolonged. The following morning there was a message at the hotel. The representative from Varadero's culture office had received a phone call from the people at the Pioneer Camp requesting my return engagement before the week's end.

An Aspirin Big As the Sun

At the Martin Klein Middle School Víctor and I read together. During the discussion period my friend asked the kids if they thought poetry was useful. They all replied in unison: Yes! "So, what's useful about it," Víctor probed. The answers came fast and at different levels: to set an example . . . to teach us history . . . to make us happy . . . to show us how we should act . . . to evoke different emotions . . . to put us in touch with our emotions. That last response surprised me, coming as it did from a middle school student.

Garzón, Margot and I put on an activity at a place called Escuela de oficios básicos. This is where young men and women learn basic trades: carpentry, electricity, and plumbing. The kids—young adults, really—weren't overly enthused about our visit. You could tell by looking at their faces they were probably thinking: oh my god, a poetry reading! It was exciting watching them warm to us and come around, getting more and more involved until we were participating together in one of the liveliest readings I've given. I started off with Roque Dalton's "On Headaches":

It's beautiful to be a communist
though it brings many headaches.
And communist headaches
are supposed to be historical, meaning
they can't be cured by an aspirin,
only by the realization of paradise on earth.
That's how it is.
Under capitalism our head throbs
and they cut it off.
In the struggle for the revolution
the head is a time-bomb.
In the construction of socialism
we plan the headache
which doesn't make it go away, just the opposite.
Communism will be, among other things,
an aspirin big as the sun.[5]

That got them going. Some laughed while others seemed to be immersed in thought, but no one now looked bored or indifferent. I followed Roque's poem with some from the Chilean prisoners and my own "Homeland." Garzón talked about two different ways people can tell stories, then did a marvelous job of telling Onelio Jorge Cardozo's "Francisco y la muerte." Margot rounded out the event with a dramatic rendition of "Memé," also by Cardozo. The faces before us broke into dozens of engaged expressions, everyone fully with us now. We performers hadn't consulted with one another as to what we would read at any of these events. I marveled at how well chosen the offerings were and how effortlessly they seemed to complement one another.

I Had a Lot of Poetry in Me As a Child

The best activity, at least of those in which I took part, was at an oil drilling base at the edge of town. In a meeting hall lavishly decorated for the occasion, some one hundred workers welcomed me with broad smiles, but quickly made sure I knew they weren't going to be able to participate much. They'd expected Alberto Molina. "We've all read his novel," one of those assembled volunteered, "but no one has read your poetry." Alberto had been called back to Havana unexpectedly and I had been tapped to take his place.

I had no choice but to introduce myself and start reading. I began with the poem by Roque, following it with one by Chilean Máximo Gedda. Without raising his hand or waiting for me to call on him, a man in the audience began to speak. "It's extraordinary that this poem is written in the second person," he said, "it's as if the comrade was able to transcend himself in those terrible torture sessions, observe what was being done to him as if he were someone else looking on. . . ." The perception might not have surprised me in a writing workshop, but coming from an oil rigger it removed whatever anxiety about the event I still had.

By now the audience was fully attentive. After reading a few other poems I ended with "Carlota," which sparked all sorts of commentary. One comrade got to his feet and began speaking of his own experiences with the Cuban troops in Angola. His tour of duty had been a year and a half. He went on for quite a while about the people he met in the cities, in the countryside, the terrible residue of colonialism, the backwardness and—to him—strange customs. I was beginning to wonder if any of it had anything to do with my poem or if the man simply needed to share his experience.

Then he said: "In Angola there are six million people but only a million speak Portuguese or know how to read. The rest speak fifty-four different dialects. And Comrade Agostino Neto writes poetry and his poems are translated from dialect to dialect.[6] Those poems become part of the struggle there; they help people see that they have to get together and unite to fight their common enemy. In Angola poetry is a weapon. And more than one world leader has used it in such a way. Take Ho Chi Minh, for example. . . ."

Before I left the oil drilling base a woman came up to me and said: "You know, I had a lot of poetry in me when I was a child. But they beat that poetry out of me. Everyone in my family laughed when I'd show them my poems. . . ." Another spoke of how important the way a poem is read can be. "I could feel the oppression of slavery in your poem," she said, "and at the end I could feel the chains breaking apart in your voice."

Another—again a woman—talked about how she wished people would come more often to their workplace to talk about contemporary literature: "literature written by people our age. I go to a bookstore and I want to buy books by people of my generation, my contemporaries, but I don't know what's good so I always end up buying something by Balzac or someone like that!"

The week ended with a big open air activity in the central plaza. The whole town turned out. Lots of local performers were eager to show off for the

Left to right: Bladamir Zamora, Antonio Castro, Margaret, metal worker, poet Angel Peña, and unknown person at the Manuel Piti Fajardo foundry, Matanzas, 1976.

International Women's Day panel. Left to right: Olga Lima of Angola, Margaret, Marta Santotomás of Cuba, Jane McManus of the United States (moderator), Le Hang of Vietnam, and Isabel Larguía of Argentina. Havana, March 8, 1971.

invited guests as well as to offer their talent to neighbors and friends. There were some not so good and other really excellent musical groups. The cultural part of the evening ended with a fabulous performance by Marta Jean Claude, the powerful Haitian singer who has kept alive the Creole cultural tradition that came to eastern Cuba with the nineteenth century cane cutters. It was clear Varadero wanted to leave us with something to remember.

Then the first secretary of the Matanzas Communist Party thanked everyone who had come together to make the week so successful. Varadero will soon have its first public library, he said, and there will be books in five languages: Spanish, English, French, Russian, and German. He also surprised and delighted the town's inhabitants by announcing that the elegant mansion on Eighteenth Street, which had served as this week's command post, would become a center for cultural activities and classes.

Their Male Co-Workers Served Them Lunch

March 8, 1978. International Women's Day was celebrated enthusiastically in Cuba. During my years on the island, each time the date approached I and others known for our interest in so-called women's issues were asked to participate in several events, ranging from neighborhood or workplace gatherings to more formal public presentations.

Mother's Day was also celebrated. On that holiday hundreds of thousands of postcards featuring one of several different floral arrangements were printed and delivered by the post office or by hand. Every mother was sure to receive many such cards. To Cuba's credit they didn't include syrupy preprinted messages but had room for more genuine personal notes from their senders. Like all mothers I enjoyed getting my collection of cards, not only from my own children but from their many friends and others for whom I played a mothering role. But International Women's Day was the holiday I preferred.

International Women's Day, like International Workers Day (May 1), traces an important part of its origin to events that took place in the United States. But both dates are more likely to be celebrated elsewhere.

On March 8, 1857, women textile workers in New York first protested poor working conditions and low wages. On the same day in 1908, fifteen thousand marched to demand shorter hours, better pay, and the right to vote. Honoring these and other demonstrations, at the first international women's conference in Copenhagen in 1910 the German Socialist Clara Zetkin proposed the date as one on which women workers should be honored throughout the world.

The following year, 1911, one hundred forty women perished in the Triangle Shirtwaist Factory fire in New York City. And so this event too is often linked to the collective history. The factory owners had locked the sweatshop doors, and when the fire broke out the women were trapped. Some jumped to their deaths, others died in the flames or expired from smoke inhalation. That year more than a million marched for women's rights in Austria, Denmark, Germany, and Switzerland. During the First World War the yearly marches also became cries for peace. After that war the demonstrations gradually lost energy and numbers. They were revived with the rise of feminism in the 1970s.

On March 8, 1978 Antonio and I were invited to the huge Construimport reception center where all foreign parts for the construction industry come into the country and are allocated to the different worksites. We were to entertain the women workers there by singing and reading poetry. This was one of hundreds of such workplaces I visited during my years in Cuba, all beautifully organized events with an enthusiastic and grateful audience. Artistic expression in celebration of all sorts of achievements and special dates has become an important part of the new revolutionary culture.

When Construimport's more than one hundred women workers had come on shift that morning they'd been greeted with individual floral bouquets. And that was just the beginning. Little or no work was waiting for them on this, their special day. Their male co-workers served them lunch. It was right after that midday meal that Antonio and I were scheduled to perform.

Actually our contribution was only a small part of the afternoon's activities. Over the preceding month the workplace had organized a poetry contest. Entries were to be on the theme of women's participation in the new society. The judges had been chosen from among the workers themselves and the first thing I noticed was how interesting the four winning poems were. Neither facile nor trite, they may not have constituted great literature but showed originality and addressed difficult issues—issues relevant in the Cuba of those years.

The winning poems were read aloud and these readings, too, showed the care that had gone into the whole affair. One poem mentioned a number of women who had been outstanding in Cuban history. Each time one of their names was read, those listening broke in with shouts of ¡Presente! Groups of responders were situated in different parts of the auditorium and each name met with a louder response. One of the poems dealt with internationalism and I suddenly realized someone had added a soft background soundtrack of "The International."

There was a wealth of local talent: singers, guitarists, comics, or just a fellow-worker with something to contribute. As all this was going on the women were being served a lavish snack of ham, cheese, and red wine. This was at the height of scarcity in the country and such a treat definitely required sacrifice.

I initiated our part of the program by telling my audience what it felt like to be celebrating International Women's Day in this kind of setting. I said that this year I was thinking especially about my own sisters in the United States as well as the women of Chile, Nicaragua, South Africa, Ethiopia and, of course, Vietnam. I read a few of my own poems, ending with "Carlota."

We Are Brothers and Sisters of Africans, and for the Africans We Are Ready to Fight!

When he announced Cuba's decision to answer the Angolan call for military aid, Fidel had told the more than one million people gathered in Revolution Square: "We are not simply a Latin American nation; we are also a Latin African nation. African blood runs abundant in our veins. From Africa many of our ancestors came to this land as slaves. . . . We are brothers and sisters of Africans and for the Africans we are ready to fight!"

These words became the epitaph for my poem, which mixes hundred-year-old texts, statistics from then and now, testimonies, and current events, all linked by a chorus that repeats allusions to the cowry shell, the currency with which human beings were bought and sold. New stanzas and this chorus alternate through one long poetic tribute to the dual history. The stanzas about Ester Lilia Díaz Rodríguez refer to a teacher and militiawoman, the first Cuban female to see battle in the campaign.

> . . . Esther Lilia Díaz Rodríguez
> an old teacher at twenty three
> and member of the Revolutionary Armed Forces
> since 1969
> was the first Cuban woman to go into battle.
> In Angola she met her three brothers:
> César, Rubén and Erineldo.
> There, all four discovered
> they had told the same story to their mother:
> . . . we're going to Camagüey
> to the military maneuvers . . .

Each time I'd read this poem, across the length and breadth of the island, I'd known it was likely that one or more of my audience would have served in Angola. Perhaps someone had recently returned or still had a family member at the front. Thousands of Cubans had begged to be sent over. Many were turned away. More than six hundred Cuban soldiers would soon be ambushed and killed in a single battle at Cuito Carnavale.

Angola, for the Cubans, became a powerful symbol of their own identity, of what their lives might have been like, perhaps, had their ancestors remained in Africa rather than being taken to the New World as slaves. Here their grandparents and parents carved a particular history, suffered a particular humiliation; their lives still carried its scars. In Africa, who knew how they might have lived or who they might have become.

The day Fidel announced Cuba's intention to respond to Angola's plea for help by sending a fighting force I remember—despite the painful claustrophobia I always experienced in such crowds—feeling I was witnessing something profound. The silence was absolute, almost ominous considering the large number of people. Even that slight shifting of bodies was absent. There was no breeze.

For many it was a blood link. Cubans were generous in their internationalism and rarely hesitated when asked to serve on a humanitarian aid or fighting front anywhere in the world. But they were more than usually eager to go to Angola. Even after the first stories came back—of horrifying physical conditions, lack of discipline, and cultural differences that were often anathema to the Cuban sensibility—people continued to beg to be allowed to go. Reading "Carlota" always elicited attention, immersion, connection. Still, I wasn't prepared for the impact it would make that March 8, 1978 at Construimport.

When I came to the part of the poem about Esther Lilia Díaz Rodríguez and her three brothers there was a sudden hush, followed by a chorus of listeners audibly shifting in their seats. It turned out that one of Esther Lilia's brothers, Rubén, was employed at this center. Of course the whole factory knew about Esther Lilia and her brothers!

Now, stuck between the dusty pages of my journal from these years, I come across an article from *Granma* dated March 17, 1978. It notes the attendance of Minister of Culture Armando Hart and his wife Haydeé Santamaría at the opening of *Carlota*, a play based on my poem. A theatrical company in the small eastern city of Manzanillo had staged the production. I remember the group's director writing to ask permission for the adaptation and his description of the collective process by which actors and technicians came up with the script. I may have been invited to a rehearsal or two; my memory is vague on that point.

My pleasure around my words being transformed into another medium, though, remains vivid. I've always loved this sort of artistic crossover: a poem set to music, a theatrical production or happening involving audience participation, a mural painted by many hands or using facial expressions from photographs in the search for authenticity, a play drawing on poetry or song, a film born of memory or the collaboration of interviewer and informant in the oral history I began doing around this time. In combination, two or more creative endeavors can become much more than what each was alone. The Cuban revolution, with its extraordinary support for all artistic genres, was a great venue for this sort of experimentation.

Back at Construimport it was as if I had been startled awake by an almost overwhelming sense of gratitude. Gratitude at connection: across cultures, despite translation, beyond any awkwardness I still felt reading my work in a different language from that in which I wrote.

Antonio got up to perform. His beautiful folk songs from his native Colombia and adoptive Venezuela were well received, as always. He had an immediate rapport with every sort of audience. As his fingers flew across the strings of his cuatro and his full voice captured the hearts of everyone in the room, I took a breath, sat back, and relaxed. I needed this respite in which I could allow myself to feel everything we'd just experienced. Frequently Cuban cultural events—especially those in places such as this one—came with their own rush of complex emotions.

Luz Began to Speak about Life in the Concentration Camps

Even more moving, if possible, than the event at Construimport, was that year's International Women's Day celebration on our block. Our local Federation of Cuban Women chapter had adopted Chile as its sister nation, so the group focused on Chilean women in resistance. Our block-level FMC and Defense Committee often worked together and on this occasion the CDR said it would take responsibility for the social part of the festivities.

I'd been working with some of the Chilean refugees and had gotten women from the Chilean Committee to lend us a flag, posters, a doll dressed in one of the indigenous Chilean outfits, and interesting texts for our mural. My friend

Luz de las Nieves Ayres Moreno came in representation of her Chilean sisters in Cuba. Several men on the block had managed to obtain a public address system and someone had talked El conejito, the nearby rabbit restaurant, into contributing a delicious spread.

When nine-year-old Ana got home from school and saw the preparations underway she decided she, too, wanted an activist role. She got a little notebook, made a list of all the Pioneros on the block, and visited every last one of them. She got them to promise to be down on the street in cleanly pressed uniforms at 8:30 sharp. They made an impressive honor guard on either side of the Cuban and Chileans flags.

For the first time in my memory our neighborhood FMC and CDR succeeded in getting everyone out for an event; even those who didn't belong to either organization. There must have been a couple of hundred people. I read a short statement I'd written about women in Chile and a Uruguayan woman who just moved to our block contributed a similar piece about women in her country. Carmen, our CDR's ideological chairwoman, read a brief biography of Clara Zetkin.

Then Luz de las Nieves rose to her feet. I don't think any of us knew what she would say. Perhaps most of those present thought she, too, would read a short greeting or express her gratitude for our attention to her country's struggle. But Luz began to speak—informally, from the heart—about life in the concentration camps. One of the most severely tortured women to have survived this recent period in Chilean history, she endured time in thirteen camps over three years.

Luz said that during a particularly rough torture session she'd found herself thinking of the 1972 May 1 celebration in Havana. She had been in Cuba then and remembered the energy unleashed. Luz told us that at Tres Alamos she and her comrades had a clandestine radio and listened to Radio Havana and Fidel. The transmissions strengthened their resolve.

One International Women's Day the male inmates sang to their sisters. The women as well as the men were punished for this show of solidarity. Luz spoke about the workshops the women prisoners organized, how they got bits of colored cloth and yarn and made their famous *arpilleras*, squares of cloth upon which a variety of scenes were appliquéd. Some depicted prison venues, others snippets of the life that had been taken from them. All, explicitly or implicitly, carried a message of justice and peace. As she spoke Luz's eyes often filled with tears. I don't think there were many of us who didn't weep with her at some point during her talk.

I Did Find and Develop a New Language

In 1978 I decided to learn photography. I had been working freelance for the Ministry of Culture's monthly journal, *Revolución y cultura*. The editor would send me and a staff photographer on assignment to different parts of the country to cover an artistic event, review a theatrical production, or interview someone doing something interesting in the arts. We'd come back with my story and his or her pictures. Increasingly I felt dissatisfied with the images the photographers assigned to me obtained. Telling them to shoot this or get a better angle on that was not something I could do; it would have felt disrespectful. The solution was to take up the camera myself.

I've always learned better from watching and experimenting than from conventional study. So I searched out a photographer whose work I admired and asked if he would be willing to take me on as an apprentice. Ramón Martínez Grandal was a wild man, particularly when he'd been drinking, but a magnificent artist, sensitive teacher, and eventually a very good friend.

The bargain we struck included turning what had once been a maid's bathroom off our back wash porch into a makeshift darkroom where he and a couple of other photographer friends could also work. Grandal's wife Gilda Pérez apprenticed alongside me. She, too, became a fine photographer.

Our darkroom didn't have a door, which meant we could only use it between about eleven at night and three in the morning when the lights of the city dimmed and the sheet we hung was enough to sufficiently darken the miniscule room. It didn't have running water but a stone wash sink just outside the room was only feet away. And it didn't have much usable shelf space; there was barely enough for two trays of chemicals: developer and fix. A stop bath would have been a luxury. Sometimes we had no water. Sometimes the electricity went off for hours. Despite these problems the room became a refuge.

I no longer remember how I acquired my first enlarger, a rudimentary Besseler. The smaller implements—developing tanks, trays, film, and paper arrived with foreign visitors. In the Cuba of those years ready-made chemicals weren't available, so my education included learning how to mix them from scratch. We got many of the raw compounds from pharmacies, as I remember, along with the precious gallon-size amber bottle in which we mixed and stored developer.

A moment still vivid in memory involves my accidentally cracking that bottle against the rough stone of the washboard sink, rendering it unusable. For several days Grandal went from one Havana pharmacy to another until

Ramón Martínez Grandal ("Grandal") and Gilda Pérez.

he found a replacement. That he didn't go crazy and tell me off showed he cared for me more than I knew.

The photographers—Grandal, Gilda, Macías, Rigoberto Romero, Gory, Tito Alvarez, Raúl Corrales, and sometimes one or two others—did understand the creative me. Working with them, learning from them, our endless discussions about movement, the photographic moment, the picture plane, the outer edges of the image, timeliness and meaning, went a long way toward filling my need for creative communication.

In the context of writing this book, I decided to google Grandal. We'd lost touch years before. I'd asked about him on several visits to Cuba and friends told me he and his family had left the island, but no one knew where they'd gone. I found them in Caracas. They'd traveled in 1993 with permission to be away two years and had stayed. Life has been rough and they're now in the process of returning home. On a December 2006 visit, Cuban cultural authorities received them well. Theirs represents one of the less publicized stories of Cuban exile: people who leave and then want to go back.

In the late 1970s I started making pictures, among other reasons because I needed a communicative form that didn't involve words. I did find and develop a new language. Still, the images didn't resolve my longing around that other language, the one composed of sound, intonation, syntax, inflection. Words had always been my currency, nurtured from earliest childhood. Now my deeply rooted English sparred with the Spanish I'd learned in everyday give and take. A hole in my creative heart remained.

And Now for the Cultural Part

From my journal: September 20, 1976.

Saturday night we all went out to see the Granados—Alberto Granado is the comrade who accompanied Che on that early motorcycle trip the length of Latin America. He stayed on at a leper colony in Venezuela and Che continued into history. Granado married a Venezuelan woman, they had children, and in 1960 the family came to Cuba. Che convinced them to stay and Alberto now works at one of the animal genetics plans. These people are friends of Antonio's. It was a great visit, and the best part was little Ana's contribution. She has been coming out with these monologues of late, at home as well as wherever she finds an audience. She calls them her lectures:

"I know the birth dates of all the stones in the world," she began, then continued to spew forth an unbroken stream of consciousness: "Before the revolution here in Cuba it was just stone stone stone stone. I was walking around and there was nothing but stone. No people, no animals, just snakes. But I wasn't afraid of snakes. And this big house: it was pure stone. Then the Spaniards came and they mistreated their maid so that one day she just couldn't stand it anymore—she was Spanish too—so she got in her rowboat and set off for the Soviet Union. There she was a heroine. They presented her in Red Square and all that. But the bad Spaniards took all the food from our refrigerator, yeah, everything was stone except there was this refrigerator, and they put the food under the mattress on one of the Spaniard's beds. They filled the refrigerator with messages and sent it flying off to the Soviet Union. When the woman who was a maid and a heroine received that refrigerator filled with messages sent by the Spaniards she didn't know what to do. But Lenin was still alive then and he gave her some advice. He told her: take my advice and burn all those messages. Don't even read them. So that is what she did. . . ."

Ana's monologue went on for a while. Everyone was attentive. At one point Alberto brought her a stone, a piece of black marble to illustrate the poetry. She took it, smiled, and said she also knew the birth dates of all the volcanoes. "Now that someone's brought me a stone, very good! Will someone please bring me a volcano?"

No volcano was forthcoming. Because Antonio had brought his cuatro and was planning to play and sing, Ana must have remembered this was to be part of the evening. She smiled again, looked around and said: "All right then, and now for the cultural part."

Ana was seven at the time.

One of the Prisoners Would Pick Me Up at the House

I cannot remember when I started teaching poetry to Cuban political prisoners. I recall Ana accompanying me, and she is six or seven in my mind's eye. So it must have been mid-seventies. The Ministry of Culture and UNEAC both had outreach programs through which established poets volunteered to perform and teach in schools, workplaces, military units, and on collective farms. Gradually prisons also became venues for such work and I remember a series of evening visits to El combinado del este, the large fairly modern prison complex on the outskirts of Havana where a number of political prisoners were serving out their sentences.

Left to right: Antonio Castro, Alberto Granado, and Ana. Havana, 1978.

La cabaña was the much older fortress-like prison that also housed political prisoners. It had become the popular reference in interviews with some of the major counterrevolutionary figures who'd been released from what they described as medieval dungeons complete with the usual privations, including torture. The Cubans have always claimed they don't torture. I suspect it depends on one's definition of the term, and also—as is true elsewhere—on the fact that policy and practice may not always line up.

The Cuban government claims freedom of dissent is permitted and protected and only when someone commits a crime in defense of his or her political beliefs is that person brought up on charges that may result in a trial, condemnation, and imprisonment. There have been enough examples of the imprisonment of those who have spoken out against government policy, though, that this claim seems somewhat suspect.

Whatever the case, the men in my poetry workshops at El combinado del este referred to themselves as political prisoners. They never spoke about the convictions leading to their imprisonment. Many seemed to possess rather high intellectual levels and had read a great deal of literature—both Cuban and from other countries. I remember a particular prisoner who told me he spoke, read, and wrote eleven languages, all of which he had taught himself while incarcerated. We didn't speak about the lengths of their sentences but I had the impression many had already served a number of years. Would some be out soon? I didn't know. Did they deserve be in prison? I had no way of knowing that either. My intention, as when I've worked with prisoners in the United States, was simply to provide contact and an outlet for creativity through artistic expression.

I structured these workshops by devoting the first fifteen or twenty minutes to getting acquainted. This usually meant my telling them something about myself and their saying their names and perhaps offering a brief reference to their own lives. Then I read three or four poems—by others as well as myself—that I thought might get them going. Those who had work they wanted to share did so, followed by some discussion, including working on a particular poem if its author wanted that.

Unaccompanied by guards, one of the prisoners himself would pick me up at the house and later drive me home. I remember riding in an old school bus which must have been the available vehicle. I preserve a mental image of a particular evening, little Ana and I sitting together on the seat just behind the driver. The three of us talked the whole way. This was clearly a prisoner trusted by the authorities. Ana loved these outings and was always eager to come along.

One night in the prisoner dining room where the workshops were held the lights went out and we were all immersed in blackness for more than an hour. It was just that group of men—perhaps twenty or so—and Ana and I sitting in the dark on long cement benches at long cement tables. Gradually our eyes became accustomed to the scant light. We continued talking and workshopping. No guard ever took part in our sessions.

The well fed, articulate, and relaxed sense I got from these men belied the many stories I heard—especially from the hard core of outside detractors of the revolution—that Cuba kept hundreds of political prisoners in subhuman conditions in cells they shared with rats and other vermin. I cannot say these conditions didn't or don't exist. But the men with whom my youngest daughter and I shared those evenings showed no evidence of such treatment.

The sense I conserve of those visits to El combinado del este is one of poetry as a social tool; the best poetry, the most evocative and compelling, coming from the many different poets whose work I read and occasionally as well from one or more of the prisoners. A vibrant echo of Roque Dalton's assertion that poetry, like bread, is for everyone.[7]

Spontaneous demonstrations in defense of the revolution were frequent. This was Havana, October 10, 1980.

Children playing in Santiago de Cuba, 1980.

Street scene, Camagüey, 1980.

Pre-revolutionary cars are called fotingos. *This one is in Havana, 1980.*

CHAPTER 11

EL QUINQUENIO GRIS

So Familiar, Yet So Eternally Other

The term *quinquenio gris* (five-year gray period) is a common reference for those Cubans who stayed and those who left, for those most painfully repressed and those who managed to remain at the margin of events. It loosely refers to a period beginning at the end of the 1960s and running through the early seventies. Perhaps because those affected generally remained silent about what they were going through, perhaps because the art world was so exciting (despite the restraints), or perhaps because I was slow to grasp certain cultural cues and many of us came to understand the era better in retrospect, I was barely aware of the excessive control and what it meant for Cuban creatives at the time.

A few years ago, Arturo Arango published a brief chronicle in the University of Havana magazine *Alma Mater*. It accompanied a photograph taken in 1976 or 1977. Arturo refers to each person in the photograph, reminiscing about how they met and the years they shared. In this context he mentions La Brigada Hermanos Saíz, the brigade of young writers where Bladimir offered me my first poetry reading among peers. His piece also gives his vision of me within the cultural climate of the times:

> Margaret Randall was close to the brigade. She had led an adventurous life, for many years linked to the Latin American revolutions, and had lived in Cuba since the late 1960s (her opposition to the massacre of Tlatelolco

forced her to leave Mexico). But . . . Margaret had fallen out of favor. She'd befriended every guerrilla fighter who passed through Havana. Ideologically she was closer to the Chinese than to the Soviets. People like Ernesto Cardenal, Julio Cortázar, and Mario Benedetti frequented her home. This was too much for the orthodox canon we refer to today, perhaps too kindly, as the quinquenio gris. Margaret was isolated, they had her on a sort of blacklist, and we took it upon ourselves to provide her with the human warmth and intellectual ambience they'd taken from her.

Thanks to Margaret we were able to put into practice Ramón Vidal Chirino's idea that we produce a bulletin for our poetry workshop. Chirino was a short story writer and engineer, and Alex's brother-in-law; he died in an accident not too long after this. *La gringa*, as we called her behind her back, had a ditto machine, and Alex and I filched the stencils and paper from the offices of the Federation of University Students (FEU) or Young Communists (UJC). We would type our poems and stories and run them off on Margaret's ditto; her generosity only balked before the insistent hunger of those students raiding her refrigerator.

To complete the picture of those who hung out at Margaret's apartment I must mention Antonio Castro, a poet and excellent singer who played the Venezuelan cuatro and was Margaret's partner at the time. And all the rest of our friends from campus or from the brigade who belonged to our poetry workshop: Roberto Méndez, Jorge Luis Arcos, Leonardo Padura, Norberto Codina, Alfredo Prieto, Orlando Alvarez Godoy, Pedro de la Hoz (sometimes with the hammer, sometimes without) [note: *hoz* also means sickle in Spanish], José Luis Ferrer, and others now lost to my bad memory.

When Roque [Dalton] was killed, the workshop already existed. . . . We held the first public tribute to him, at least the first in Cuba, at the Sala Talía. We prepared a bulletin with previously unpublished texts by the poet which Margaret had in her possession. Prestigious cultural institutions attempted to stop the event. The confusing circumstances surrounding Roque's death delayed Cuba's public recognition. Still, the university authorities authorized our tribute. On barely audible tapes we listened to the poet's voice. His widow and sons and two people we didn't know attended as well. Later we found out they were José Benito Escobar and Daniel Ortega. (Every once in a while, when something we were copying got caught in Margaret's ditto, we would extract a bit of paper from the machine. It might have been from a proclamation by the Sandinista National Liberation Front (FSLN), the Farabundo Martí National Liberation Front (FMLN) or, as Alex liked to say, The People's Front for the Liberation of the Fiji Islands!

Memory, as we know, is selective. Yesterday, February 27th, 2002, I attended the event commemorating the School of Arts and Letters' fortieth anniversary. Only two others from my class were there, only one from the poetry workshop. I said hello to many beloved professors. But today, when I try to comply with *Alma Mater's* request to write about my college years, these are the memories that surface. I received an excellent basic literary education. . . . But the poetry workshop, like the brigade, gave me my cultural life, that other sort of knowledge which the academy cannot bestow—a living culture, one that soars, bursting with humor and the pleasure of heresies. And, of course, the unique knowledge that fosters friendships; that which is truest and most lasting.[1]

Unnecessary and Sad

As a poet, writer, and photographer I am most familiar with how issues of power have played themselves out within Cuba's intellectual and artistic milieus. During my years on the island, and since, there have been times of great openness in which conflicting ideas and rich discussion were encouraged, and others of a more repressive nature in which certain groups gained control and individuals and/or categories of persons suffered greatly. Not infrequently these repressive periods prompted great talents to leave the country, forcing them to start over in cities around the world. A terrible collective frustration, a chilling of the creative spirit, and several suicides resulted.

A succession of U.S. administrations also provoked and took advantage of the contradictions. From Operation Peter Pan (December 1960–October 1962), in which fourteen thousand Cuban children were airlifted to the United States in the wake of rumors that communism would take them from their families, to the 1980 exodus of 125,000 people through the seaport of Mariel, these emigrations have been plagued by political intrigue on both sides, and have mostly resulted in demoralization and long-term pain for all involved.

In thinking about this history—and although decidedly unfunny in retrospect—the old chicken and egg joke comes to mind. Did the increased controls respond only to pressure from the outside (as the revolution tried to make us believe) or did censorship perpetuate self-censorship, creating an evolving culture of repression? Undoubtedly both scenarios were true. With the perspective of time, the latter becomes more obvious.

The Cuban revolution, represented by those who stayed, has moved through a variety of attitudes toward those who choose to leave. For years the response was one of blanket repudiation. In a society where there was so little of everything, from food and medicines to housing, I think people especially resented those who'd spouted revolutionary slogans and then, from one day to the next, were packed and ready to go. They'd kept their intentions secret until the very last moment, pretending loyalty and partaking of reward. When they left, then, it was felt as betrayal. Those who had been most vociferous in their support of the revolution drew the most ire; those who had never shown any interest were allowed to leave in peace.

The émigrés were called *gusanos* (worms). During one mass exodus after another those who were found to have their names on exit lists were taunted by angry neighbors, sometimes even out–of-control mobs. The Party tried to control this anger but was never wholly successful. Perhaps it didn't want to be wholly successful.

In the creative world many great talents chose exile because their lifestyles, ideas, or artistic expression were in opposition to or out of step with the official line. They felt cornered, menaced, suffocated, or hopeless. Homosexuals were among those most vilified and it took years for the revolution to review and rectify its treatment of those it saw as "sexually different." The Cuban Party subscribed to the traditional Communist idea that homosexuality was a pathology, one that did not belong within its ranks.

To keep this in perspective, at the time homosexuality was still considered pathological by the American Psychiatric Association. And many other noncommunist institutions held the same position back then. But those institutions didn't pretend to stand for justice, and the Cuban revolution did.[2] This ideological distortion not only proved devastating for the country's lesbians and gay men, but kept the revolution from thinking about gender in ways that would allow for a feminist analysis of Cuban society, greatly limiting women's self-knowledge and access to power.

Religious belief was another difficult area. Early on, the Catholic Church positioned itself in opposition to a revolution ideologically rooted in secularism. Some denominations actively worked against revolutionary policy. In response, the government closed the country's religious schools. Many priests and nuns left the island. This also affected revolutionaries who held convictions of faith; they were barred from joining the Cuban Communist

Party and marginalized in other ways. Jehovah's Witnesses were declared illegal because of their refusal to do military service or allow their children to receive blood transfusions or inoculations.

Not only Catholics and some minor Protestant sects, but members of the African religions also suffered persecution. To add insult to injury, Cuban cultural institutions promoted Afro-Cuban song and dance as authentic cultural manifestations even as they marginalized their religious practices. Vatican II and the upsurge of liberation theology throughout Latin America eventually brought the Cuban party around to a more inclusive position on matters of faith. Cuban schools continue to offer a materialist education but a measure of accommodation with believers has been achieved.

Without public discussion or any acknowledged shift, the Cuban revolution has also gradually softened its attitude toward intellectuals and artists wishing to live elsewhere. Many have been given permission to spend months or years in other countries studying or working. Those with permission can return when they wish.

Some who left without permission have also been permitted to return, to visit and—very occasionally—to stay. Cuban artists and writers in exile have attended conferences, both on and off the island, with their counterparts who remained. Over the years there has been a coming together that has defied the strict regulations originally imposed by the Cuban government. This softening, also largely initiated by Cuba, has been more or less visible however, depending on the moment and who may be involved. It cannot be seen as the resolution to a skewed immigration policy.

Restriction of movement, long waits for permission to come and go (in other words, immigration policy used as political coercion), and the fact that Cubans are not allowed access to the internet, are measures that have always seemed shortsighted to me, an abuse of power—unnecessary and sad. Like the North Vietnamese separated for years from their South Vietnamese families, like the arbitrarily divided North and South Koreans, like immigrants to the United States separated by cruel immigration laws, regulations of this sort fly in the face of shared cultural roots, a global oneness, and single humanity.

El Quinquenio Gris

Cuban intellectuals and artists frequently refer to the quinquenio gris mentioned by Arturo Arango in his *Alma mater* piece. During the period a Stalinist rigidity was applied to those who wrote, painted, acted, sang, danced, or took part in other of the arts; and to those who were ideologically or sexually different. Despite its name, most agree that this period lasted longer than five years—some would argue that vestiges remain—and that gray is too pale a description. One of the most visible moments of el quinquenio gris was when Luis Pavón Tamayo, a military man who had previously edited *Verde olivo* (the magazine of the Armed Forces), was tapped to head a National Culture Council. Heads began to roll.

Among Pavón's initial victims were singer-songwriters Silvio Rodríguez, Pablo Milanés, Noel Nicola, and Sara González, the founding members of what would come to be known throughout Latin America and the world as La nueva trova, The New Song Movement. These are exceptional talents. Yet when they first appeared on the Cuban scene they were greeted hesitantly. Some time later they were prevented from performing on television, radio, or in the country's theaters. Their music was perceived as too different, somehow threatening. This was a time when the Beatles were considered counterrevolutionary in Cuba, and young men with long hair and young women with short skirts were told their look was unacceptable.

Hippies and other rebellious youth around the world were protesting the status quo but were seen by the Cuban leadership as emblematic of an out-of-control drug culture, the very opposite of what it wanted its own young people to be. Those who thought, acted, or dressed like their foreign counterparts were mistrusted, ostracized, and repressed. A rigid and misconstrued decolonization rejected any vestige of what could be considered cultural penetration.

One of the revolution's saving graces has been the fact that when it comes to freedom and repression, parallel tendencies have generally competed. Men and women with a profoundly analytical sensibility have vied with mediocre, often ignorant or unthinking middle management types who revel in using their quota of power against others. The cultural scene is no exception.

While the Culture Council restricted artists in all genres, and some of the avant-garde were denied exposure on TV or in other venues, forward-looking institutions such as ICAIC (The Cuban Institute of Film Art, under the brilliant direction of Alfredo Guevara) and Casa de las Américas (presided over by Haydeé Santamaría's exquisite sensibility) took it upon themselves to give refuge and support to the most vulnerable artists. They were able to perform, and the sheer genius of their art gained them an enthusiastic audience. In a few years they were considered valued ambassadors of the revolution, immensely popular in their home country and throughout the world.

Pavón and others—Jorge Serguera, ex-director of Cuban television, and Armando Quesada, once head of the National Culture Counsel's theater section, to name only the most visible hatchet men—decided to cleanse the major theater and dance groups of their homosexual members. Some were unceremoniously fired. Others were told they could not represent their country in international venues. Some of these men and women had the courage to take their grievances to labor courts, where a few won reinstatement. This speaks to the viability of revolutionary labor law even in times of criminal abuse of power. But many artists eventually chose exile. Rectification came late for such victims.

One incident which gained international attention during my years in Cuba was the Padilla affair. Heberto Padilla was a well-known poet, then in his late thirties. We had published him in that issue of *El Corno* dedicated to the art and poetry of the island. Padilla began to draw negative attention when a book of his, *Fuera del juego* (Outside the Game) was awarded first prize in the 1968 UNEAC poetry contest. The poems in *Fuera del juego* were critical; some saw them as counterrevolutionary, while others deemed them revolutionary precisely because of their critical stance.

The three Cuban judges and two from outside the country agreed this book deserved the prize.[3] The revolution, represented by the Communist Party and the National Culture Council, tried to dissuade the judges. Despite threats against the Cubans involved, the judges refused to back down. The prize was awarded and the book was published—but with a preface noting UNEAC's opposition.

Several years later, in 1971, state security agents went to Padilla's home and took him into custody. Accused of misrepresenting the revolution to foreign journalists and intellectuals, he spent more than a month in detention in what he described as constant discussion with officials who tried to show him the error of his ways. During this time he was also taken to the beach, received medical attention, and—by his own admission—was not physically mistreated. When released, he appeared at the UNEAC in a carefully orchestrated meeting where he read a long statement admitting to counterrevolutionary behavior and urged his fellow poets not to follow his example.

In the wake of these shocking and somewhat contradictory events, Padilla remained in Cuba for about a year. He worked in publishing and translating. He must have been more than eager to leave however, and was finally issued an exit permit. When he arrived in the United States, Senator Ted Kennedy personally met his plane. The poet was now an international figure, a cause célébre. He taught at Princeton for a while, traveled the international literary circuit, and died of a heart attack in 2000.

When the Padilla affair happened I took the revolution's side against the poet. I believed the threat to Cuba's security was such that everyone must do his or her part to defend the vulnerable project. I believed that Padilla had been treated well while in custody and took at face value the statement he made upon his release. Looking back, I should have realized that someone in his position would say what he was told to say—play the game to the best of his ability until he was able to get out. Many poets and writers of international stature protested the action taken against Padilla. Among them were some who supported the revolution. One of these was the Argentine Julio Cortázar, although he soon changed his position of protest to one of tempered support.

A few years after this incident I too came to believe that the Cuban revolution had overreacted in the Padilla affair. I saw it as overreaction because I felt a single poet writing poems that were critical of the revolutionary process or hobnobbing with critical western journalists was exercising his inalienable right to hold and express opinions contrary to the official line. I also saw a single poet's behavior as relatively unimportant in the grand scheme of things, and thought the Cuban party had done itself more harm than good by making such a show of Padilla's activities.

Now my criticism of the revolution's action goes much farther. It is qualitative rather than simply quantitative. With the wisdom of hindsight I believe Cuba should have honored a broad range of expression among its artists and writers. A truly revolutionary position demands nothing less.

The quinquenio gris was neither the beginning nor end of these repressive measures. Early in the 1960s homosexuals and others had been sent to the UMAP (Military Units for Antisocial People), work camps where it was presumed they would be rehabilitated—where they would be "made into men." Eventually these camps were denounced and closed but their existence was never publicly discussed or critiqued. As recently as the late 1990s, the poet Raul Rivero and other writers were imprisoned for alleged counter-revolutionary activity.

Many Cubans inside and outside the country point out that repression goes far beyond the creative milieu. Those protesting human rights abuses on the island are routinely sanctioned, even jailed. It is clear some repressive policy has been reversed but the control such measures reflect and the perception that danger lurks are still part of the official Cuban psyche. None of this has ever been adequately addressed.

As I say, visionary and dogmatic tendencies within the revolution's leadership constantly compete for dominance. The pendulum swings slowly at times, sharply at others. The *pavonato*, as some have called the artistic repression of the early seventies, came to exemplify the worst abuses. But Pavón did not act alone. His orders came from above. And although he was demoted in 1976, when cultural policy was raised to the ministerial level and Central Committee member Armando Hart was appointed Minister of Culture, no public discussion of this repression and its residual chill ever took place.

Until now.

Telephone Calls and Emails Began to Fly Back and Forth

On Friday, January 7, 2007, some thirty years after his ignominious fall from grace, Luis Pavón suddenly returned to public view in a primetime television interview devoted to his life. In a program that surprised and shook Cuba's artistic community, the interviewer listed the man's accomplishments, virtually ignoring his repressive role so many years before. Pavón, aging and feeble now, was shown with a chest full of medals and in the company of revolutionary leaders; the implication being that when all was said and done the man had contributed positively.

Viewers at first wondered if the interview had simply been a matter of bad taste, responding to some producer's ignorance, or whether it might foreshadow a return to unwelcome cultural policy. But then there were a couple of other interviews, with other villains of times gone by. For whatever reason, the bad guys were enjoying some sort of resurrection. These events may have seemed more ominous in light of the fact that Fidel's brother Raul was acting head of state at the time and some believed he had been behind the repressive measures two decades earlier.

Telephone calls and emails began to fly back and forth, first in Havana, then in the provinces, and eventually also among expatriate writers and artists. All expressed outrage. Desiderio Navarro, Arturo Arango, Renaldo González, Antón Arrufat, Miguel Barnet, Senel Paz, Zenaida Romeau, Waldo Leyva, Ambrosio Fornet, Mario Coyula, Alfredo Guevara, Humberto Solás, Pablo Menéndez, José Prats Sariol, Juan Carlos Tabío and Reina María Rodríguez were among those who took the lead. Quickly these were joined by others, and by Cuban writers and artists in exile: Amir Valle in Berlin, Eliseo

Alberto Diego in Mexico, Magaly Murgurcia in Argentina, Duanel Díaz in Madrid, Abilio Estévez in Barcelona, Pedro Pérez Sarduy in London, among others. The messages kept coming. It was as if Pandora's Box had suddenly blown its lid.

The communications varied. Some were simple two or three line expressions of repudiation of what had been perpetrated on Cuban TV. The famed musician Paquito de Rivera, long in exile, sent a dismissive one-liner saying he "could care less about what Cubans on the island thought." Others wrote long diatribes, some including painful personal histories.[4]

The short story writer Ivette Vián broke years of silence: "I was twenty-three years old. And I spent the next twelve ostracized. They canceled my membership in the UNEAC and in the Cuban Journalists Union. I worked for four years as a teacher's aide at the Káspar day care center and eight in construction. . . . I thought I would never be able to publish again, but kept hoping. I didn't understand what had happened to me or to my country's government."

Another woman wrote in defense of her mother, now deceased, a brilliant pianist who had been prevented from performing publicly. Her words held more grief than recrimination. In a telephone interview Antón Arrufat, Cuba's best known playwright, told Reuters News Agency: "I lost my job and spent nine years in the basement of the Marianao public library, packing books."

Some writers accused others of hypocrisy or opportunism for not having spoken out when things were rough. Others were self-critical. Many evoked the names of the great Cuban poets, novelists, essayists, painters, actors, musicians, puppeteers, and others who died in or far from their beloved homeland with neither redress nor vindication. "The fact that I live in Barcelona doesn't make it easier," wrote Abilio Estévez from Spain. "Remember, I experienced the horror firsthand because I accompanied Virgilio Piñiera during the worst years of his life. And his was not an ordinary death. It was a long, drawn out assassination." One exile contends that for months he has been soliciting a visa to return to Cuba and hasn't been able to get a simple answer to his request.

One of the most interesting letters to date, and one that vividly illustrates the competing lines of power within Cuba's cultural milieu, comes from film director Enrique Colina. He describes his thirty-two year tenure at the head of a program called "Twenty-four per Second," a feature that takes Cuban films and produces them for television. "The program was conceived of at ICAIC [the Film Institute]," Colina explains, "and broadcast by ICRT [Cuban television]. The latter had to approve the weekly transmissions. . . ."

This presented a problem. The Film Institute has always represented a vital creative space, one in which avant-garde projects have been encouraged. Cuban television was and is conservative, often repugnantly so (as in the offending TV specials). Colina's lengthy letter traces a problematic history in which TV censorship prevented a broad public from viewing some of the best Cuban movies made during almost half a century of cinematic production. Among the censored films were *Alicia en el pueblo de maravillas, Adorables mentiras, Fresa y chocolate, El elefante y la bicicleta, Suite Habana, Amor vertical, Nada, Tres veces dos, Guantanamera, Lista de espera, Diario de Mauricio, Maria Antonia, Papeles secundarios, Techo de vidrio, Hasta cierto punto, Miel por Ochún*—the list includes more than thirty titles.

Colina explores the absurd reasons given for canceling one or another of his programs. Sometimes the subject was simply not deemed appropriate, a foreign actor was featured or the director was known to have "counter-revolutionary tendencies," too much sex or violence were displayed (although violent and/or sexually explicit films from other countries were routinely shown), "bad language" was used, or the film in question embodied an overall attitude that "might offend our sister socialist nations."

In his letter Colina refers to the period 1977–1979 as one of tremendous openness and creativity in film; one in which extraordinary directors, under the guidance of the great Cuban documentary filmmaker Santiago Alvarez, produced weekly newsreel shorts dealing with all manner of social and political concerns. "Viewed today," Colina writes, "these newsreels remain absolutely pertinent. They attack institutional disorganization, carelessness, irresponsibility, misuse of public funds, and other types of corruption. Due to the enormity and persistence of these problems the critiques became ever more bitter and ironic, until the order came down to stop producing the newsreels. The economic, social and political consequences of failing to address these issues finally exploded in the Mariel exodus. . . . "

Colina also describes a time in the 1990s when the Cuban Film Institute was almost closed, attacked by the Council of State for "ideological weakness." "This happened at the revolution's moment of greatest economic and political vulnerability," he goes on to explain, "and if it hadn't been for the resistance of Cuba's most important filmmakers—who opposed the move guided not by any governmental mandate but by their own consciences—ICAIC would have been reduced to an appendage of ICRT." The filmmakers won the battle, the censored films were shown, and ICAIC lived to fight another day.

Cuban Intellectuals and Artists Should Not Fear
a Change in Cultural Policy

On January 16, 2007, with emotional messages still flying back and forth among the artists, the UNEAC issued an unsigned declaration which was published on the front page of *Granma*. In the somewhat stilted political language characteristic of such documents, Abel Prieto (prestigious writer, bright intelligence, member of the Party's politburo, current Minister of Culture and the statement's presumed author) assured Cuban intellectuals and artists that broadcasting the televised interviews had been a mistake and they should not fear a change in cultural policy. The deeper issues of censorship and self-censorship, the up and down history of artistic freedom in the country, the need to openly analyze a repressive past and what intellectual freedom means, were not addressed. Some involved in the current discussion decried this use of the same old superficial verbiage. Poet Reina María Rodríguez responded:

> I'm deeply troubled and left with a bitter taste in my mouth after reading the note by UNEAC's secretariat which was published in today's paper. It in no way reflects the spirit and tension we've all felt in recent days, during this open and unusual debate that just might be capable of resolving . . . so many dark dilemmas. We have to move beyond our personal resentments, cowardliness and opportunisms, to a place where this issue that affects us all . . . is examined in the most inclusive terms, with a language not used by some to the detriment of others. Today's note is like a mask . . . reminiscent of so many written years ago, in whichever period we would be loath to relive.

A group of concerned writers and artists then met with Prieto. One of their fears was that if the discussion remained limited to those relatively few intellectuals with email access, a broader public would be denied the opportunity of addressing issues vital to continuing policy development—including a necessary analysis of past mistakes. Opening the circle was imperative. And so invitations to a series of lectures on these subjects were issued to interested artists and writers and to the public at large. The first took place in February at Casa de las Américas. Ambrosio Fornet, one of Cuba's most respected and thoughtful intellectuals, opened his talk with these words:

We thought the nightmare belonged to some remote past, but the truth is when we woke up the dinosaur was still there. We haven't been able to find out—we may never know—if the media event in question signaled an insidious return to darker times, reflected some capricious example of favoritism, or was a simple question of irresponsibility. It doesn't matter. Seen from today's perspective . . . it was a suicidal act.

A Language Inhabited by All

The following month, a second lecture was given by Mario Coyula at the Instituto Superior de Arte. Coyula is an architect, urban designer and critic who headed Cuba's School of Architecture in the early 1970s, was a visiting professor at Harvard (2002) and Vienna's University of Applied Arts (2006), and is a recipient of his country's National Prize for Architecture (2001). His lecture addressed the deepest issues of cultural policy. Although the entire talk is well worth reading, I will transcribe a fragment that is particularly revealing:

There are principles essential to the sustainability of ecosystems which are also valid for all human activity and its institutions. These include addressing today's needs without compromising the ability of future generations to resolve theirs, even those we cannot yet envision; working within the system's ability to act in order to encourage self-regeneration; and permitting one element to serve several different functions and a single function to be served by several different elements. All this requires respect for diversity and plurality. We must nurture everyone's active and conscious participation so they will be able to identify and solve their own problems. Curiously, in Cuba these healthy principles once provoked envy among the most dogmatic.

Tolerance, that shameful acceptance of diversity, was considered morally lazy, unbecoming to revolutionaries. Rigidity became a virtue rather than a defect. A provincial xenophobia refused to accept that which was different or came from outside the country, including styles and tastes considered to be distorting influences, a form of "cultural penetration" by the decadent capitalist world. Ironically, those who had this mindset tried to impose models from another world, one that was geographically and culturally even farther away and less attuned to our sensibilities. This attempt lasted longer than a single lifetime. That other cultural penetration

by a brand of socialism that had the temerity to proclaim itself "real,"[5] has
left us but a few dusty manuals, a collection of mundane and deformed
figures who insist on paying homage to unworthy heroes, and a host of
innocent Ivans and Tatianas who are every day more relegated by the later
hemorrhage of Yosvanys and Yumilsleidys, where overuse of the letter Y
reflects an aura of escapism.

After his humorous reference to Cuba's mangling of Russian names,
Coyula goes on to describe how this intolerance did irreparable damage to
the country's architecture, criticizing initial examples of brilliant design,
multiplying the dull and the dreary and—most disturbing—deforming the
teaching of building and industrial design to the detriment of the human
landscape as well as producing generations of stifled talent. Early promises
of a vibrant national architecture gave way to monotony and poor quality.
Contractors took over where architects showed themselves to be too innovative. Much was sacrificed.

Coyula's talk is particularly interesting because architecture affects so
many more lives and so much more directly than poetry, painting, or theater.
Of the expressive arts perhaps only music reaches larger audiences—and this
is true only of the most popular musical genres. Although the Cuban revolution has done an exceptional job of bringing the arts to great masses of people,
some forms of expression remain of little interest to the average citizen.
Architecture, on the other hand, creates a landscape in which everyone lives,
studies, works, and plays. The man- and woman-made horizon embraces
the human being who assimilates that horizon almost without realizing it.
Architecture is a language inhabited by all and as such powerfully shapes a
population's collective identity.

ONLY FRIENDSHIP AND POETRY CAN ERASE HATRED AND RESENTMENTS

Coyula's lecture brilliantly traces the move away from a series of interesting
buildings constructed in the revolution's first years: the National Art School,
the Copelia Ice Cream Parlor, Pabellón Cuba, and others. These buildings
were designed by foreign architects or by Cubans influenced by the best
and most innovative of what was then going on in the wider world. They
imprinted their works with a uniquely Cuban style. These first gems gave way
to the prefabricated blocks of cement reminiscent of what was then popular
in the Soviet Union, or of Miami's ugly 1950s style.

In the classrooms and at building sites, architects were replaced by contractors. In an effort to resolve the acute housing problem, high-rises began springing up in towns and cities; it became a badge of honor for every provincial capital to have one or more. These buildings were not only anathema to Cuba's visual history but inappropriate for its climate. Local materials and ideas were abandoned while imports were deemed acceptable—as long as they weren't considered to be expressions of cultural penetration by the country's principal enemy.

It is hard to know how this discussion will end. What seems evident and immensely healthy is the honesty of most of the missives and talks, the willingness to bare painful personal histories, and the tendency on the part of many of those writing to want to go beyond specific incidents to examine the core issues. Important as well is the fact that the Cuban Communist Party reopened a cultural department at the end of 2007, after seventeen years without one. Eliades Acosta is its director, and he is respected, indeed beloved, by every Cuban intellectual and artist with whom I've spoken.

Acosta has been quoted as saying that Cuba "aspires to a society in which people feel free to speak about their problems out loud and without fear, in which the press no longer publishes only good news, in which errors are discussed publicly and with an eye toward finding solutions, in which people can express themselves honestly, where the economy works, where there are adequate public services, and where Cubans don't feel like second-class citizens in their own country because of past measures that may have seemed necessary in their moment but are obsolete and untenable today."[6]

I want to close my summary of the current discussion among Cuba's writers, artists, filmmakers, musicians, theater people, architects, and others with excerpts from one more letter. There have been numerous contributions worthy of quoting at length. This one shines, though, for its reference to little publicized events, its raw honesty and self-critical tone. It is again from the poet Reina María Rodríguez.

> . . . I think now of Mandelshtam, of Pasternak, of Ajmátova, of Marina who didn't even have a cemetery. After having read these authors and knowing how they lived and died (Mayakovski, for example, and Marina who hanged herself at Yelábuga), I cannot remain unmoved before something—as distant as it is from those other events, and on this island in the middle of the Caribbean—that seems to me to be a tragedy for the Cuban people, who've already lived through expulsions and censorships in the 1970s and continue to live with them today.
>
> "Favorable conditions," wrote Marina, "we know these don't exist

for artists. Life itself is an unfavorable condition ..." But conditions can became even harder, and this is what I've felt these past few days. In Stockholm, in 1994, when I met with our writers in exile, I understood that the tragedy of separation cannot be resolved in meetings or dialogues. The pain (an open wound) was there where shame and remorse had created a pus-filled sore, impossible to heal. Participants on one side or the other insulted each other in the formal sessions and then embraced one another in the halls.... My innocence was a bridge that allowed me to hand Heberto Padilla a sheaf of poems by young poets unknown to him ... which Heberto later used in a lecture on Cuban poetry he read in Madrid that same year, at an event called The Whole Island.

Because I've always believed in writing as salvation or therapy, I think only friendship and poetry can erase hatred and resentments. We've all been sick with paranoia (even those who, because they are too young to have participated in the tensions and ruptures of the seventies, shouldered the ghostly burdens and the guilt of "not acting like revolutionaries" when they dared utter oppositional opinions or espoused attitudes that went "beyond the norm").

Cuban poet Reina María
Rodríguez, Havana, 1979.

How can we deal with the causes of these problems without examining the motives? . . . I write this letter recalling other scenes in which neither Pavón nor his acolytes took part but where they were present nonetheless. One is complicit retroactively. One is complicit (without wanting to be) in the future. There are images from which we must rid ourselves; they are engraved on the interiors of our minds. Observe and Punish is a model we must put aside. It reflects fears we must overcome so we can approach the risk of truth. . . .

Loss to the Whole When Some Voices Are Silenced

All my life I have intuited these truths. I have lived by them as I have been able. In some instances—I can see now—my own condition of privilege made it hard for me to consider freedom of expression as an inviolate principle rather than specific to a particular situation. I remember, in 1978, being privy to an argument between my mother and father. Members of the Ku Klux Klan were marching in Skokie, Illinois, and there was vehement discussion about whether or not they should have been issued a permit. My mother came down passionately against the permit. My father, who hated bigotry of any kind and certainly despised the Klan, argued that if our enemies were denied permission to march it would leave those whose ideas we favored open to such silencing as well.[7]

In Mexico, *El Corno Emplumado* brought together diverse authors, belief systems, lifestyles, and forms of writing. This was one of the journal's hallmarks. As long as a poem advocated life instead of death (i.e. some form of humanism rather than fascism, classism, racism, or sexism), and as long as it was a good poem—well crafted, innovative, its use of language original and evocative—it was welcomed on our pages.

During the journal's last years I came to believe that the most exciting poetry, at least in Latin America, was being written by those poets whose lives as well as work evoked the new. The new on that continent at that time was revolutionary struggle. At the 1968 Cultural Congress of Havana I met several Latin American poets who criticized *El Corno* because it featured, in their words, "poets who defend the old order." In their lives and in their poems they believed they were creating a new order, one of equality and freedom, and they wanted the journal to showcase this.

My experience in Cuba, at least at first, made me believe that the freedom to live with dignity—to have work and shelter and food and health and education—was the primary freedom and that all others would follow: freedom of expression, freedom to fully be who one is, freedom to dissent. I subscribed to a pecking order of freedoms, not understanding that freedom itself is an inviolate principle. When I think of how partially I saw this then, it doesn't seem all that different from the idea that we women would gain our freedom when society as a whole was free, and that attending to the so-called women's issues before national liberation could be fully achieved only divided men and women in struggle.

Fully grasping power equations and a real commitment to diversity show this idea to be flawed. Through my own experience I learned respect for difference has to be built into every phase of struggle. Where gender, race, and sexuality are concerned, feminism helped me see this. And my personal pain, during those years of semi-marginalization, made me think about the danger in marginalizing those who don't follow a prescribed line, the loss to the whole when some voices are silenced.

Still, I was living in a tiny island nation valiantly battling to survive. Daily I was in touch with the multiple ways in which international capital worked to destroy the Cuban revolution: by continuing the blockade and penalizing nations that dared break it, luring professionals with promises of high salaries and luxury living, encouraging defection and illegal emigration, and offering special treatment to those managing to reach U.S. shores. Propaganda such as that aimed at the island via Radio Martí, ongoing germ warfare, and attempts against Fidel's life were also staples of the campaign.

I loved what I saw about me: creativity, experimentation, and courage in the face of such enormous odds. Each small victory felt important. Frequently we were warned against open criticism of one thing or another, and made to feel we would be giving grist to the enemy if we spoke out. I tended to believe what I was told. Sometimes I was right to believe; often I wasn't.

Sometimes I went along with rigid dictums or arbitrary measures because I accepted them as necessary. Sometimes I didn't understand the puzzle, how things fit together or didn't. Sometimes I'm sure I followed the Party line because of a misplaced but understandable guilt; I was, after all, from the country that continued to attack the revolution, my origin one of petit bourgeois and racial privilege. Always I believed in what the Cubans were working so hard to build.

I continue to believe.

What was more difficult was being able to differentiate between the revolution's objectives and the conduct of certain leadership cadre who put their own needs before the collective. Often someone in a position of power would engage in clearly counterrevolutionary conduct. People would complain. And then that person would be removed from his or her position. We were satisfied that there was an honesty of intent that provided the necessary checks and balances. I still accept that overall honesty of intent. I also know that power, held too long by an individual or group of individuals, leads to systemic abuse. Until we launch a comprehensive discussion of the system itself—especially with regard to its way of dealing with power—nothing will change.

In the early 2007 exchange of letters, Desiderio Navarro addresses the issue of power and the danger implicit when one social group fails to make space for others. Recalling the repressive 1970s he writes:

> With few exceptions, heterosexuals (including those who weren't homophobic) ignored what was happening to gays; whites (including those who weren't racist) ignored those blacks who were fighting for their rights; traditionalists ignored those in the vanguard; atheists (including the most tolerant) ignored the way Catholics and other religious believers were being treated; pro-Soviets ignored what was happening to those artists who refused to work in the socialist realist style or those Marxists who objected to the Moscow party line; and on and on. It might be worth asking ourselves if this lack of moral responsibility could repeat itself among Cuba's intellectuals today.

I Think of Martin Niemoller

I think, as I have so often, of Martin Niemoller, the German pastor who supported Hitler early on but then broke with the Nazi doctrine to become one of the most articulate antifascist voices for equality and peace. He was captured, accused of treason, and spent time in the Sachsenhausen and Dachau concentration camps. Near the end of the Second World War he narrowly escaped execution.

After the war Niemoller emerged from prison to preach the words for which he is best known: "First they came for the Communists, and I didn't speak up because I wasn't a Communist. Then they came for the Jews, and I didn't speak up because I wasn't a Jew. Then they came for the Catholics, and I didn't speak up because I was a Protestant. Then they came for me, and by this time there was no one left to speak up."[8]

In an equitable distribution of power, an inclusive social construct, no one would come for the Communists or Jews or homosexuals. No one would come for blacks or women or for those with different ideas or ways of expressing themselves that go beyond a prescribed mindset or party line. This oversimplifies the issue, but it would be a beginning. More importantly, it would set the tone for a different society. If people enjoyed equal conditions—creative as well as material—the first step toward a just distribution of power would already be a reality.

I have mentioned how, from the beginning of the Cuban revolutionary process, surfacing from time to time and in different contexts, parallel influences have vied for control: on the one hand those mediocre minds that managed to achieve some sort of power-wielding status and on the other the more creative visionaries capable of a more complex interpretation of reality and change. When the revolution felt most threatened it tended to pull in, assume defensive attitudes and positions. When it was more confident the atmosphere was more expansive, more conducive to encouraging a breadth of perspectives.

For years Fidel himself seemed to lead the most profound analysis, the most open and intelligent discussion. It was, after all, the Cuban leader who insisted on more than one occasion that the revolution must not talk down to the population but raise people's educational level so they could appreciate, understand, and produce the most sophisticated science, technology, art, and ideas.

In other political processes the "safest" or most conservative and rigid tendencies have succeeded in defeating the more creative, innovative, and riskier proposals. The coexistence of these parallel and competing influences may have been one of the Cuban revolution's salvations, one reason it lives, in the face of so many attempts to destroy it.

CHAPTER 12

THE SANDINISTAS

Two, Three, Many Vietnams

"Two, three, many Vietnams," cried Che Guevara, the Argentine doctor who came to international prominence when he joined Fidel's group of exiled revolutionaries in Mexico, went on to play a major role in the Cuban war, and then disappeared from public view to go off to lead guerilla forces in other impoverished countries. He was in Congo before Bolivia. Polemics continue to this day about the strategy he modeled.

From July 31 through August 10, 1967, just after my first visit but two years before our family moved to the island, Cuba hosted the first conference of the Organization of Latin American Solidarity (OLAS). This was an effort to promote and consolidate revolution throughout the continent. Cuba favored an armed guerilla movement as the inevitable means to political change, and OLAS provided the forum for discussion and support of that option.

Che, unbeknownst to all but a small circle of comrades, had been fighting for months in the mountains of Bolivia. At the conference his absence became a powerful presence and he was named its honorary president. Haydeé Santamaría was its functioning on-site executive. One hundred sixty-three delegates, representing twenty-seven Latin American countries, plus one delegate from the United States and sixty-six observers, thirty-eight invited guests, and two hundred eighty-one journalists attended OLAS.

In January of that year Regis Debray, a Frenchman who would later be captured and imprisoned on his return from a meeting with Che's guerilla, had published an essay called "Revolution in the Revolution?" It would become the authoritative text of the foco theory, putting forth the idea that a small irregular army of combatants, operating in a region where people had nothing to lose but their poverty, could win over a population that would become the nucleus of a successful fighting force. Cuba pushed the theory hard. Many of us believed the concept could work.

Throughout the developing world, legal or democratic roads to political change had long shown themselves to be ineffectual: too vulnerable to cooptation, sellout, and corruption, and much too slow. Those liberals who bemoaned the violence of armed struggle ignored the violence implicit when hundreds of thousands died of poverty, hunger, curable diseases, and abandonment.

A small guerrilla force had succeeded in Cuba but had retreated into relative isolation or failed elsewhere. Each country had its unique history of struggle, culture, physical terrain, and political balance of powers. Living in Cuba during the years in which the foco theory was favored I was privy to very little opposing argument. I can only remember questioning the theory with my friend Roque Dalton, who, eight years later, would himself fall victim to a criminal faction in El Salvador's guerrilla movement.

Cuba was living proof that armed revolution could succeed and its authoritative voice carried great weight. Delegates to OLAS who disagreed with the Cuban position were either silenced, refrained from openly opposing their host, or didn't voice divergent views until they were back in their home countries. In retrospect it seems tragically obvious that a white Latin American among black Congolese fighters, or a small group of Cubans in the midst of Bolivia's indigenous population would be seen as intruders.[1]

As I write I am struck by a particularly dramatic timeline. Debray's treatise on the validity of the foco theory appeared in January, 1967. The OLAS conference opened in late July. Guevara's *Bolivian Diary*, published posthumously, includes this July 31 entry:

Tonight I explained the errors of our action [to the group]: 1. a badly situated camp, 2. bad timing, which allowed [the enemy] to attack us, 3. excessive confidence, resulting in the deaths of Ricardo and then Raul, 4. inability of safeguarding our gear. We lost eleven knapsacks with medicines, field glasses, and some very sensitive items such as the tape recorder with messages from Manila [note: Manila was code for Havana]....

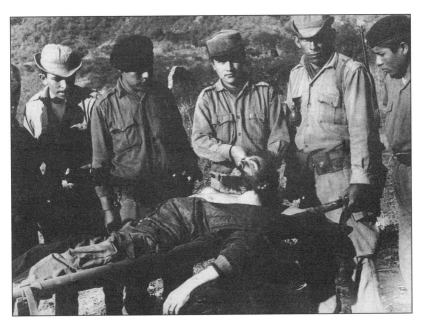

Ernesto "Che" Guevara, murdered in Bolivia. An image I cannot wipe from memory. Las Higueras, Bolivia, October 9, 1967. Photographer unknown.

Eight weeks later Che Guevara was dead. The photograph of his lifeless body surrounded by young Bolivian soldiers circled the world; an image I cannot wipe from memory. Of his embattled fighting force only a handful survived. In Bolivia, at least, the foco theory had failed. For several more years, however, the one successful revolution in the Americas continued to insist upon it as the most viable strategy and to favor revolutionary movements with a similar line. Salvador Allende's Unidad Popular electoral victory in Chile in 1970 broadened the panorama, although it too finally met a tragic end.

In the coming years I would get to know men and women from a number of the Latin American and Caribbean insurgent movements. They came from Mexico, the Dominican Republic, Peru, Bolivia, Venezuela, Chile, Brazil, Argentina, Uruguay, Colombia, Guatemala, El Salvador, Haiti, and Nicaragua. Some had emerged from the ranks of their countries' Communist parties; others were members of independent armed struggle organizations. Each espoused his or her vision of struggle, in line with a particular history and culture and with conditions on the ground. It is only from today's perspective that I am able to unravel some of the knots and understand which movements had more of a chance and which were doomed from their inception. The human sacrifice in all these efforts, the deaths of so many brave men and women (some of them close friends), haunts me to this day.

None of us truly understood the ruthless power wielded by a succession of U.S. administrations, all dedicated to preventing "one, two, many Vietnams." One Vietnam, and of course Cuba itself, were more than they could tolerate.

I Remember a Childhood Indignation

It is 2007. I am growing old in the New Mexico of my childhood, this place that daily reenergizes my spirit, continually reestablishing itself as home. Last year my partner Barbara and I celebrated our twenty-first anniversary. It's been almost that long since I won the immigration case that made it possible for me to begin to relax back into living once again in the country where I was born and received my first indelible cultural impressions. It's been more than a decade since I stopped teaching. Retirement, they call it, although for me that's mostly meant less structure—and less income. I work as much and as hard as I always have, albeit on projects of my choice.

One of those projects is this book about my years in Cuba. I must get it down, I keep telling myself, before I forget the events, the meaning, but especially the feelings. Those are the most elusive and perhaps the most important.

My childhood indignation at injustice may have had its origin in the fact that I was sexually abused by my maternal grandfather when I was very young; I learned injustice in my cells. My father's devotion to fairness was also an influence. But my conscious dedication to fighting for social change probably began in New York with my earliest protest activities. Ban the Bomb. Civil Rights. The movement against the U.S. war in Vietnam. It continued in Mexico, where a deeper experience of struggle, resistance, and initial recognition of the lengths to which power is willing to go enveloped me in the student protest of 1968. At the end of 1974, just six months before the United States was defeated in Southeast Asia, a visit to Vietnam moved me profoundly. But my political education consolidated itself in Cuba. It wasn't only that small island nation and its people; witnessing and participating in an experiment that was daily changing people's lives. There were also the dozens of revolutionaries from other countries who found shelter, encouragement, and support in the country.

The Dead Do Not Die Completely

I wake unsure of where I have been. The impression of my body on the mattress, the wrinkled sheets and bunched covers say I have been asleep, in the bed I share with my life companion. Barbara reaches her hand out to touch my shoulder, welcome me to another day. My pounding heart tells me I have been far off, out there somewhere as the poet says.[2]

If I walk, following the path that winds through canyons and across valley floors, if I walk slowly and patiently, eyes attentive to features of land and markers along the way, will I find the memories I am looking for, be able to retrieve them and carry them back into my life? Will I fill my basket? Or will the basket always be too small to hold all the memories? Where will I put them? How will I order them? How make sense of so much? Must one revisit the places themselves? And what of those visits where everything has shifted, where even the reference points have disappeared or morphed into something else? My chest constricts. It is harder and harder to breathe.

The other day I was listening to a local jazz station. Suddenly a male voice interrupted the improvisation. The brief monologue sounded as if it might have been part of the piece but there was only one interruption of this kind. The voice said: "the dead do not die completely until the last person with a memory of them is gone. Until then they exist in a semi-dead state. It is not until all those with memories of them have died that they finally move on—to the land of the completely dead." The voice stopped speaking. The music continued.

I wake now remembering the Sandinistas with whom I shared work and deep friendship during my last years in Cuba. I speak of them here because an important and generous part of Cuba's identity in the 1970s was the haven it provided for revolutionaries from all over the world. Their energies and dreams, combined with those of the islanders themselves, filled everyday life with the sense that we were indeed creating a new world; one that would be healthier and more just for greater numbers of people. I also speak about them because they impacted my life in important ways.

A Catholic Priest Saying Mass for a Communist Poet

Ernesto Cardenal must have been the first Sandinista I knew, although he was not yet a Sandinista when we met and it would be a while before I left Mexico and moved on to Cuba. I'm talking early 1960s. Ernesto moved in and out of the group of poets—Latin and North Americans—who gathered at Philip Lamantía's Zona Rosa apartment to read our poetry to one another. A slim figure but powerful of voice and presence, the beard that hid his receding chin already beginning to gray, Ernesto was one of six poets who read at a benefit for *El Corno Emplumado* in the neighborhood of San Angel around that time.

This was the period of Ernesto's poem about the European conquest of his native land, "El estrecho dudoso," which we published in *El Corno's* first issue. And "Canción para Marilyn Monroe," in which the Hollywood icon dies with the telephone receiver in her hand, God waiting on the other end of the line. The magnificent "Hora cero," also from this period, remains one of his greatest works and the one that put Nicaragua on the map for many, including me.

At the time Ernesto was debating his vocation for the Catholic priesthood. He was in correspondence with the Trappist monk and well-known philosopher and author Thomas Merton about founding a contemplative community somewhere in Latin America; and would soon join Merton for a year at the Trappist Monastery near Gethsemani, Kentucky. Merton died before they could realize their shared vision. Ernesto ended up studying for the priesthood at a seminary in Antioquía, Colombia, and taking his final vows in his native Nicaragua. He went on to carry out his and Merton's dream on a small island in the archipelago of Solentiname, near the border with Costa Rica.

I vividly remember attending a mass Ernesto offered for *El Corno*. He was already a priest, so this must have been on one of his subsequent visits to Mexico. The chapel was a small one in a large city hospital where a friend who was a nurse allowed him access. A dozen of us attended, including Sergio and me, and the Cuban poet Roberto Fernández Retamar, who was visiting at the time. My body experiences once again the hard wooden pew. I was immersed in ancient ritual but fully focused on the new.

This mass was not only for *El Corno* but also in memory of a young Nicaraguan poet named Fernando Gordillo, who had recently succumbed to a heart condition. We had published Gordillo's work and that of his girlfriend Michele Nájlis. I remember the tiny ID pictures they sent when we asked for images of contributing poets, and their place in a display of such photos that covered one wall in our home. Ernesto said something to the effect that this was a unique situation, but indicative of the times, in which a Catholic priest was saying mass for the soul of a Communist poet.

Indeed, despite the hierarchical Church's message to the contrary,

Ernesto Cardenal would come to represent for us and for many the idea that Christianity as understood through Jesus' teachings and social revolution understood as the Sandinistas envisioned it need not be incompatible. We had entered the era of Vatican II when great masses of peasant and worker Catholics began to look for God not in ritualistic dogma but in the lives of the poor. Liberation theology became a powerful force for social change; so powerful that in less than two decades the popes who succeeded John XXIII would do everything possible to erase his legacy, effectively reversing much of that healthy openness.

In the figure of Fernando Gordillo, Ernesto taught us what was going on in Nicaragua, and introduced us to the young student leaders and guerrilla fighters who were beginning to stand up to the Somoza dictatorship. He told us about the Sandinista National Liberation Front (FSLN), just then beginning to organize. Its first military and political successes were still far in the future. Soon Ernesto himself would join the FSLN. By that time he was at Solentiname. After the Sandinista victory the dual allegiance of a number of politically committed Nicaraguan priests would prove an embarrassing challenge to Rome's authority.

"¡Qué Se Rinda Tu Madre!"

Later, in Cuba, Ernesto would also introduce me to the poetry of Leonel Rugama, the twenty-one-year-old ex-seminary student who died fighting Somoza's army in the city of Managua in 1970. The house where the young man hid was surrounded by tanks. Realizing there was no escape, Rugama answered the soldiers' call to surrender with the words for which he is best known: "¡Qué se rinda tu madre!" he is said to have shouted, as he emerged from the house, his sad weapon blazing. (The line has been translated literally as "Tell your mother to surrender!" I believe "Up yours!" may be closer to its Spanish meaning.)

On July 20, 1969 we were still in hiding in Mexico. In the home of the friend who had taken us in, Robert, the children, and I watched the first moon landing on a small black and white television screen. Apollo Eleven hovered above the celestial surface, the landing capsule descended, and Neil Armstrong stepped onto lunar dust and into history. I had no idea at the time that a young Nicaraguan poet named Leonel Rugama was watching the same scene and would write a poem called "The Earth is a Satellite of the Moon." It is still absolutely relevant to our world situation:

Apollo 2 cost more than Apollo 1,
Apollo 1 cost enough.

Apollo 3 cost more than Apollo 2,
Apollo 2 cost more than Apollo 1,
Apollo 1 cost enough.

Apollo 4 cost more than Apollo 3,
Apollo 3 cost more than Apollo 2,
Apollo 2 cost more than Apollo 1,
Apollo 1 cost enough.

Apollo 8 cost a fortune, but no one cared
because the astronauts were Protestant.
To every Christian's delight
        they read the Bible from the moon
        and when they returned Pope Paul VI gave them his blessing.

Apollo 9 cost more than all the rest combined
Including Apollo 1 which cost enough.

The great-grandparents of the people of Acahualinca
        were less hungry than the grandparents.
The great-grandparents died of hunger.
The grandparents of the people of Acahualinca
        were less hungry than the parents.
The grandparents died of hunger.
The parents of the people of Acahualinca
        were less hungry than the children
        of the people who live there now.
The parents died of hunger.

The people of Acahualinca are less hungry
        than the children of the people who live there now.
The children of the people of Acahualinca
        are not born because of hunger.
They hunger to be born, only to die of hunger.
Blessed are the poor, for they shall inherit the moon.[3]

Acahualinca was an impoverished shantytown on the fetid shores of Lake Managua. I would learn more about it and those who lived there several years later when I worked with Doris Tijerino on her life story.

As we became friends Ernesto introduced me to the Sandinistas—so many of them poets—and to his country's extraordinary history as it moved into one of its most turbulent and heroic periods. The community he founded at Solentiname became a center of resistance, as did many Christian communities throughout the country. When Somoza's forces closed in, Ernesto was forced into exile where he continued to do important support work. When the Sandinistas took power he became his country's first Minister of Culture.

Poet in a Nation of Poets

By that time I had been living in Cuba for a decade. In August 1979, just after the end of the war, Ernesto invited me to come to Nicaragua to interview the women who had played such an important part in overthrowing the dictatorship. He had read my book on Cuban women and believed I might write an equally useful one about their Nicaraguan sisters. *Sandino's Daughters* became, in fact, my most widely read work. It awakened the interest of tens of thousands of mostly young U.S. Americans in what was happening in Central America.[4]

Before I left Cuba for Nicaragua—first to do the fieldwork for *Sandino's Daughters,* and later to live and work there—Ernesto and I shared a number of experiences on the island. The first of these was when we worked together on the poetry jury of the 1970 Casa de las Américas literary contest. Another was Ernesto's own fieldwork for his book *En Cuba* (In Cuba).[5] As *Sandino's Daughters* would later do for Nicaragua, *En Cuba* encouraged readers to see beyond the anticommunist propaganda that painted the Cuban revolution as quasi-Stalinist, two dimensional, rigid, and irrelevant. It became iconic in the social struggle literature of those years.

Ernesto knew that Robert and I had chosen to use the ordinary Cuban ration book. My small contribution to *En Cuba* was taking him with me to our neighborhood supermarket, showing him how the system worked and what each family unit received in the way of food. The rationing was rigorous and often tedious but certainly adequate. Cubans, with their legendary ingenuity, devised all sorts of creative ways of compensating for individual preferences and needs.

Ernesto's book was composed of a series of conversations with Cubans of all ages and social origins. Most praised the revolution; some were critical. He presented his chorus of voices largely without editorial comment but arranged them in such a way that the portrait he wanted emerged. It was a powerful book.

I remember being slightly annoyed at Ernesto's apparent enthusiasm for scarcity: closer to the concept of voluntary poverty espoused by certain Catholic saints, I thought, than to the hopefully temporary but necessary hardship that comes with equal distribution of basic goods. The first was a choice, I argued. As production levels rose the second would give way to healthier, more satisfying fare. Cubans hoped for and worked toward the day when consumer products would be plentiful. *En Cuba* seemed to embrace the idea that equality of hardship was a good thing in and of itself.

Ernesto embodied the very essence of what it was to be a poet in a nation of poets. After the Sandinista victory, when he became Minister of Culture, one might address him as Minister, Father, or Poet. This latter was his title of choice: Poeta Cardenal. I remember once returning to the country from a trip abroad, and a Nicaraguan customs officer asking my profession. "Poet," I responded, "I work at the Ministry of Culture."

"¿Con el poeta Cardenal?" the man inquired, clearly impressed. After asking if I happened to be carrying a book of my own poems, and happily accepting a signed copy, he waved me through without a glance at my luggage. Such was the respect for poetry in Nicaragua. It preceded Cardenal by generations but during the years of Sandinista rule was largely focused on his persona.

A Poet's Voice

My friendship with Daisy Zamora began in Cuba. Shortly after the Sandinista victory she traveled to the island as Cardenal's Vice Minister. It was Daisy who passed on Ernesto's invitation to interview Nicaraguan women. I remember receiving her in our ample but shoddily furnished living room, gazing for the first time upon her clear face, being stunned by the calm depth of her very blue eyes and listening to her talk about the nation she and her comrades were already busy turning inside out.

An accomplished poet in her own right, Daisy had also studied psychology. It showed. She looked straight at you and spoke in quiet tones, had a way of making you feel you were the only two people in a room. During the last months of the war against Somoza, Daisy's was the voice heard on Radio Sandino, the underground station that kept the Nicaraguan people apprised of the revolution's progress. What more powerful use of a poet's voice?

Gioconda Belli, another of Nicaragua's excellent writers, was also one of my early Sandinista friends. I hadn't heard her name before her *Línea de fuego* (Line of Fire) won the 1978 Casa de las Américas poetry prize. But by then she was well known in many political circles as one of the Sandinistas' most effective ambassadors at large. Her beauty and seductive playfulness belied a quick mind and hard work ethic.

Gioconda and I crossed paths once or twice in Havana, but after I moved to Nicaragua we got to know one another better. I ended up working for her at the FSLN's Department of Political Education, known as DEPEP,[6] commiserating with her about the pain of unrequited love, comparing an occasional encounter with the same lover, and eventually sharing a podium or two when our paths crossed on our generation's reading circuits throughout the United States. "Our generation" may be a bit misleading when speaking of Gioconda and myself; she is a dozen years younger than I. Still, I think of us as having shared some of the same history, albeit in different roles.

Some of Gioconda's poems have been set to music and sung by tens of thousands in Managua's 19 of July Square. Her novels have been published in many languages. But the book of hers that means the most to me is *The Country Under My Skin*, an autobiography of her early years of struggle and so also a history of the FSLN during the same period.[7] It is a brilliant and courageous book, an insightful and honest telling and a must read for all young women embarking upon the road of revolutionary struggle or persuaded to follow the lead of powerful male figures in whatever endeavor.

Can Someone Come Over to Use the Ditto?

Daniel Ortega was exceptionally quiet, almost pathologically so; quite possibly traumatized by his years in prison, much of it spent in solitary confinement. Perhaps also just socially awkward. Being around an older North American woman may have made him uneasy.

Throughout the second half of the 1970s we'd often get a call from the group of Sandinistas in Havana asking if someone could come over to use our ditto machine. On a number of occasions Daniel would show up, wearing a simple white t-shirt and levis. He'd have a battered brown leather briefcase with him. I'd show him into the wood-paneled library, termites leaving their tiny piles of sawdust on all the built-in shelves, ask him if he wanted something cold to drink and retreat to whatever I was doing at the time. Daniel was almost monosyllabic, seemingly uncomfortable in any but the simplest conversations. We rarely exchanged more than a few words.

Once Daniel's brother Humberto showed up in his place. While the former was quite ordinary looking, neatly attired, somewhat absent, the latter was a kind of caricature of himself: uneven featured, louder, slightly jaunty. More talkative, Humberto might crack a joke or make a bit of small talk. One hand was healing from a bullet wound incurred in his escape from a Central American prison; sometimes he wore a brace on it, sometimes not. I thought he might need help positioning the waxy ditto master over the roller or feeding the paper into the tray but refrained from offering in deference to the possibility that the material might be internal, a document not for my eyes.

If I could have imagined then that the Sandinistas would soon roll to victory in Nicaragua—and I couldn't—it still would have seemed improbable that Daniel would be named that country's president and Humberto its Minister of Defense.

Later, Jacinto Suárez also came around to use the ditto. He was very different from the Ortega brothers, more cultured and open. Also reciprocal in his interests. We conversed easily and became friends. Back then I didn't know his name was Jacinto Suárez. I called him Mauro, which was what he was calling himself at the time. Even after I went to Nicaragua to live it was a while before I learned his real identity.

Shortly after my arrival in Managua I attended the wake for Carlos Fonseca, by then several years dead. His body was being moved from the mountain grave near where he'd been ambushed—a local farmer had tended to it since his death in 1976—to a permanent mausoleum in the capital. I'd been asking about my friend but with only the name Mauro I was reduced to vague descriptive phrases: You know ... kind of tall, light eyes—I think. Broad forehead. Curly hair. Suddenly someone came up behind me and placed his palms over my eyes. It was the man I'd known by his pseudonym. Silently I rejoiced that Jacinto Suárez had been one of those who'd survived.

Before getting too far ahead of myself, let me go back to that ditto machine for a moment. I'm no longer sure how we came to possess it. Certainly we didn't bring it from Mexico so it must have been a gift from someone in Cuba. I want to say it was given to us by a Canadian couple who worked for an NGO called Canadian University Service Overseas (CUSO). They became our friends. Much later, the Cubans called me in to tell me the husband was an enemy agent and was being expelled from the country.

This was hard for me to believe but I felt I had no choice at the time but to take Cuba's word. The ditto machine stayed with us, was used during those years by friends from a number of different liberation movements who resided in Cuba, and also to run off copies of poems for our Roque Dalton Poetry Workshop.

To the Mother I Loved So Much

The undisputed leader of the FSLN, Carlos Fonseca was unique. Tall and thin, exceptionally tall for a Central American, his piercing blue eyes were magnified by the thick round lenses of his wire-framed glasses. Glasses and all, he couldn't avoid the myopic gaze of someone who had been half blind since childhood. Carlos would show up not to use our ditto machine but to visit. He enjoyed conversing, especially about his country's history—about which he knew a great deal. Sometimes he had his young son and daughter with him. They were thin, quiet children, exceptionally well mannered. They would sit beside him on our threadbare living room couch until I succeeded in luring them with some of my own kids' books or toys.

The most salient of Carlos' social attributes were his unfailing seriousness and total focus on his people's struggle. He was well educated, though not intellectually sophisticated. He was highly versed on a number of subjects, but whichever of them one raised in a matter of minutes he would manage to steer the conversation to the Sandinistas' efforts to rid his country of a half-century-old dictatorship.

When I think of Carlos a particular conversation comes to mind. He appeared one day, took his usual place at one end of our couch and pulled a couple of folded sheets of paper from his shirt pocket. He handled these as if they were gold. On them he had copied the letter Rigoberto López Pérez left for his mother before going off to make his attempt on the older Somoza's life. He had just found it in a Havana library and his emotion was palpable.

The event had taken place in 1956. The scene was a gala state affair: uniformed waiters walking among the guests as they offered platters of rich tidbits, musicians, dancing, the cream of high society dressed in its finest. Rigoberto, a poor young student, somehow made it into the private hall. He pulled his gun but was quickly overcome by members of the dictator's security guard. They didn't hesitate to shoot him on the spot.

Finding this text left Carlos stammering. His weak eyes shone. He seemed deeply impressed—moved might be the better word—when he pointed out the past tense in the way the young man had signed his letter: "To the mother I loved so much." Predicting and accepting his own death, Rigoberto must have known he was unlikely to succeed. At best he probably hoped he would have a shot at the dictator before he died. Carlos had transcribed the letter word for word but had added line breaks, turning it into a poem.

On another occasion Carlos told me:

Ours is a revolutionary movement without propaganda, without publicity. We ourselves are learning as we go along, analyzing Nicaragua's reality. In our country it was the victory of the Cuban revolution that introduced us to Marxist thought. Nicaragua didn't have the great European immigrations that helped populate Argentina, Brazil, or some of the other Latin American nations. In Nicaragua, all our last names were bequeathed us by Columbus.

We went to the mountains to educate the peasants and the peasants educated us. Imagine: only two generations have passed since Sandino's time and in those two generations it's as if Sandino has been lost, his struggle forgotten by our country's intellectuals. But in the mountains Sandino's struggle lives. There's a real tradition of anti-imperialism in the mountains of my country. The peasants of Nicaragua know they won a war against U.S. intervention!

"We took up arms out of rage," Fonseca told me, "and now we're beginning to learn about our country, its history and idiosyncrasies." He talked a lot about the Jesuit invasion, as he called it, which he blamed for the deeply Catholic aristocracy of intellectuals. I find these direct quotes from the leader of Nicaragua's Sandinista revolution in my journal from those years.

When I worked with Doris Tijerino on the book about her life I learned much more about that first, short-lived Latin American victory over the U.S. Marines, about William Walker, the man the United States government appointed president of the Central American nation, and about Sandino's triumph and betrayal. Augusto César Sandino was the early-twentieth-century Nicaraguan revolutionary who organized an army of peasants and workers against Somoza's father, the first in the dictatorial dynasty. His ragged army succeeded in ousting the U.S. Marines from Nicaragua, but he was quickly betrayed and murdered by Somoza himself. Doris told me stories about peasant families who kept old photographs of Sandino in proud frames on the walls of their shacks, and what happened to those families if Somoza's National Guard happened upon their devotion.

Carlos Fonseca must have visited our Havana apartment fifteen or twenty times over the few years he remained in Cuba before returning to Nicaragua, ambush, and death. Yet he called us, we never called him, and I would say we were more acquaintances than friends. His staunch formality, the way he held himself and his absolute single-mindedness didn't invite a casual relationship. I felt I could have counted on him, though, and always enjoyed our talks.

Nicaraguan poet and priest Ernesto Cardenal, Managua, 1979.

Nicaraguan revolutionary Doris María Tijerino with her daughter, María Doris. Havana, 1980. Years later, in her adolescence, María Doris would die in a plane crash between Havana and Managua.

At a school in Havana province. Margaret and Jacinto Suárez ("Mauro") giving a presentation on the Sandinista struggle. 1976.

Carlos Fonseca's funeral. Left to right: Víctor Tirado, Daniel Ortega, and others guide the casket into the mausoleum. Managua, 1979.

I Wanted to Retrace José Benito's Last Moments

My relationship with Alvaro was different. Doris Tijerino brought him by one day and his warmth and quiet compassion quickly won him the love of everyone in the family. I'd been working with Doris for more than a year, recording her life story for the book that would become *Somos millones*.[8] More than the academic texts then available, I believed a book about a single woman's life might capture the interest of U.S. readers, and hoped it would build solidarity for the Sandinista cause. I also wanted to take advantage of the United Nation's designation of 1975 as International Year of the Woman.

For months Doris and I taped every weekday morning; I'd transcribe in the afternoons and have pages ready for her to go over the following day. This was my second book of women's oral history; I'd already published *Cuban Women Now*. I remember how desperately I wanted to structure this project differently, attempt a circular telling rather than a strict chronology. Although it fell short of what I envisioned, I think of *Somos millones* as the first effort bearing something of my future oral history style.

When we started, Doris had just learned of the death of Ricardo Morales, her partner and the father of the daughter she carried in her womb. He had been gunned down in a firefight days earlier. Those first sessions after she received the news were hard: she the resolute revolutionary, numb, reserved, and accepting her tragedy—at least with me. I the sympathetic outsider, devastated but at a loss as to how to be there for her. Now, months later, it seemed clear that she and Alvaro were becoming a couple.

Not until shortly before I went to Nicaragua myself, after Alvaro too had been shot down in Estelí, would I learn that he was José Benito Escobar, a comrade beloved and respected across the splits that beleaguered the Sandinistas in those years. José Benito was a man whose modesty and simple demeanor belied his organizational stature. My memories of our brief but deep friendship in Havana later compelled me to travel to Estelí to visit Doña Leandra, the elderly woman from whose home, an FSLN safe house, he'd set out on the day he was killed.

I wanted to retrace José Benito's last moments, understand how he fell into the ambush that took his life. A longtime Sandinista supporter, Doña Leandra made and sold sweets in the local market. She herself had lost a son in the war and often hid fighters in her humble home. She told me how José Benito left her home one afternoon, and how he was gunned down less than an hour later. She took me to the place where he died. A few flowers were strung around a simple cross. I raised my camera to photograph the cross and some neighborhood children moved in to embrace it. Doña Leandra and I remained in touch during my years in Nicaragua. Years after her death I received a surprise email from her grandson. He found me on the internet. He'd been two years old when I first visited, he wrote, but had grown up with the stories. The stories, apparently, included me.

What I shared of José Benito's time in Havana remains significant to my sense of what the best of these guerrilla fighters were like: their ideological clarity, selflessness, genuine kindness, and concern for others. He and I did some outreach together, going to Cuban schools in the countryside to talk about the Nicaraguan struggle. Those were rich experiences. But my last image of him is more personal.

Two of my children slept on lumpy mattresses, the only ones available when we'd been assigned our Havana apartment almost a decade before. Their backs were beginning to resent the discomfort and I feared they might suffer permanent damage. José Benito noticed. He mentioned that because of his status as a member of a political organization recognized by the Cuban Party, he had access to a special store. They sold mattresses, he said, and he'd be glad to buy a couple for the children.

We lived on the ninth floor of a building with two elevators. Frequently one or both were out of commission and since replacement parts were almost nonexistent they might remain that way for days. I can still see José Benito, weighted down but determined, struggling up the front stairs with both mattresses awkwardly balanced on his head. I had heard his heavy tread and opened our front door to see what was going on. At that moment he overcame the last step, letting his load slide to the granite floor, a broad smile breaking across his usually stoic face.

After the Sandinista victory of 1979 the revolutionary trade union movement was named for José Benito Escobar, the quiet working class man who'd been born into extreme poverty and followed his conscience into death.

TODAY WE FEEL MORE LIKE EQUALS

Two other Sandinistas we came to know well in Cuba were Jaime Wheelock and his then wife Gladys Zalaquett. Gladys' pseudonym at the time was Ruth. Jaime was Jesuit educated. His knowledge of economics was obvious. Gladys was no less bright, no less competent, although as the wife of one of the *comandantes*, leadership was not to be her role. She was Chilean, of Lebanese descent, vivacious and embracing, one of those truly special human beings. Gladys had met Jaime in her home country. Actually two sisters became involved with two brothers: Gladys and Mónica Zalaquett with Jaime and Ricardo Wheelock.

When we knew them, Jaime and Gladys were living at the Hotel Nacional, a short walk from our apartment. We spent a lot of time together. Once they found a stray kitten in the hotel dining room and brought it over for the children. I remember Jaime carefully cutting the kitten's claws so it wouldn't scratch our youngest. Ana remained wary of that small bundle of fur, though, and they had to find it another home.

Gladys and I developed a friendship that continues almost forty years later. We spent time together in Nicaragua and have seen one another in Chile, where she returned several years after the Sandinista defeat. She and Jaime had a daughter, also named Ana, but separated before the rebel victory. Back then I saw Gladys as older, wiser, much more experienced. I felt young and immature by comparison. In reality, I am more than a decade older than she. Today we feel more like equals, but she is someone I would call a mentor as well as a friend.

I remember envying Gladys's membership in an organization not of her home country. I wished I belonged to a political organization capable of more formally channeling my revolutionary work. When I confessed this to her one day, she said that being a Party member wasn't everything I imagined, that there were as many complexities and difficulties as there was a solid base from which to work. I also have more superficial but equally vivid memories, such as the purple gentian she used on her toenails to combat a fungus she'd picked up somewhere; and how vain she was about what she thought of back then as that purple medicine ruining the way her feet looked. Even in Havana's tropical heat she always wore closed toe shoes.

I still chuckle when I remember asking Jaime why in the world he would have chosen such an English sounding pseudonym, then discovering it was the name with which he'd been born. As the surname implies, Jaime was a member of Nicaraguan aristocracy, traditionally anti-Somoza. He had gone to Chile to study, became a well-educated Marxist, and when the Sandinistas split into three tendencies emerged as one of the leaders of the Proletarians. Jaime became one of the nine comandantes (three from each tendency) and Minister of Agriculture in the new Sandinista government. The project of land reform was largely developed by him.

The Seeds of Decadence and Power Abuse

I don't mean to imply that the entire Sandinista leadership turned out to be less than we hoped. This wasn't the case, not at all. A number of men and women—Carlos Núñez, Luis Carrión, Jaime Wheelock, Doris Tijerino, Henry Ruiz, Victor Tirado, Sergio Ramírez, Dora María Téllez, Gioconda Belli, Daisy Zamora, Ernesto and Fernando Cardenal, Mirna Cunningham, Carlos Fernándo Chamorro, and Sofía Montenegro to name just a few—retained their integrity throughout. Today a number of these men and women represent what is left of the old *sandinismo*. But some, like the Ortega brothers and Tomás Borge disappointed by betraying—in one way or another—the ideals for which they once stood.

Tomás Borge was brilliant, a capable tactician and writer but misogynist far beyond the parameters of the most stereotypical Latin conditioning. Victimized by torture and then propped up by power, both probably combined to stunt his development. During his years at the pinnacles of Party and Government, he did things like conspicuously vacate the mansion he'd taken as his own, claim he had decided to live like the people and then move into a small house in a working class neighborhood of Managua. The catch was that he occupied not just that house but several blocks of similar structures, their lots connected behind walls that put them out of sight, all the while pretending a modest lifestyle.

Daniel Ortega is a study apart. After the decade of Sandinista administration his stepdaughter Zoilamérica Narváez publicly accused him of having sexually abused her over a period of nineteen years. He, of course, denied the charge and his wife, Rosario Murrillo, took up his defense. Zoilamérica's ex-husband and many others, however, support her claim. The evidence seems compelling. This is a case in which a man moved from humble beginnings through difficult struggle and prolonged imprisonment to victory and ten years in a position capable of corrupting all but the strongest individual. Who knows what unresolved demons have plagued him along the way.

Explanation is not justification, though. Ortega and his followers made a mockery of the revolutionary movement that held such hope for Nicaragua. He refused to entertain the slightest challenge to his command, including questions about his stepdaughter's abuse. Honest Sandinistas had to leave the Party and build an alternative structure in order to keep what they stood for alive. Denigrating and invalidating all challengers, Ortega continued to run for president of Nicaragua in every election after the 1990 defeat. In 2006 he once again became president.

Today's Ortega is not the Ortega we admired and supported twenty-five years back. He uses some of the familiar rhetoric but his actions speak louder than those tired words. In order to retake the presidency he entered into pacts with neofascists and with the conservative hierarchy of the Nicaraguan Catholic Church. He rejected anyone who challenged his authority, from inside as well as outside the Party. In the National Assembly he pushed through the most repressive antiabortion bill anywhere in the world; it criminally penalizes women who seek reproductive rights as well as abortion providers. During his presidential campaign his program for tackling the serious problems of a nation that had regressed to pre-Sandinista levels of misery included such vagaries as forgiveness and loving one another. He and his wife, Rosario Murillo, have made a mockery of the project they and their comrades once achieved and betray the thousands who died during the years leading up to their decade in power.[9]

Although Daniel Ortega inspires anger, revulsion, and sorrow in those of us who knew his early history, many who voted for him—especially in the rural areas—undoubtedly believed they were voting for the Sandinista platform, a history of defense of the impoverished. This may be the positive side of his victory. Ironically the Bush administration seems to think it faces another revolutionary in Central America. Only time will reveal how all this unfolds.

Humans are always humans, whether or not they are also leadership cadre in a revolutionary movement capable of defeating a dynasty of horror. We wanted to see them all as larger than life. Some of them were; others weren't. It can be difficult to separate personal and political judgments, to understand that a man or woman may be brave and committed enough to wage unequal war, conquer the seemingly unconquerable, propose to create a new society—and then show him or herself to be just as damaged by the old society as those we reviled without hesitation. Looking back, it's clear that the seeds of decadence and power abuse helped doom the Sandinista revolution of the 1980s.

A PAINFUL PERIOD IN MY LIFE

But I'm getting ahead of myself again. During most of my years in Cuba, a Sandinista victory still belonged to an unknowable future. There were many foreign revolutionaries in the country and most never achieved their ultimate goals. I can't even remember how I first met the Sandinistas who moved in and out of Havana—arriving to cool off for a while after some brilliant escapade or prisoner exchange, to receive military training or just to meet with their comrades in a safe and supportive environment. During the years I lived there, Cuba provided refuge to thousands of liberation fighters from all over Asia, Africa and Latin America. This was but one facet of its extraordinary internationalism, which also included taking in and educating hundreds of thousands of young people, sending highly trained personnel anywhere in the world that requested their expertise, and responding with immediate medical aid wherever there was a natural disaster.

However it was that we met, with the Nicaraguans there was a special bond. And this bond became dramatically apparent to me late in my time on the island, when they took a stand that made a great difference to my life back then, and moves me to this day. During my last three or four years in Cuba I confronted a mysterious and extremely difficult personal situation. Perhaps because I had been friendly with the CUSO representative cum spy, perhaps because I was outspokenly critical on issues of gender and sexual identity, perhaps because my friends included revolutionaries who did not subscribe to the Cuban line, perhaps for some other reason or all of these, there came a time when some in Cuba began to distrust me.

I lost my job, and was not told why. The Cubans never stopped paying my salary or using my work in their publications, which was reassuring but also made the situation more difficult to understand. Doors closed, but I could never claim I had been marginalized completely.

Cuban writer Eduardo Heras León describes this sort of oppression succinctly when he remembers his own experience of the 1970s:

> There was nothing to be done. No way of defending myself. No way of talking with anyone who might have been open to dialogue, investigation, polemic. I must confess: at the time I felt as if I were reliving the conflicts of Joseph K. in *The Trial*. I was being accused of something I could not understand, and some monstrous mechanism prevented my access to justice.[10]

Heras León's words describe my experience as well. This was an extremely painful period in my life. I knew I could be trusted, and tried to keep my spirits up. So much of my situation seemed contradictory and its complexities made it harder to fathom. Through my trade union I tried to find out why I had been fired and was told that as a foreigner I didn't belong to the union. This was particularly hurtful because by then I had paid union dues for a very long time and had even held a union leadership position at my workplace my first few years on the job.

When I tried other channels, the person with whom I spoke would invariably point out that I continued to draw a salary, try to convince me that nothing was wrong and that I should simply accept the situation. I was writing books and was indeed grateful for the unearned income and ample writing time. Still, in a worker's society people work, and I was confused and saddened by having been so unceremoniously let go. No description written today can adequately speak to the anguish I felt then.

Chilean friends admitted they had been warned by the Cubans against working with me. They told me this after their own investigation convinced them I was worthy of their trust. But it was the Nicaraguan comrades who stood by me unfailingly. They too said they had been told that I might be an agent of some kind. But they had worked with me and knew this wasn't so. And, despite their deep respect for their Cuban comrades, they showed me complete and uninterrupted support.

(Years later, and in a much more public venue, the Sandinistas would again demonstrate their independence. In 1989, when Cuba staged a rigged trial condemning Arnaldo Ochoa and executing him along with three others, the Cuban Party asked the Sandinistas—still in power at the time—to take back the high honor they had bestowed upon the Cuban general. The Sandinistas respectfully refused.)[11]

For an activist there are probably few things worse than losing the confidence of your political comrades without reason. Because you have done nothing to lose it, there is nothing you can do to gain it back. Because you have given up so much to work for social justice and this work has become your identity, you feel as if your life itself may not be worth living. In the years about which I write, false accusations were often whispered about people—out of jealousy, vindictiveness, the rumor monger's desire to build him or herself up, sometimes even out of the conviction a warning was necessary. Although I cannot remember a specific instance, I am ashamed to say that however unwittingly I too may have aided and abetted some half truths or lies about others.

When this happened to me my optimistic nature came to the fore, at least at the beginning. Guilelessly, I went from office to office following all leads. As time went on, though, I became despondent. I shed many tears of frustration. I remember long walks along Havana's malecón, some of them alone and some with my son, Gregory. Gregory was a great support. His belief in me never wavered. There did come a time when he urged me to leave the country, go somewhere I was appreciated and wouldn't be forced to fight such invisible demons.

I always refused. I couldn't conceive of giving up. It seemed to me tantamount to admitting those making my life miserable had some valid reason for doing so. Then too, what I knew about myself gave me reason to believe the issue would eventually be resolved. On the one hand it could be argued that the Cubans were trying to get me to leave of my own accord. On the other, something would always come up that made that seem absurd. I wanted to believe I would soon wake from a bad dream.

The larger issue of mistrust generated many smaller ones. I would speak with someone I believed could untangle the mystery, that person would express shock and promise to investigate and get back to me right away, then no further contact would be forthcoming or—in cases where the person risked a degree of honesty—they would call to tell me they, too, had hit a brick wall. On the more personal front, some friends remained loyal and close while others kept a distance or stayed away altogether. At the time, each such experience was a gift or wrenching disappointment. In retrospect I find lessons in all these responses: lessons about individual courage and cowardice; but also about the ways in which authoritarian bureaucracies stimulate unexamined actions, arrogance, opportunism, paternalism, sexism, and social climbing. At the time I often experienced physical pain along with the frustration.

Gradually, during my last years in the country, things got better. And then one day I was called in to the office of State Security where I received as close to an apology as the Cubans were willing to offer. The man with whom I spoke claimed an unfortunate combination of events had conspired against me. There had been the return of Cubans studying abroad who needed the jobs being held by foreigners; he said that had been one of the reasons I'd lost my job. There had been our family's friendship with the CUSO representative. And xenophobia, perhaps some of my independent opinions or outspoken critiques, and the fact that some people in power respected me while others were jealous, resentful, or simply had their doubts.

The meeting was brief. I now wish I had asked more questions, primary among them why I alone had been punished for a friendship shared by Robert. Questions about the agent himself—what made them suspect him, what he had done—were off-limits; that I knew. I remember leaving that office a bit dizzy, juggling a strange mixture of confusion and relief. My name cleared, I was free to move on. And I chose to go to Nicaragua, where I had already done three months of fieldwork, knew many of the leaders of the new revolution, felt I could learn a lot from a process in its early years, and also had a lot to give.

The Nicaraguan comrades in Cuba never lost faith in me. They continued our work and in fact wasted no time in alerting me to what was going on. I was moved and grateful that these men and women who had only known me a couple of years were willing to defend me in this way. Perhaps their own experience of struggle had taught them how dangerous such unfounded accusations can be.

CHAPTER 13

A QUESTION OF POWER

I Remember

I am sitting in the Willard Reading Room at the University of New Mexico's Zimmerman Library. A small audience has gathered to listen to Dr. Teresa Eckmann lecture on the Jane Norling / Lenora (Nori) Davis Collection of Latin American—mostly Cuban—posters that Jane has donated to the library's vast Sam Slick collection.

Jane and Nori met in a women's cancer support group in 1988 where they discovered both were graphic designers producing imagery and print materials for the people's struggles of those times. Nori succumbed to breast cancer in 1990. Jane and Nori's widower eventually married and are together today.

Nori's husband wasn't all Jane inherited from her activist artist friend. She gained an expanded studio and Nori's poster collection. Added to Jane's, it represents a visual, in depth history of ideas, causes, anniversaries, events, and iconic figures. After visiting an Albuquerque show of one hundred thirteen posters from the Slick collection, Jane felt the University of New Mexico would be a good repository for what had become their combined collection.

"Well, not really a collection," Jane insists. "As artists we didn't think of ourselves as collectors. We acquired our posters from trips to Cuba and other Latin American countries where we were given them by colleagues and organizations we met or worked with. We then made them available for community events where we lived—Nori in Chicago, I in the San Francisco Bay Area. We kept the posters in flat files and portfolios and when we

*Jane Norling planting tomatoes in
Havana's green belt. December 1971.*

displayed them we put them up with tape or push pins." The corners of many
are mutilated; one poster has a large square cut from the center, perhaps used
as a color chip, Jane speculates.

Jane is in Albuquerque for the collection's acquisition lecture. She is an old
and dear friend, someone with whom I have shared more movement years
than I can remember. We often reminisce about the work we've done and
the change it has brought or failed to bring about. Eckmann, who negotiated
Jane's donation, speaks about the value of these posters, their importance
to all those interested in the politics as well as the art and culture of an era
today's young people don't remember.

I remember. And, as so often happens at this sort of event, viewing the
material on display moves me to think about power. What idea of power
do these posters project? How does the message, from a time now all but
forgotten, strike me now? Is how we think about and exercise power any
different today? And what role, if any, does art play in political struggle?

During the talk my mind keeps wandering from Eckmann's words to
long-ago places, people, events. The images and texts send me back to a time
when they were familiar and urgent: "Two, Three, Many Vietnams!"; "To
Love Life is to Fight for Peace"; "The Guerilla Christ"; "Ten Million Tons of

Sugar Will be Harvested"; "People Teaching People to Read"; "March 8th: International Women's Day"; and "The Sun Rises So it Can Get Out and Vote." There were the protests: "Against Apartheid"; "Against Imperialist Aggression in Nicaragua"; "Down with Repression in Guatemala." And the tributes to beloved figures: Fidel, Amilcar Cabral, Uncle Ho, Mandela, Simón Bolívar, José Martí.

Some of the phrases continue to resonate. "If You Love Life, Fight for Peace" is still one I see on cars (the artistic poster now so often reduced to commodity bumper sticker). Others evoke a time long gone and, sadly, from which few struggles were successful. Following ten years of Sandinista administration, Nicaragua was overcome by imperialist aggression and its own internal shortcomings; that country has gone from its heroic, decade-long period of dramatic social progress to once again being one of the poorest in Latin America.

In Guatemala new and widespread incidents of repression recall the protracted period of terror and loss. And a guerrilla Christ? In the decades since these posters were produced the idea of a loving and compassionate Jesus has mostly given way to one of a wrathful and punitive God. The power nuclei that control most of the world's major religions today speak threatening languages of hierarchy, domination, intolerance, and war.

This May Feel Like the Worst of Times

George W. Bush has gone so much further than previous U.S. presidents in his assault upon other countries and his rollback of social progress at home. His imperious refusal to listen to dissenting voices and strategy of pretending ignorance or paying rudimentary lip service to critics characterize these times. It is a tactic that has become a model for people at all levels of government, the corporate world, and society at large. Indeed, the constitutional changes Bush has imposed upon the presidency itself, if not reversed, will reshape the office, perhaps for generations to come.

This may feel like the worst of times but it's important to remember that humanity survived the Crusades, devastating plagues, the assaults upon Native peoples, the Middle Passage, the Armenian holocaust, European fascism and the annihilation of six million Jews, the launch of the world's first nuclear bombs, the U.S. war in Vietnam, the Cold War, and the horrendous slaughters in the Balkans, Rwanda, and Darfur. Before the current U.S. administration, presidents of both political parties waged unjust wars and engaged in criminal policies. But several things are different today. One is an extent of damage from which there may be no return. Another is surely the weight our own failures impose, a weight that often robs us of the confidence that we may yet be able to bring about change.

I think of the values and struggles captured in these posters. I remember some of our victories and linger with memories of how it felt to operate under the assumption we were helping to make the world a better place. And I am overwhelmed by sadness. It is discouraging, exhausting, to witness the painful upsurge in violence and the sophisticated ways in which so many have been conditioned to accept that violence as inevitable, even defensible or necessary. The rapacious strategy of the preemptive strike validates and applauds this solution, from the highest levels of government and the corporate world on down, making it increasingly difficult to try to teach values of honesty, solidarity, fairness, and cooperation to the youngest among us.

I remind myself that some of my generation's efforts did succeed, or at least managed to push the overall struggle forward. In the United States, although much remains to be done and despite recent setbacks, the Civil Rights, women's, and LGBT movements have achieved tremendous progress toward equality. Latino, Native American, peace, and immigrant rights movements have made important strides.

South Africa finally did defeat apartheid. Next door, though, Zimbabwe is devastated by poverty and repression. Angola and Mozambique, two nations whose liberation movements came to power in the years evoked by these posters, have been reduced to new levels of misery and despair. The Palestinians, so many thousands of lives later, don't seem much closer to having their own state than they were back then. And the Bush administration, the Israeli government, and other extremist governments and groups have kept the whole Middle East in an ever-worsening mire of political and religious upheaval.

VISUAL MESSAGES NOW CIRCLE THE GLOBE IN SECONDS

I focus on Cuba. That country did teach its citizens to read and today, despite the revolution's complex problems, has one of the best educated populations in the world. The ten million ton harvest of 1969–1970, on the other hand, failed. To the detriment of every other economic goal, that country's largest-ever sugar harvest came in at just eight and a half million tons. The power abuse inherent in ignoring the critics and insisting on the impossible goal points to a painful lesson. At the time some believed the lesson worth the failure. Today some wonder if it really was a lesson learned.

Today's U.S. war of aggression in Iraq reminds me of the wars in Vietnam and Korea that shaped my own young adulthood; but rather than urging the creation of two, three, many Vietnams, the current cry is a more rational (albeit also more desperate) plea to avoid such conflagrations—which in today's hegemonic world can only lead to a destruction that would threaten life everywhere. Combating the damage to our planet from man-made climate change and global warming must take precedence among today's struggles.

Today we have the internet, a communicative tool we couldn't have dreamed of back then. This phenomenon—with its 'zines and blogs and potential for political campaigns that can rally millions of people and raise hundreds of thousands of dollars in minutes—has completely changed the graphic art medium and capability. Visual messages now circle the globe in seconds; they are more immediate and effective but lack the tangible presence which once made them such sensuous, substantive objects. The flyers we once taped to the refrigerator door and saw each time we prepared a meal now flash briefly and disappear into the hidden recesses of cyberspace.

The internet also delivers a message about power. It separates those who have access to computers from those who still transmit information person to person or for whom radio is a luxury. Globalization brings some together while making it easier to control large sectors of people, and everywhere pushes rich and poor farther apart. As I write this I am reminded that none but a very limited number of Cuban intellectuals and scholars has access to the internet today: a policy of political control that has kept most Cubans isolated from the modern world. To my mind this is disingenuous and dangerous.

In the posters from the 1970s and 1980s a unity of form and content was achieved. Art served a message, but wasn't diminished or diluted by that message. On the contrary, in the best of that political art there is a balance that deepens both. Form and content merge. Color, design, movement, juxtaposition, surprise, emotion, the sure brushstroke of conviction, and clean line of uncluttered reason speak to us with the same power and urgency they did back then.

Nuance and sophistication are also present: in the classic African sculpture shouldering a semiautomatic weapon; in the *Vogue* model wearing wild animal skins and pictured beside a bloated, gaunt-faced African child; or the deceptively tranquil vision of Vietnamese farmers moving across a flowering field. Vietnam: that extraordinary country whose ravaged people nonetheless have always been concerned with portraying the essence of life rather than the horrors of death. Flags become letters, Middle Eastern oil transforms itself into dollars for U.S. coffers, washed hands urge the prevention of contagious disease. The image of a single stylized lavender rose on a yellow background framed in tones of green, one thorn issuing a single drop of blood, symbolizes the worldwide protest song movement even today. (We had used this image as the cover for *El Corno Emplumado* number twenty-six.)

POWER IN THE HANDS OF PEOPLE

These posters evoke a sense of power in the hands of people: artists committed to rendering the urgent issues of the day with brilliance, energy, and passion. But power, then as now, was most often concentrated in the hands of closed groups or individuals. The theory of revolution we inherited from Lenin was that a relatively small group of revolutionaries, if they could garner enough popular support, would be able to seize state power and proceed to transform society.

What if it turns out there is a fundamental problem with this way of seizing power? What if it inevitably leads to over-centralization, and centralized power becomes the problem rather than the solution? Maybe there needs to be a much longer period in which people's consciousness, behavior, culture, and cooperation with others can be transformed before revolutionaries take over the state. What if the seizure of state power should be the last step in social transformation, not the first? Although we as yet have no long term example of this, the Zapatistas in southern Mexico may be involved in a social change project more weighted in that direction.

Memory pulls me back in time, and I feel again the pulse of all these images, their seductive quality—to inspire and spark productivity, as well as humiliate or destroy. The enemy clearly understood the possibilities as well. During my years in Cuba a single poster folded in four was inserted between the pages of each issue of *Tri-continental Magazine* and sent to thousands of subscribers. One of these, in support of the Black Panther Party, featured the open, fang-filled panther's mouth: black on white, unnerving. In a particular press run I remember that poster was removed from every single copy of the magazine and replaced with an alternate version which at first glance proved impossible to distinguish from the original.

The difference was that the forgery included a phrase written to provoke internal strife between two Panther factions: raging jealousy took its toll and internal disagreement weakened the organization. I no longer remember the phrase nor whom or what those different factions represented. I do remember how closely the copy resembled the original and how stunned we were when we discovered the ploy. In those years mail from Cuba had to travel a circuitous route on its way to other countries. I don't know if anyone ever figured out where the switch was made.

It Was a Landscape That Inspired

Jane Norling and I met in 1972. People's Press, the San Francisco print and publishing collective with which she worked, sent her to Cuba for two months to work at OSPAAAL (Organization of Solidarity with the Peoples of Asia, Africa and Latin America, the group that published *Tri-continental*). There she was surrounded by the clever, stylized, combative, and evocative images created by dozens of Cuban artists. They appeared on posters and were magnified on billboards and the sides of buildings. The images of the revolution itself, in its everyday dimension, surrounded us all; creating a graphic backdrop that functioned as another landscape. It was a landscape that inspired, influenced our ideas and allegiances, and greatly affected our capacity to question.

Jane looked me up, as did countless North American visitors who filled our Havana apartment. We hit it off right away. My most enduring memory of our early friendship is of the morning I took her to my bodega, the neighborhood market where our family's ration book was registered. Visitors were often interested in what food shopping was like in Cuba then, what was available on the ration book and how one obtained one's share. After spending some time with me inside the store, Jane sat on the curb that bordered the market's parking lot, making quick sketches of people going by and of the pastel poverty of old houses along this block: their weathered columns and peeling paint.

Jane's mentor at OSPAAAL was the fine Cuban artist and graphic designer Alberto Rostgaard. He chose her to execute a poster in solidarity with the Puerto Rican people's fight for independence. Aside from Jane's obvious talent, the fact that she was a U.S. American must have prompted him to give her the assignment.

Now that poster is featured in this 2007 show. The Puerto Rican flag—single white star on a blue triangle at the left, red and white stripes flowing right, and two lines of exuberant blue combatant fists rising from the red bands in energized splashes of paint. The top line frames the poster's uppermost extreme and is upside down, a mirror image of the lower line where the arms and fists move right side up in profile across the picture plane. At the very bottom is OSPAAAL's logo and the words "Día de solidaridad mundial con la lucha del pueblo de Puerto Rico / Day of worldwide solidarity with the Struggle of the Puerto Rican People."

Jane is the only non-Latin American represented in this show. As art the living breathing movement in her poster has stood the test of time; it is as effective today as it was when she designed it in 1972.

Apart from the visual images, what do the words, if any, say to us now? Do they sound as crisp and clear as they once did? Have they become clichéd or perhaps even embarrassing in a period in which so many of those earlier struggles have been transcended or we see them as having been naïve or futile? Do the posters hold up beyond their historical value? Can art, as a signifier of alternative cultural consciousness and engagement, push us to renewed action and hope?

I am talking about power here, and about the mechanisms through which we organize power.

Most of these posters do remain beautiful, compelling. Successful art carries its own energy. But the test of time can be applied as well to the issue of power. What seemed necessary to those of us who lived in Cuba in the sixties, seventies, and eighties in retrospect may seem righteous but only sporadically viable, sometimes laced with intolerance, misjudgment or error, in an overall sense perhaps even skewed by a lust for domination or control.

I look at these posters and ponder each of the efforts or causes they portray. I have become accustomed of late to analyzing these causes from a more complex, nuanced point of view. Did I not understand, back then, that power in the hands of a single man or small group of men would necessarily become vitiated, that decolonization must stretch to address internal as well as external distortions? Why was it so much easier for me to defend national or class struggles than struggles having to do with race or gender? What construct of social hypocrisy kept me from even articulating the rights of homosexuals, or elderly or disabled people? Did I really believe that the lives of women, peoples of color, lesbians and gay men would be addressed once the new society had been consolidated? How long would that take? And who would be sacrificed along the way?

Power Kept Its Own Vigil

Of course one might argue that our failure to acknowledge other groups and their needs was simply indicative of the times. Decolonization was and is the Cuban revolution's driving force. Our consciousness had yet to evolve to the point where it could embrace struggles we did not yet understand. But I wonder if blind loyalty to a leadership that refused to allow dissenting views may not have kept us from grasping more inclusive concepts.

Power kept its own vigil.

I was living in Cuba when I and many others discovered that the leaders of the Khmer Rouge, Cambodia's so-called revolutionary movement, were not liberating their country but committing genocide. How could I have been tricked by Cuban rhetoric, and the rhetoric of much of the rest of the socialist world? Then again, why should I have believed the stories by members of the western press when they lied about so much else?

Should I also have been able to detect the suspicious attitudes of certain Sandinistas or the murderous jealousies of some in El Salvador's FMLN leadership? When were the seeds of Soviet glasnost or China's turn toward a market economy sewn? How could I, an individual without access to information only revealed much later, have known that some of the projects which so vehemently demanded equality would ultimately end up betraying their own loudly-proclaimed goals?

We could not be in all places, experience every struggle. And few of us were social anthropologists, economists, or political scientists, with the scholarly tools to carry out an in depth analysis of so many different situations. So we relied on the opinions of those we believed could guide us. This hierarchical dependency was dangerous. A truly democratic system must provide access to the information needed to understand the important issues, and guarantee people's participation in the decisions that affect their lives.

I lived in Cuba for eleven years. There I worked, raised four children, wrote books, translated, and made photographic images. I was close enough to some of the revolutionary leadership and conscious enough of policy decisions and how they were being developed that I fancied myself an insider of sorts. What decisions, unnoticed by me at the time, should have raised flags, warning of later derailment? Should I have questioned certain tendencies, been more skeptical of particular directions? I myself became a target of unfounded suspicion. Yet it took me years to find out why, and I was only occasionally or partially able to discern repressive attitudes against others.

There are so many more questions than answers. My family and I were privileged in the sense that we had access to outside communication and a range of ideas. We could travel and eventually leave without having to break with our roots and generations of family. Some Cuban friends who once shared our ideals eventually opted to work elsewhere, temporarily or permanently. Some were able to maintain their ties to the island. Others became virulently counterrevolutionary. Still others stayed. It would be interesting to be able to trace each person's process, to understand what careful analysis or spontaneous urge motivated each decision.

THE ABILITY TO MANIPULATE THROUGH COERCION AND SHAME

One of the weapons those in power often wield is their ability to manipulate through coercion and shame. Victims are corralled into a compliant silence; in families, communities, schools, workplaces, religious and political organizations, and nations. And it is this silence that, far from protecting them or helping them extricate themselves from unjust situations, actually keeps them isolated and disempowered. One of feminism's great lessons is that by talking to one another, revealing the secrets and naming our oppressor, we gain the strength to empower ourselves. One of feminism's gifts has been the ability to distinguish between power and empowerment.

National allegiances beg similar questions. When has each progressive government made an alliance because it truly identified with another government's goals, and when were such alliances purely strategic or tactical? Fidel's speech in defense of the 1968 Soviet invasion of Czechoslovakia comes to mind. The images of those tanks rolling into Prague shocked and repelled us. I, in particular, held a memory of similar tanks rolling down Mexico City's Avenida Universidad not that many months before.

In the Cuba I inhabited in the 1970s we waited for Fidel to speak. Absurdly (I think in retrospect) we always waited for him to explain a situation, to point us along the correct analytical path. And his speeches were magnificent, moving as they did from the general to the particular, veritable history lessons that remain exquisite, even through today's lens. I go back to those speeches and am again stunned by the man's brilliance, by his ability to talk to a diverse population with neither platitude nor condescension. Still, I cringe when I remember how utterly we depended upon a single analysis, a single political line. Missing were the tools, and the freedom to use those tools, which might have encouraged analyses of our own.

When Fidel addressed the Soviet invasion of Czechoslovakia he spent some time conceding that invasion is always wrong. He applauded the Czech people's defense of their sovereignty. But then he went on to talk about the United States' imperial designs and the necessity of defending the Socialist bloc. There were times, it seemed, when one country's sovereignty must be sacrificed to the collective good. I remember that I and others considered the fact that Fidel didn't simply defend the invasion without a caveat indicative of political independence. How extraordinary, we thought, that the leader of a tiny island nation has the courage to stand up to the Soviet Union; not how tragic that no one in the socialist world can risk unequivocally supporting a sister nation's rejection of outside domination.

Feminism Has Taught Us about Power

Feminism has taught us a lot about power and it has done so primarily by revealing the personal as political and the political as a reflection of the personal. It is now much easier than it was back then to understand the dynamics implicit when an abusive father tells his daughter that going along with the abuse is what will keep her safe, or an administration tells its citizens they must go along with invasion, occupation, torture, and wiretapping of its own citizens in supposed defense of national security. It is easier, as well, to understand the connection between these two manifestations of domination or control.

Governments are privy to behind the scenes evidence, tradeoffs, promises, and crimes. Individuals without particular specializations know only what we can discern from the information to which we have access, the level of skepticism or admiration we have for those providing the information, and the analyses we are able to make. It helps to possess a well-developed theoretical understanding. I always believed that living and working on site gave me some sort of access. Knowing the character, intelligence, and apparent generosity of spirit of a series of revolutionary leaders, I trusted they were telling the truth.

Often they were. But I took a great deal at face value when I might have looked more closely at systems, alliances, deviations. From where I stood (and stand), David's brave effort was infinitely more attractive than Goliath's voracious greed. I was unable to separate structural concentrations of power, sometimes bearing a dangerous resemblance to dictatorship, from the brilliant and seemingly modest men (and some women) defending them.

Decades have passed. Many socialist or revolutionary experiments have failed (Nicaragua, Grenada). A few are barely hanging on, pale reflections of their original projects (Vietnam, Cuba) or have changed so radically we can no longer consider them socialist (Russia, where the Soviet Union imploded and the Communist Party ceased to rule; and China, where the Communist Party continues in power but a kind of state capitalism has evolved). From this distance it is easier to see where these efforts went wrong, where equality may have been sacrificed to other presumed gains. Theoretical understanding is important not only in order to assess history, but when considering current political projects, such as those in Venezuela, Bolivia, and southern Mexico.

Today it is clear we need to think about power in new and different ways. When we understand that feminism doesn't demean but in fact deepens and enhances the struggle against neocolonialism, we will be able to design a power equilibrium more immune to verticality, super-concentration, and corruption; more inclusive of all the different social groups, more transparent, and with better safeguards against abuse. I am not advocating for the positions held by so many western social critics who are all too quick to point out socialism's failings. Such positions almost inevitably lead to a blanket defense of the capitalist market economy with all its cruelty and exploitation. Some of the positions held by anarchists 150 years ago seem more interesting today.

From Each According to Their Ability, to Each According to Their Need

For most of my adult life, socialism with communism as its ultimate goal seemed the answer. From each according to their ability, to each according to their need. What other division of resources and labor could be fairer or more equitable? I still believe in socialism; but today would like to see a version that honors a broader range of ideas, nurtures freedom of dissent, acknowledges difference, and seeks some formula which addresses individual identity as well as collective concerns. Perhaps the only way to achieve a change with these characteristics is to promote a shift in consciousness before—or at least concurrent with—the struggle to seize state power.

In Cuba and the other socialist states, Communist parties took seriously their responsibility for citizens' well-being. Work, housing, food, health, education, and other areas of basic human need were centrally organized, equitably administered, and guaranteed. The collective took precedence over the individual. What was good for the greatest number of people was deemed good for all. For eleven years I experienced and contributed to Cuba's version of such democratic centralism.

There was also the all-important issue of a Socialist bloc as opposed to separate, often isolated, and to varying degrees developing, socialist economies. In the global marketplace both socialism and capitalism were complex systems, and they were also necessarily interrelated. One country depended upon another. One bloc operated in opposition to, but also in conjunction with, the other. The solidarity between nations was important but international production and trade affected them all. When the socialist bloc disintegrated in 1989 its member states collapsed. Each sought its own route to survival.

Cuba declared a "Special Period in Peacetime," requiring a tightening of the proverbial belt and demanding ever greater sacrifice from a people who had sacrificed for several generations. The question is: has this sacrifice been accompanied by appropriate ideological work, and the in depth structural or systemic changes capable of saving the socialist project?

Today there are new and ever more dangerous threats to human life: the still growing pandemic of HIV/AIDS, which in some countries is killing entire generations; the resurgence of diseases that had been eliminated or controlled, such as malaria and certain drug resistant strains of tuberculosis; the hegemonic power of a single nation—the United States—with its flagrant disregard for the rights of others; and, of course, climate change and global warming, which disproportionately affect the poorest nations but if not reversed will lead to the death of our planet.

WHICH OF SOCIALISM'S ORIGINAL PROJECTS HAVE SURVIVED?

Which of socialism's original projects have survived? I ask this question with particular regard to Cuba.

There are many reliable sources to which we can go for a statistical analysis of Cuban society. We can look at gross national product, calories per capita, educational levels, employment, infant and maternal mortality, life expectancy, eradication of curable diseases, and all the other indexes used to determine a society's well-being. We can look, as Lenin and other theoreticians have urged, to women's integration in society as a way of measuring overall social achievement. We can examine suicide rates, incidents of post-traumatic stress, other forms of mental illness, and additional areas that reflect a population's health. We can also assess areas in which cause and effect may be less quantifiable, such as the links between pollution of air, food and water, and overall fitness, stress levels, curiosity, creativity, happiness. We can take a nation's pulse and try to get some sense of a people's state of mind and heart by listening to stories and paying attention to diversity and respect for difference, demeanor, mannerism, humor, creative output, and the presence or absence of fear.

Contemporary Cuba presents a picture often painted in colors that are just a bit too one-sided. Fictitiously pale when described by the most vociferous in the exile community, because they will always feel they must justify having emigrated by exaggerating the scarcity, oppression, and desperation left behind. But irrationally bright when put forth by many who stay, because they have been conditioned by a radical system to project self-righteousness, prioritize an unconditional loyalty (my country, right or wrong), applaud the single choice, and overlook complexity. Irrationally bright, as well, by some on the international left who still believe that criticism gives weapons to the enemy.

On February 19, 2008, Fidel Castro announced he was stepping down from the positions of President and Commander in Chief, and wishes only to remain "a soldier in the battle of ideas." The transition long desired by some and feared by others, moves into focus.

A Tragic Waste

In Cuba, the decision to nurture and expand tourism has proved both salvation and curse. A tropical climate and beautiful beaches, other inviting natural landscapes, an excellent year-round climate, coral reefs and tropical fish have brought hundreds of new luxury hotels and other multinational investments. These are joint economic ventures in which foreign capital and its consumer ideology necessarily exert an important influence. Tourism has brought hard currency. But it has also brought elements of a market economy and a series of devastating social setbacks.

Most obvious among these are the resurgence of prostitution (including a de facto sex tourism), hustling, and drugs; recreational areas closed to the poor (often also meaning to darker skinned Cubans); and commercial advertising (much of which is denigrating to women). Many highly trained doctors and other professionals have left specialized jobs to work in the tourist industry where they have access to dollars. This is a tragic waste of education and reflects serious policy problems.

To successfully compete with other Caribbean destinations Cuba has had to loosen many of its hard won standards. It is clear that too little in depth ideological work had been done before these survival-motivated changes became necessary. A one-dimensional press offered little more than the official viewpoint and failed to stimulate useful discussion. The population hadn't effectively dealt with race, gender, and sexual inequality so couldn't successfully unite against such threats.

I cannot begin to imagine what a black Cuban must feel when he or she is stopped from entering one of the island's lavish beach resorts. On one of my visits in the 1990s I got a glimpse of what this might be like. I was leading a group of U.S. American women, one of whom was black. We arrived at a Varadero beach hotel eager for a brief swim. Everyone but the black member of our group was warmly welcomed; she was stopped and asked for her passport. Not until it was discovered that she wasn't Cuban was she allowed to proceed. Profuse apologies couldn't begin to erase the humiliation to which she was subjected or the racist impression we received.

Volumes of statistics and analysis exist and I'll leave the in depth analysis to others. I will say that despite the extreme problems provoked by the dissolution of the Socialist bloc (in which Cuba, literally from one day to the next, lost the Soviet Union's vital support), the country has seen steady economic growth over the past several years. Beginning around 2005 there has been a notable improvement in energy distribution, all but eliminating the frequent blackouts suffered over the previous years by an ever more frustrated population. Public transportation has improved. Renovating rundown schools became a priority, new health centers were built, and a number of bureaucratic bottlenecks, such as some unnecessarily complicated customs regulations, were eliminated. In the summer of 2007 the vast resources and expert organization preventing death and destruction during Hurricane Dean stood in sharp contrast to the U.S. government's wavering will to protect its own population from natural disasters.

Food is generally available, but nutrition remains problematic for Cubans who do not have access to hard currency. The very existence of dual currency is a concern. Housing construction has not kept up with population growth and overcrowding continues to be a huge problem, also generating other social ills. A badly deteriorated infrastructure makes for a degree of stagnation. The progressive turn of oil-rich Venezuela and other Latin American governments has helped break through the island's imposed isolation and has provided new goods and trade opportunities. Without profound changes in Cuba's current system of government, however, these opportunities can only act as Band Aids.

In an online analysis of Cuba's current situation, social commentator Soledad Cruz points out how important it would be to promote popular discussion of these issues rather than simply try to resolve them behind the scenes. "Now is the time to analyze what affects us," she writes, observing how useful it would be if the open discussions in the cultural arena could be extended to other areas of concern. "To conceive of unity as unanimity may be one of the impediments standing in the way of every questioning attitude," she asserts.[1]

When we speak of Cuba's current system of government we must point out that it is not the government those of us who love the revolution once defended with such energy, but rather a version of state-centered neocapitalism with some socialist remnants. Its extreme economic centralism requires excessive control, breeds bureaucracy, and makes the country vulnerable. This is what produced the implosion of European socialism. Many Cubans are asking how many more years they must endure before they emerge from the oft-referenced Special Period, and if the Special Period will simply have delayed defeat or provided a bridge to better times.

Cuban political scientist Pedro Campos Santos writes:

> Socialism, to remain valid, must be participatory, democratic, self governing, inclusive, and integrationist. Participatory because it must allow the broadest participation in the important economic, political and social decisions that affect people's lives; democratic because the mechanisms through which decisions are made cannot be based on top-down politics; self-governing because self-government and cooperative projects alone are capable of creating the collective conditions for the development of a truly democratic society; inclusive because all social groups, including the most marginalized, must be mobilized in support of the great socialist plan; and integrationist because socialist nations must trade and collaborate with other socialist nations above and beyond their relations with international capitalism.[2]

Campos Santos quotes Italian theoretician Antonio Gramsci: "If the governing class loses consensus it cannot govern. It will only retain its coercive force, only dominate. This leads to the great masses separating themselves from traditional ideologies, no longer believing in what they once believed." This, Campos Santos maintains, is what is happening in today's Cuba. He argues as one who believes the revolution can be saved but insists urgent action is necessary.

Even as we applaud the survival of certain socialist principles, even as we marvel at a small island nation capable not only of overcoming the disintegration of the Socialist bloc but of actually improving its economic indexes and standard of living, I am also troubled by that other side of Cuban life: the vast amorphous place where information remains tightly controlled, travel and internet access severely restricted, the press ludicrously shallow and one-sided, an aging infrastructure all but immune to renovation, the most vicious characteristics of capitalism can so easily resurface, and the same small male-dominated group has held power for almost half a century. Religious freedom has been expanded in recent years, but individual spirituality often remains suspect.

The Human Spirit Requires Freedom

Let me be clear. I love the ideals of the Cuban revolution. I have always respected its right to exist and shape its country's future. I have actively worked in defense of that right, vigorously protesting the U.S. embargo of the island and every overt and covert U.S. government action aimed at bringing the Cuban process down. I reject as deceitful, even criminal, U.S. government policy which encourages illegal emigration and privileges those Cubans who manage to make it to our shores over those from countries who are fleeing civil wars, torture and death. I have supported and continue to support the Cuban revolution.

I also have my own ideas about Fidel Castro, the man and revolutionary. I believe he was one of the twentieth century's most brilliant visionaries and extraordinary teachers. His passion, courage, intelligence, and early analysis were exemplary. In general terms I also agree with much of his assessment—especially his early assessment—of regional and global politics. I'm not one of those naïve critics who claim the Cuban leader betrayed his supporters when he pronounced the revolution socialist in 1961, or insists that U.S. hostility pushed Cuba into the arms of the Soviet Union.

At the same time, I see a detachment that comes from age and entrenchment, a rigidity resulting from having been in power far too long. Nothing and no one can justify a failure to recognize that change is necessary for growth and that a new generation of leaders, with new ideas, must be trained and encouraged to emerge. I remember Nicaragua's Dora María Téllez once telling me that a political leader should be replaced every five years, simply because new ideas will always be fresher, more creative, and progressive than the old ones.

The human spirit is resilient. But it requires freedom. There is no other way to say this. Individuals must be provided a diversity of information, connection, and experience. People must be taught to recognize a variety of choices and allowed to make those which are in their best interests. Difference must be respected and the voices of difference heard, evaluated, taken into account.

People must be permitted to experiment, disagree, even be wrong—without fear of reprisal. Only in this way can we explore a range of thought and feeling, move back and forth among life's options, and develop the analytical skills all individuals and societies need.

POWER AS A POLITICAL CATEGORY

I remember, throughout the 1960s, 1970s, and 1980s, the Left's endless discussions between those who claimed that class was the major social contradiction and those who prioritized race or gender. Whichever position we defended, we generally mouthed a concern for the other. But our particular political practice didn't allow us to fully understand that other. Of greater concern, believing we were addressing the important issues we failed to look at the overarching issue of power itself. Concentrating on bigotry or inequality in one particular area, we avoided looking at power as a political category.

Although Cuba's Communist Party has been more independent than many, it is still part of the international Communist movement; in most cases sharing that movement's criteria and goals. Some policies didn't translate easily, either historically or culturally. Until the 1989–1990 implosion of the socialist world, Cuba's Marxism in Spanish was also to an important extent Marxism in Russian. And when the break came, the sudden withdrawal of Soviet economic support threw Cuba into a crisis that required drastic decisions. Once again it seemed inadvisable to prioritize such issues as broad-based access to information, race and gender relations, sexuality, and spirituality. The nation's survival required unity and sacrifice. In the context of a half-century history of revolution this was seen as just another setback and one that the revolution was able to put behind it—but at what cost?

Fidel Castro emerged as the natural and logical leader in Cuba's war against Batista. He didn't grab power so much as earn it. But somewhere along the way, at some point in these almost fifty years, I believe it would have been healthier for Cuba's future for him and those in his governing circle to have understood that power too tightly held becomes power entrenched. I am not suggesting that Fidel became a dictator along the lines of a Pinochet or an Idi Amin. I argue that systems in which power is so jealously guarded are dangerous, and stifling to organic social development. The Ochoa case brought this truth home with painful force.[3]

Cubans on the island hold their opinions of Fidel close. Some will brook no criticism of the leader. An undercurrent of raucous humor also lies beneath a public unease which refrains from any suggestion that conflicts with the Party line. At the same time, Cubans in exile often speak of Fidel as embodying everything they despise about the political system that took possession of their homeland almost half a century ago. Neither attitude reflects reality or promotes useful dialogue. Neither is a viable starting point for looking at the best and worst of the Cuban experience, an open-ended discussion of that which should be discarded or preserved.

I Long to See Diverse Visions and Unique Talents

We would not wish on any people the vitiated democracy we have in the United States: where the obscenely rich get richer, the poor become more numerous and with less access to life's necessities, and the rhetoric of representational government masks a range of unchallenged inequalities and lies. While other industrialized societies evolve, the current U.S. administration continues rollbacks in equality, women's autonomy, social services, support of public education, access to health care, the rehabilitation of prisoners, welfare assistance, and support of the arts.

Nor is it ethical for us to speak of what is good for others while we continue to attack, invade, and kill around the world. This is power abuse at its most criminal. Some degree of central planning and socialist regard for people's need are important in designing a life that is more equitable for greater numbers. I believe states must assume responsibility for their citizens' health, well-being, productivity, education, art, and recreation. I also believe it is imperative that people have access to what goes on in other parts of the world and can participate in the global marketplace of ideas.

I dream of a society in which respect for difference is recognized and promoted. One in which individuals and groups of people are informed, encouraged to speak and act on their own behalf, and do not live subservient to some vague greater good (which translates to a few living at the expense of many). I want a society in which income differentials are minimal and do not mean that some have private jets while others go hungry. I suggest that organized religion is almost always hierarchical, coercive, destructive and damaging to rational thought; but that personal spirituality is endemic to the human psyche. I long to see diverse visions and unique talents coexisting with state responsibility for people's basic needs: health, education, work. I do not believe that imagination must be forfeited to unity. Rather, it is necessary to a people's well-being.

The Cuban revolution, for my generation, represents the experiment that came closest to achieving this dream. What may have been lost and what remains are not academic issues for us, for me.

Jane Norling and I often speak about what's happened in our world, the excruciating losses of the 1980s and 1990s, the degree to which the profit motive, legitimized violence, mean-spiritedness, and lies have surged ahead of compassion, solidarity, and recognition of the fragility of our planet. Perhaps it is our generation's lot to bemoan the hegemony and greed that have rolled back so many of our successes and threaten peoples across the globe. As artists, we often face the dilemma in our own work: how can we continue to hone it as a tool for change while remaining true to its internal memory, need, structure, texture, and voice?

I speak as an artist, which is why I have chosen to use the Cuban political posters of the years I lived on the island as a point of departure for discussing power dynamics and empowerment. I speak as a woman who lived and worked in Cuba during the decade of the 1970s, raised four children there, suffered repression, and experienced the joy of helping to create a new society. I speak as a lesbian, intimately familiar with what hate can do to human beings. I speak as someone who contributed to and benefited from one of the twentieth century's great sociopolitical experiments.

When I think about the Cuban revolution, its almost half-century effort to deconstruct colonialism and neocolonialism, its extraordinary resistance in the face of continuous attack from the north, its exuberant successes and painful failures, generous internationalism, split families, defensive stances and underlying push for justice and equality, I always end up thinking about power. How power has been distributed and managed, earned, or usurped. How power and empowerment coexist and unfold will be key to under-standing which aspects of the revolution survive and which crumble beneath the inevitable rush to reaccommodation likely to surge when the current governing structure no longer exists.

CHAPTER 14

EPILOGUE

THERE WERE SOME CHALLENGES

I left Cuba for Nicaragua at the end of 1980. Except for Ana, who was eleven at the time, my children were old enough that I felt I could give them the choice to come with me or remain in what had become their home.

Gregory was twenty. He was already living with Laura Carlevaro, the woman who, two and a half years later, would become his wife. They had their own plans but for the moment opted to stay on in the apartment on Línea. Sarah was just finishing college, getting her degree in chemical engineering. She too chose to stay. Ximena was in her last year of high school. She stayed through graduation, joining Ana and me the following summer. I hadn't given Ana a choice and she packed up and headed out with me that December, ready or not for the challenges ahead.

And there were some challenges only someone who'd spent the better part of her young life in Cuba would be called upon to face. Widespread poverty was the most dramatic. Although many in Cuba lacked adequate housing, no one was homeless. No one was hungry. Driving through Managua's streets, stopping at a traffic light and experiencing the dozens of kids clamoring to wash the windshield or sell some trinket was disconcerting at best. Soon the threat of counterrevolution could be added to the list. In Cuba attacks to the revolution's integrity had long been controlled or erased. In Nicaragua they were just beginning.

Last photograph of the four siblings together in Cuba. Margaret leaves for Nicaragua with Ana; Gregory, Sarah, and Ximena stay behind. Havana, 1980.

Religion was also something new. I remember the first time a classmate at her Nicaraguan school invited my daughter to a birthday party. These often included a Catholic mass. Ana wanted badly to make friends and was excited about the invitation, but the idea of the mass frightened her. In Cuba religion had been portrayed as residual ignorance or worse. A wonderful liberation theology priest in a lively working-class parish helped Ana acquire a tolerant if skeptical attitude toward that ritual so much a part of the country's culture, revolutionary as well as traditional.

In Cuba I had been close to many of the Sandinistas who had lived there on and off throughout the 1970s. I was interested in how they were grappling with the problems inherent to radical social change. Twenty years separated the two revolutionary takeovers, twenty years signaling a before and after in terms of the international women's movement as well as the within Catholic church. Because the Nicaraguan revolution came to power in 1979 instead of 1959, the Sandinistas were able to think about feminism and faith quite differently than their Cuban comrades.

Gregory and Laura. Havana, 1979.

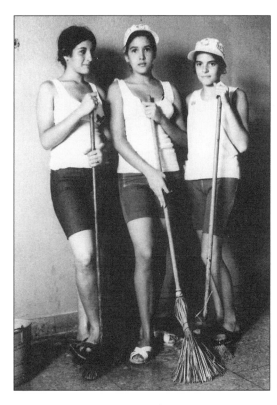

Ximena and friends Odalys Fonseca López and Idayma Quijano doing voluntary cleanup work. Havana, 1979.

Following the Cuban victory a number of Batista criminals had been put to death. Capital punishment continues to exist in that country. In Nicaragua, in contrast, progressive Christian input prevented this form of punishment. From the beginning, in Cuba abortion was considered neither more nor less than an aspect of public health: accessible, safe, and free. In Nicaragua a powerful Catholic hierarchy succeeded in keeping the practice illegal. In that country, too, there was a strong indigenous culture which the European conquest had obliterated in Cuba.

Cuba was enormously supportive of Nicaragua and offered aid in the form of teachers, medical personnel, military advisors, and more. Ana's own fifth grade teacher had joined the thousands laboring in the Nicaraguan countryside. When I worked at the Ministry of Culture in Managua I remember comrades from Havana's Graphics Workshop who had come to teach Nicaraguans to craft handmade paper. But each revolution retained its autonomy and independence. From my arrival in the Central American country I was fascinated by the cultural differences and by the contrasting lines taken by the two processes.

Working first at the Ministry of Culture and later with the Sandinista National Liberation Front's ideological department, I spent four years among the brave and creative men and women working hard to remake their country. I continued to write: about Nicaraguan women, poets, even the revolutionary Catholics who were playing such an important role in social change. All this is for another book. Here suffice it to say that my experience in Nicaragua proved as profound and exhilarating as my years in Cuba had been.

THE UNITED STATES WASN'T ABOUT TO PERMIT
ANOTHER CUBA IN LATIN AMERICA

Faced with such a pluralistic process, the Reagan administration might have adopted a wait and see policy with regard to Nicaragua. But Reagan dubbed the Contras (anti-Sandinista forces) "freedom fighters" and supported them from the beginning. We and other foreign residents demonstrated once a week in front of the U.S. Embassy in Managua; we wanted to tell the world not to fear what the Sandinistas were building. Once again the hawks prevailed. The United Sates wasn't about to permit another Cuba in Latin America.

Even before the Sandinista victory of July 19, 1979, the CIA began training an army of dissidents and funding anti-Sandinista groups. The U.S. Congress cut off money to the Contras but the Reagan administration encouraged Oliver North and company to funnel the aid covertly. By the end of 1983, when the Contra war began to make its presence felt in Managua, I was over-worked, overwhelmed, and stressed beyond my ability to handle everyday life. Sometimes I found myself crying for no apparent reason. I wasn't the only one in such a state but, in my late forties, I lacked the resiliency of many of my much younger Nicaraguan comrades.

Approaching midlife, I was tired. I longed for some down time. Increasingly I realized the work I was doing, although stimulating and sometimes important, could be done by others—perhaps much better than me. I longed for time to write, not after a ten or twelve hour day at the office but as a priority in my life.

I wanted my language, my culture, a reconnection to my earliest memories. I also began to feel a deep need for the northern New Mexican landscape of my childhood: the red rock canyons, vast space and intensity of light. My parents were growing older; for the first time I knew they would not be around forever, and if I wanted some quality time with them that time had to be now.

I decided to go home.

The Shift in Temperature Paralleled My Emotional State

I returned to the United States in January of 1984. After a quarter century abroad, my reentry wasn't destined to be easy. After so many years outside the country, home was a complex weave of place, culture, language, and family. Ana traveled to her father in New York. Ximena decided to go to Mexico where her father lived. I packed what I still had of belongings acquired in Mexico, Cuba, and Nicaragua, and prepared to send them via ship to Albu-querque. The Nicaraguan port of Corinto was mined around that time and I had to dramatically reduce what I owned in order to send it by plane.

On a January morning in Managua I myself boarded a flight in tropical heat that must have ranged around 104 degrees Fahrenheit. That night I deplaned in the bitter cold of an Albuquerque winter. The shift in tempera-ture paralleled my emotional state. My parents and brother, as well as a friend with whom I had been having a long-distance relationship, all met my plane.[1] I was still in shock, and would be for a while. I remember asking my father to accompany me whenever I had to enter a large department store or supermarket; the affluence and profusion of consumer items was one of several aspects of U.S. life that unnerved me.

The first years home were intense. So much was recognizable while so much else kept me off balance. Hearing the sound of everyday English was comforting. Childhood images reached out and drew me to their familiarity. On the other hand I had never before had a credit card or used a bank machine. Because I had taken out Mexican citizenship in 1967—while married to Sergio and expecting to remain in that country—I entered the U.S. on a visa. I had to legalize my residency, recover my citizenship, figure out how I might earn a living and so much else.

And there were issues I hadn't expected: the deep sense of loss I experienced living without any of my children for the first time since the oldest was born; the U.S. government's eventual refusal to allow me entrance and the emotional cost of my immigration case; the discovery, in therapy, of childhood incest at the hands of my maternal grandfather; getting through menopause; coming out as a lesbian. Each of these challenges required strength—and a centeredness I fought hard to achieve.

The immigration battle took my most immediate energy. After a drawn out series of interviews and a court hearing in El Paso, Texas, the U.S. Immigration and Naturalization Service ordered me deported in October of 1985. The government invoked the 1952 McCarran-Walter Immigration and Nationality Act. It accused me of "being against the good order and happiness of the United States." Its agents focused on opinions expressed in a number of my books, opinions contrary to U.S. government policy in Vietnam and Central America. Apparently it had become a crime to publicly disagree with the ideas of Reagan and (George H. W.) Bush.

Clearly the larger issue in my case was the fact that I had lived in countries like Cuba and Nicaragua, written favorably about them, and transcribed the voices of ordinary people from both places, particularly women. This was the sort of information absent from the U.S. press and it was considered dangerous, even subversive.

Another strike against me was my refusal to say I'm sorry, to play the good girl and promise never to utter such opinions again. During my El Paso hearing I was asked such questions as why my children had different fathers, if it was true that I'd posed nude for artists in the 1950s, or waitressed in a gay bar during the same decade. Many aspects of my immigration battle revealed the double standard to which women are routinely subjected in public as well as private life.

Although my basic political ideas had not changed I was embarrassed by some of the ways in which I'd expressed myself twenty or thirty years before. I never said this, though. I was determined to defend my opinions, even those I might have modified as I'd grown and matured. Many of the government lawyer's questions in El Paso revealed an anticommunist subtext reminiscent of the 1950s. Tell me, Ms. Randall, did you ever write a poem in praise of free enterprise, was one of the more ludicrous.

Following a struggle that went on for almost five years, and with the help of many good people throughout the United Sates and the world, I won my case at the end of 1989. If I gloss over the events of those very intense years it is because this is a book about Cuba. I've written elsewhere about coming home,[2] retrieving the memory of incest,[3] my immigration case,[4] and may yet write about Nicaragua.

I Believe They Come Up with a Positive Tally

Each of my children has his or her own memories of life on that crocodile-shaped island in the Caribbean. They have built on the experience in their own way. The girls, especially, carry its rhythms in their bodies: the beat of the conga drum and joy of salsa dancing. After her move to the United States, Ana would sometimes take a quick trip to Miami just to be able to listen to Cuban music and taste Cuban food. Sarah and Ximena also retain memories and good friends in the country they left as young women. Both have been back a number of times.

Gregory assimilated the best of the revolution's ideas of justice and equality, even as his subsequent experience gave him a critical eye for the problems that have plagued the process. He and Laura have raised their three children deeply influenced by Cuban revolutionary values. As a university professor, Gregory has also taken aspects of his own education and modified them to fit the Uruguayan reality.

In a film about my life all four of my children have spoken about growing up in Cuba.[5] In any case, their stories are their own; they will tell them in more detail, or not, as they're ready. What I would add about their growing up on the island is that they enjoyed drug- and violence-free childhoods in a city where a child taking a bus home alone at one A.M. from the movies or a party was never cause for concern. They had free education and the best health care, also free. The revolution's values and priority attention to the well-being of young people gave them a sense of self and a confidence today's youth often lack.

Honesty, fairness, and justice were celebrated attributes and attitudes; and reality lived up to rhetoric more often than in most places I know. Social hypocrisy was minimal. Whatever limitations Cuba may have had for Gregory, Sarah, Ximena and Ana, whatever their unmet needs, I believe they come up with a mostly positive tally when thinking about their Cuban childhoods.

STILL ALIVE, STILL MOVING AND CHANGING

The Cuban revolution continues to be one of the great social experiments of the twentieth century, still alive, and still moving and changing in the twenty first. It enjoys the distinction of being the only country in the western hemisphere where socialism as a political system remains operative. Modified, having made concessions necessary to its survival, but operative.

There are those who point to the many years of Soviet aid as if that somehow invalidates or discredits the process. The Soviet Union and the Socialist bloc greatly influenced the revolution; for years they provided economic backup, sometimes with mixed results. Just as the implosion of the Soviet Union and European socialism thrust Cuba into chaos and required spectacular creative innovation almost from one day to the next.

But every small country is dependant on a more powerful country for trade and connection. The United States jealously guards and controls its sphere of influence. China reaches out to the African nations. Venezuela, under Hugo Chávez, is becoming a country able to affect its partners. In its first years the Cuban revolution could have caved to U.S. pressure or turned to the Socialist bloc to survive. It did the latter, which proved its salvation, occasionally its albatross, and eventually, perhaps, its nemesis. Given the international panorama at the time, the circumstances and pressures, I don't believe it could have done otherwise.

In 1992, long after coming home to the United States, I returned to Nicaragua to do the fieldwork for another book on that country's women.[6] There I had an experience which points up as well as any the contradictory nature of the Cuban process. With overt and covert interference from the United States, the Sandinistas had been voted out of office in 1990. The Central American nation was already on its way to losing the important social gains it had made throughout the preceding decade. Nicaraguan revolutionaries were desolate, many of them numbed. A number of the country's leading intellectuals were involved in discussions, both public and private, about what had happened and how.

It was in this context that I had the opportunity of attending a gathering at the Cuban Embassy in Managua. Several important journalists from the island had invited their Nicaraguan counterparts to talk about a single issue: what roles had Cuba's controlled press and Nicaragua's more pluralistic journalism played in their respective revolutions' ability or inability to remain in power. Each country's participants were profoundly interested in what their counterparts had to say. No one disagreed about freedom of the press as an ideal, or the importance of high quality journalism. At issue was: how far can a revolutionary government safely go in allowing diversity of opinion?

Because one side was represented by journalists from a revolution still in power while those from a defeated revolution spoke for the other, it was a debate impossible to resolve. I had been enthusiastic about the Sandinistas' more inclusive ideological stance, the Nicaraguan revolution's respect for people of faith, derogation of capital punishment, openness to feminist values, and variety of opinions in the press. Just two years after the defeat of the revolution, though, loss of political power was already erasing every gain: in education, health, and security. The country was once again on its way to extreme poverty, corruption, everyday violence, a high rate of illiteracy, endemic curable diseases, and so many other ills that routinely plague the dependant and developing world. How much of the country's vulnerability could be traced to what the Cubans considered ideological weakness?

The Nicaraguans at that meeting insisted on freedom of the press as an inviolable principle; one to which I subscribe as well, fervently. Yet if I had to choose between a country in which certain freedoms have been curtailed but a system of social justice essentially remains in place and one in which a free press stands its ground, undeniably opening the door to outside and disrupting influences, there is no question I would choose the former. Sometimes principles must be bent to meet a given situation. Then the question becomes: when will those in power reintroduce such principles? It's always about power, entrenched or open to modification.

I Am a Hybrid

I was away for a quarter of a century and by the time this book appears I will have been home for an equal length of time. Which begs the question: where is Cuba in my body, my cells? It's easy to talk about what I love or criticize about the Cuban revolution, even when my opinions are in flux, and it remains to be seen how Fidel's foreseeable death will affect the country in the near or medium term. It's harder to describe what Cuba gave me, what continues to live here, inside, in that place where all emotions are shapeshifters and the notes of a song, the tone of an argument, the look of a street, the scent of yucca in lemon juice and oil, or the taste of chocolate ice cream served only at Copelia may suddenly overpower me.

When I was forced underground in Mexico the Cuban revolution took my small children in. It cared for them in practical terms and with great sensitivity until I could get to the island. This is something the revolution did for tens of thousands of children throughout the 1960s, seventies and eighties. It is a generosity I can never repay. Cuba educated my children, shared food and medical attention with us when it had little enough of either, and opened us to the brave social struggles of peoples throughout the world—from Laos and Vietnam to Uruguay and Brazil, from Portugal to Guatemala, Angola, South Africa, Palestine, Chile, and Nicaragua.

Cuba showed me ways of conceptualizing problems and their solutions that remain useful to me today. Not every solution to every problem, not even whole solutions, as I've subsequently learned to adapt to circumstance and take bits and pieces of a variety of ideas, but enough so that the country and its revolution remain bedrock to my experience. Cuba gave me mentors like Raul Roa, René Vallejo, Haydeé Santamaría, Juan Luis Martín, Mirta Rodríguez Calderón, and Santiago Alvarez. It gave me photography in the person of my teacher, Grandal. It gave me lifelong friends, too numerous to mention without inadvertently leaving some out.

Cuba gave me a landscape of Caribbean beaches and stately palms, and a cityscape of weathered stone buildings, brass knockers against old wooden doors, and media lunas of brightly colored glass. These images accommodate themselves now alongside my New Mexico desert, Utah canyons, southwestern river corridors, and many ancient sites, to feed my deep connection to place.

Most importantly, Cuba taught me that another future is possible.

I am, by virtue of the life I have lived, a hybrid: culturally, linguistically, and where my eyes meet an ever-changing horizon. Cuba is part of that horizon, just as New York and Seville and Mexico City and Nicaragua and Vietnam and Peru are all part of the artist—the woman—I have become. I was born to some of these places, chose others. As with an adopted child and one to whom one gives birth, the connections may come from different places but can be equally strong.

This hybrid condition, though, is not always simple or free from contradiction. I have felt alternately insider and outsider, often quite intensely. Distance can give perspective. It can also hurt. Multiplicity can be difficult even as it provides a vibrant prism.

With Cuba, I was fortunate to share a particularly energized moment in its history. This implies responsibility. I will always defend the Cuban people's right to the system of their choice, observe with interest its social changes and solutions, work toward a hands-off policy on the part of the United States, and follow with joy each new turn on an unfinished map.

IMAGINATION, CURIOSITY, AND REVELATION

I want to end with a story about ordinary Cuban people, those for whom the revolution opened a window impossible for an outsider to grasp—even, perhaps, for a Cuban living in Havana. This is a story of imagination, curiosity, and revelation. I lived it in September of 1980, a few months before leaving the country for good.

A couple of years before, I'd noticed a brief article, one of those two- or three-inch fillers, in *Juventud Rebelde*, the Young Communist afternoon daily. It was about a one-hundred-and-twenty-year-old woman who lived in the eastern province of Las Tunas and remembered both of Cuba's nineteenth century wars of independence from Spain.

The story caught my attention and I wrote a letter to the general secretary of the Federation of Cuban Women in the provincial capital of Victoria de las Tunas. On some vague calendar of future possibility I wondered if I might visit the old woman. No immediate answer was forthcoming and I eventually forgot I'd written.

Until several months later, when I heard a knock on the door of our Havana apartment and opened it to find a young man standing there. He was the son, he said, of Celina Escobar Machado, general secretary of one of the Federation's zonal offices in Las Tunas. My letter had been referred to her. Now she wrote that the old woman—Ana Garcés—was her grandmother. She confirmed the newspaper story, said Ana was healthy and lucid, and invited me to visit whenever I wished. Although I answered the hand delivered letter, I didn't hear from Celina again.

Time passed. Other concerns took priority. Then, toward the end of Gregory's summer 1980 work brigade stint in Las Tunas province he called home and I thought to ask him to try to find out if Ana Garcés was still alive. When he got home he said he'd been told she was, but that she lived far from the city and he hadn't been able to get out to see her. Even such vague confirmation seemed like a sign of sorts. By this time I knew I would be leaving Cuba in December. Perhaps I should try to make the trip before then.

Armed with no more that this rather meager information, but with a great desire to get out of the city for a few days, I decided to head to Las Tunas. I flew out one Thursday morning aboard a tiny Yak-40, the Soviet jet that flies thirty passengers at a time to some of the easternmost cities. We were midway in flight when the pilot's voice suddenly came over the loudspeaker with an urgency that caused me to gasp: "Ladies and gentlemen, at the close of the second inning the score is zero to zero!" Other passengers began discussing the news. I hadn't the faintest idea who was playing.

After deplaning at the tiny Victoria de las Tunas airport I decided to begin my hunt for Ana Garcés right away. I walked over to the three or four cabs lined up to take passengers into town. When I said I was going to Majibacoa, the driver who in order of lineup should have taken me motioned to one of the others: "Why don't you take her? You know that area." This turned out to be my introduction to the first in a series of extraordinary people. The adventure was on.

The cabbie, whose name was Silvio Villagómez, looked to be in his mid-thirties; mulato with a bit of Chinese blood several generations back. I told him I needed to find Celina Escobar Machado, general secretary of the FMC in the village of San Rafael, Majibacoa. I had no street address but was sure if we went to Majibacoa it wouldn't be hard to track her down. Silvio thought our best plan would be to go to the FMC municipal office in Majibacoa; they'd be able to tell us where San Rafael was located. The fact that he, a native of the area, had no idea was my first indication we were heading into back country.

As he drove we talked. Silvio told me he'd fought with Fidel during the war of liberation. I told him what I knew about Ana Garcés. He said his own grandfather had died at the age of 112, that he'd been a slave whose mother was from Congo and father Chinese. Silvio's grandfather had died sixteen years ago, one September 4. I noted that today was September 4 and silently wondered if this might be a bad omen. Perhaps Ana, too, was gone.

I'd had no idea that Majibacoa wasn't a neighborhood on the outskirts of Victoria de las Tunas. It turned out to be a municipality some ten or twelve kilometers distant. When we arrived in the village people were setting up for their local carnival, to begin that night. It was still early—about 7:30 in the morning—and there was no one in the small wooden shack that served as FMC headquarters. Next door, at the CDR office, we heard a comrade pounding away at a typewriter. We asked for Celina and he said: "Sure, she's a member of the Party's Municipal Committee, her husband too. But they live deep in the countryside, past Las Parras. You won't be able to get that far by car."

Silvio suggested he stick with me. By this time he too was interested in what or whom we might find. We set off for Las Parras, which turned out to be a few wooden structures along an unpaved country road. A smattering of small homes, a general store and a place that advertised itself as a *comidería*, a luncheonette. We stopped at the one room police station, where Silvio ran into Peña, an old friend.

Peña must have been in his seventies or older, still working as a law enforcement officer and with two sons on internationalist missions. He hopped into the cab and the three of us continued, along a dirt trail now. We began to talk about Celina and Ana, asking people along the way if they could point us in the right direction. The closer we got the more likely we were to run into those who knew the two women. By this time Peña too was emotionally involved. We kept driving, over roads that became deeply gutted lanes, for another two kilometers. People would wave us on: Down that way; just follow the railway tracks.

Soon Silvio had to park his taxi. We continued on foot, along single-gauge tracks mostly overgrown with weeds. At one point a group of robust uniformed children appeared, walking on the ties. They were headed to school. I explained to both men that I had no problem going on alone. As long as I know I'm headed in the right direction, I said, imagining both must need to get back to work. Neither was willing to abandon me. They said they'd come at least as far as Celina's.

After another two kilometers or so we came to a peasant home and Peña said: "René here will know about Celina. Just wait a minute." An old woman peered from the doorway. "Is René in," Peña asked.

"Yes he is."

"Well, tell him to come out, will you." Renè appeared a few minutes later, and yes he knew exactly where Celina lived, some eight kilometers further along the tracks, on the right, in a pretty house with a real floor! I mentioned the grandmother and René nodded sadly as he told us she'd died the month before.

The news hit the three of us hard. Later we admitted to one another we'd each still silently hoped it might not be true. Silvio asked if I didn't want to turn back. I told both men again that I'd understand perfectly if they wanted to leave me at this point but I was going on. I explained I'd sent a telegram to Celina the previous Monday. I had no idea if it had arrived but in case it had I didn't want to disappoint her by not showing up. Furthermore, the least I could do now was to meet her and express my sympathy over the loss of the old woman I wouldn't get to know. That'll teach you, I thought to myself, not to wait two years to meet someone who's 120. As I talked, both men kept walking. We had several more kilometers to go.

Behind a crude fence the house was clearly something special. It was of brick construction, heavily plastered and whitewashed. The floors, as we'd been told, were real: made of cement. A small living room had as its only contents four straight-backed chairs, a modern treadle sewing machine, and a variety of pictures on the walls; these included a good sized portrait of Lenin, a hand-painted still life, and several calendar pinups.

Beyond the living room I glimpsed two bedrooms with beds and clothes cabinets, a dining area with a wooden table, chairs, and a large barrel for drinking water, and a tiny kitchen. There was neither piped water nor electricity in this area, one of the most isolated in the country. (Upon his return from his summer brigade work, my son had told me: "The people in Tunas don't even think of themselves as living in a real province. They say they're creating their province as they go.")

Celina had received my telegram late the night before. I could only imagine how it had reached her. She hadn't gone in to work today because she had a bad headache, and her husband had told her he didn't think I'd show up anyway. Even if I made it as far as the city of Las Tunas, he said, someone was bound to tell me the old woman was dead. Who would want to walk all the way here, knowing that? Celina looked at me through the painful pounding in her head. "But I felt you'd come," she said. "Men just don't understand the way we women are."

As she talked she busied herself in the kitchen straining fresh coffee for the three of us. "Of course you'll stay for lunch," she said, adding her intention to kill a chicken then and there. Silvio and Peña accepted the coffee, but said they had to be on their way. Peña instructed me when I walked out as far as Las Parras to stop at the police station again and he'd tell me how to get back to Las Tunas from there. As the two men prepared to leave I remembered what the meter had read when we'd left the vehicle by the tracks: just under eleven pesos. I asked Silvio how much more he wanted and he said nothing at all. I insisted he take a twenty peso note. Then he and Peña were gone.

I spent that whole day with Celina—and her kids, her neighbors, her friends. People must have heard there was a stranger in the community; they came around all day and from all directions. I took out my camera and asked if she'd mind my taking pictures: of her as we talked, of one of her daughters feeding the pigs, of others who dropped by as she readied the meal. She said

Celina.

not only that she didn't mind but it would be an honor. This was when I realized the camera was a special event for these people, some of whom had never seen one before. I made a mental note to send lots of prints.

Two of Celina's daughters all but climbed into my skin each time I finished one roll of film and replaced it with another. They were fascinated by every aspect of the process. And yet they were completely natural about all they were doing, never self-conscious, never posing. The one exception was when Celina's oldest daughter Omayda, who is studying to be a nurse in Las Tunas, asked if I'd photograph her in her good dress. I said of course and she went to change. Thus began an interesting dance in which I moved between making images I knew they would appreciate and those that most interested me. As the day wore on the two types of pictures became almost indistinguishable.

Celina was forty-three. She has four children, two sons and two daughters; plus an assortment of local kids who seem to make her house their home. During the day I spent with her, neighbors came by: to borrow a hypodermic needle, to inquire about a scholarship, to consult about an upcoming meeting, to ask for water or bring a gift of avocados. At one point an elderly woman named Iluminada Machado walked by. Celina called her in to chat.

Iluminada was in her eighties, with two sons fighting in Ethiopia. Up until this year she'd worked continually. Now she told her neighbor: "I'm not working anymore. No ma'am, no more. Well, at home of course; that's work too, and with my animals. But I've decided to take a break this year. No work for me!" I talked with Iluminada for quite a while. I asked her if she knew how to read and write. "Not a single letter," she replied, and then added: "Well, that's not completely true. I can make a pretty good O because it's so round."

As we ate Celina's delicious meal of stewed chicken in sauce, tostones (thin fried rounds of sliced macho bananas), rice, black beans, and salad, we talked about our lives, sharing our dissimilar stories with curiosity and compassion. After a late lunch we set out for Las Parras, breaking the ten kilometer stretch by stopping at one house after another to visit with friends. Shortly before we arrived at the village, we came to the compound where Celina's mother and father lived with all the rest of their offspring: five brothers and sisters, their respective spouses, and twenty eight grandchildren. This was a circular collection of *bohios* (grass-roofed shacks). I immediately felt the intensity of family.

Celina's mother, Ana Garcés's daughter, was in her eighties. She was Ana's youngest and only living offspring. Having suffered her mother's death barely a month before, she had tears in her eyes as she spoke of the old woman. Little by little I was able to piece together everyone's images of Ana.

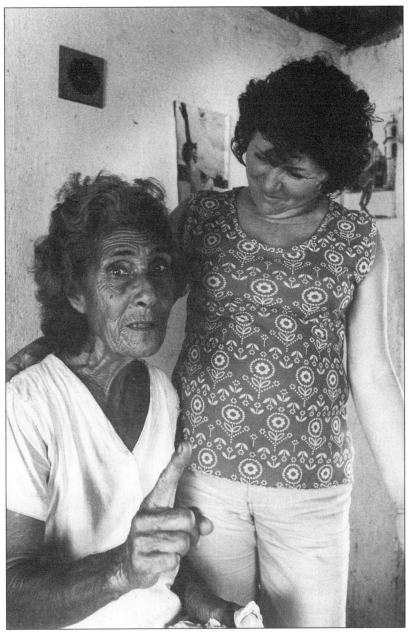

Iluminada and Celina. "I can make a pretty good O because it's so round. . . ."

Ana Garcés, they told me, was born on July 26, 1859. Her husband had indeed been a lieutenant in the war of 1868. She had her six children late. Two of them were born in the hills while she was involved in support work with the anti-Spanish rebels. Ana was extremely small of stature. The family possessed two photographs, one taken in her seventies, the other just a few years before her death. Almost all her life she wore her hair long, until several years back when she'd announced one day that she wanted "a few years without all this hair." According to these relatives she was never sick, rarely even suffered a headache. She was lucid until the end, doing her own housework and caring for her own animals until four years before she died.

Then she fell and broke a hip, an event not uncommon among the elderly everywhere. The accident sent her to a doctor for the first time in her life. After this she no longer cared for herself, but continued to regale family members and others with stories from her long life: Cuba's wars of independence, the things she had seen and people she'd known. On July 26, 1980, she celebrated her 121st birthday. Three days later, on the 29th, her heart stopped beating. Peaceful as that.

As we talked a young man rode up on a horse. He dismounted with a small white cloth sack in his hands. This was the local barber, come to cut the men's and boys' hair. Most of the younger kids didn't want haircuts but their mothers told them: "No going down to the river to swim if you don't let the barber do you." The old man, Celina's father, was first in line and had no objection to my photographing the process. Two of the youngest boys were sent off on horseback to bring back ice, which was used to cool our drinking water. Omayda had brought two of her nurse's uniforms and explained to one of her aunts that she needed them altered. Everyone said I should come back with my whole family; swimming in the local river was wonderful and they'd all be expecting us. The heat was stifling.

I had tried, before this visit, to get some documentation on Ana Garcés. I had mentioned her to a stateside friend who was writing about old people around the world, and he wanted me to try to verify her age. Now I asked if there were birth or baptismal papers. Celina and her mother told me there had been a baptismal certificate; they'd used it in the revolution's first years to obtain Ana's pension as the widow of an officer in the wars of independence. When Hurricane Flora hit this area in 1963 all their papers had been destroyed. Ana's daughter's age seemed to confirm the fact that she was, in truth, as old as she'd said she was; or at least not that much younger. In response to my request for documents, their answer was: "Well, we know from the things Ana remembered that she was as old as she said."

Celina walked with me as far as La Parras, where I stopped in to shake Peña's hand. Then I took a local bus to a hospital stop on the outskirts of Victoria de las Tunas. From there it was just a couple of stops on a second bus to the center of town. When I went to the local Cubana office to reconfirm my ticket for Saturday's flight back to Havana I decided to change it to Friday. No real reason to stay on. Around five A.M. the next morning I tiptoed from the apartment of the people kind enough to put me up, and walked across an open field to the bus stop near a huge water tank. The night before, my hosts had explained the two buses I'd need to take back to the airport.

At the first bus stop people were talking about hurricanes. One construction worker going to an early job said he'd heard on the morning news that one was moving across the Caribbean. A woman said it didn't seem to be headed their way. Someone else noted that hurricane season was usually October and November but this year they'd come earlier. The first speaker began reminiscing about Flora. "There are hurricanes and hurricanes," he said, "because you have the problem of rain and the problem of wind. Flora did a lot of damage but it was mostly the water, the floods that hit the Cauto Valley and caused so many deaths. Unless you've seen a hurricane where the destruction is by wind you haven't seen anything."

An older woman agreed. She spoke about the tragedy in Santa Cruz del Sur in 1932. "I was just a kid then," she said, "and I don't claim to remember the worst of it. But the sky was a dark dark gray. I'll never forget that sky, like coal dust it was. And when the people tried to go out of their houses to go for help, there was no escaping it. They were just blown away."

When the bus finally came, it took me as far as the train station. From there it was easy enough to get another to the airport. Compulsive as I am, I was the first in line for my flight. Just before boarding, the three or four taxis I'd seen on my arrival pulled up, ready for their morning passengers. I looked for Silvio but didn't see him. Then, a bit later, he arrived. I watched him get out of his cab and, with expansive gestures, begin telling the dispatcher a lengthy story. As I emerged from the tiny waiting room he caught sight of me and I heard him say: "Look, there she is now!"

NOTES

1. Comparative country statistics are from United Nations, World Bank and other official sites, such as http://www.worldbank.org.

CHAPTER 1 — SCARSDALE TO HAVANA

1. As the anti-communist witch hunt of the 1950s began, a leftist couple from New York, Julius and Ethel Rosenberg, were arrested and charged with conspiracy to commit espionage. They were accused of stealing the secret of the atom bomb and giving it to the Soviets. Despite having only the flimsiest of circumstantial evidence, and faced with a world-wide protest movement urging their release, the U.S. government went ahead with its macabre plans to scapegoat the couple. They were condemned and put to death in the electric chair on June 19, 1953. Research shows the government's case against Julius was sketchy at best, and that they always knew that Ethel was innocent.

2. Caryl Chessman, accused of rape and robbery in California, was on death row for many years. While there, he wrote a book which became influential in the struggle against capital punishment. Chessman always maintained his innocence, and that he knew who the real criminal was; but he refused to name that person. On May 2, 1960, Chessman was put to death, sparking indignation among opponents to the death penalty.

3. A Declaration of Conscience by American Artists and Writers, *Monthly Review*, Vol. 13, Number 5, p. 230. Our Declaration of Conscience read, in part, "The people of Revolutionary Cuba have the right to determine their own destiny without intervention from the United States government. We believe that by financing, arming, and

training Cuban émigrés and planning and participating in the invasion of April 17, 1961, the United States government has intervened and has committed an act of aggression against the people of Cuba.... President Kennedy's request that the press engage in self-censorship continues the process of suppression and regimentation of American life under the guise of 'fighting the Cold War.' ... If we are to safeguard freedom in America, we must do all in our power to oppose and prevent further aggression against the people of revolutionary Cuba."

4. Sonora matancera is a musical group that dates back to the 1940s. Some of its best known original members were Beny Moré, Celia Cruz and Alberto Beltrán. As some died or left the country, others took their places; and the group still performs and records. I use the group's name as a generic way of referring to a certain type of popular Cuban dance music with a heavy African influence.

5. El quinquenio gris.

6. Hana Volavkova (ed.), *I Never Saw Another Butterfly* (New York: Schocken Books, 1978).

CHAPTER 2 — TRANSITION

1. A peaceful demonstration, held ten days before the Mexico City Olympics, was charged by special forces with tanks and high caliber weaponry. The official death count was twenty-six, but there is evidence that more than a thousand were murdered on that October 2, 1968.

2. A few months after we were reunited on the island, Ximena had the operation for which we had been saving in Mexico. In Cuba it was free. A Czech specialist performed the delicate procedure, assisted by Cuban surgeons he mentored. The operation was a complete success; my daughter even recovered most of her hearing, something the doctors had believed impossible.

3. I had decided this collection should be where it could be enjoyed by the public, so I donated it to Havana's Museum of Modern Art. I know it left Mexico and arrived in Cuba. But for many years following our arrival on the island I periodically asked Marta Arjona, the museum's director, where the paintings were. Initially I was told they were being cleaned or treated in some way. But they never turned up, and to this day I have no idea what became of them.

4. The original Spanish, with all its spelling errors, reads "Querida mami y Robert— Espero que esten vien y Goyo me caí de una vicicleta y me erí el vraso y la pansa. No te pongas triste pues no fue grabe. Ximena se callo y le salió sangre tampoco fue grave. Y Sara no le pasó nada, a Anna no la e visto porque ella está en un círculo infantil con los amigos, Saris y Ximena en la Casa 18 de Internados y yo en la 9 de Internados de la escuela, que dijiste antes de venir, estamos vien aquí ai mucha hormiga volando que se te meten asta la naris, son mui molesta aquí y mis hermanas todos los días en la mañana vamos a la plalla yo y mis ermanas nos metemos al mar como 10 metros de la arena, yo goyo e estado tres días buscando plumón pero no encuentro y tube que aser la carta con colores. Así ves con que cariño te la escribo la carta. Por fabor ben pronto

todas las noches se lo pido a las estrellas. Yo tengo dos amigos un de Jinea y otro de Cuba. Se las escribe con mucho amor y casi lágrimas en los ojos, Goyo Saris Ximena y Anna." Gregory's nickname was Goyo, Saris was the name he used for Sarah, and we spelled Ana with two n's at the time.

5. "Del subsidio al exilio," *Revista Generación*, Mexico City, Año XVII (2005), No. 63.

CHAPTER 3 — SETTLING IN

1. These events are described in detail in later chapters.

2. At this time, Cuba was divided into six provinces. Later there were fourteen and eventually each of these had its own special middle- and high school for exceptional students.

CHAPTER 7 — WOMEN AND DIFFERENCE

1. From an article entitled "The Truth About the United States" by José Martí, July 1880.

2. With regard to women, *cubanía* defined a stereotypical tropical allure such as that which is showcased in certain 1950s-style nightclub shows. Consequently it rejected many notions or theories considered foreign imports, particularly if they came from the United States.

3. *La mujer cubana ahora*, Editorial Ciencias Sociales, La Habana, Cuba, 1972; *Mujeres en la revolución*, Siglo XXI Editores S.A., Mexico City, 1972; *Cuban Women Now*, Canadian Women's Educational Press, Toronto, Canada, 1974; and *La mujer cubana ahora* and *La mujer cubana: revolución en la revolución*, volumes 1 and 2, Fondo Editorial Salvador de la Plaza, Caracas, Venezuela, 1973 and 1974, among other editions.

4. "Hey, little mama, what a butt! Wanna give me some?"

5. During a 1997 interview between Federation of Cuban Women founder and president Vilma Espín and U.S. American writer Alice Walker, for which I interpreted, Walker asked about Magín and Espín made this unfounded accusation.

6. I describe Magín at length in my book *Narrative of Power: Essays for an Endangered Century* (Monroe, Maine: Common Courage Press, 2004), 189–190.

7. Among the various sources for Mariela Castro Espín speaking of gays and lesbians in Cuba, is the article "Cuba's sexual minorities find a champion in a Castro" by Marc Lacey, *International Herald Tribune*, June 8, 2007.

8. DeWayne Wickham, "When it comes to gay rights, is Cuba inching ahead of the USA?" *USA Today*, February 26, 2007.

CHAPTER 8 — INFORMATION AND CONSCIOUSNESS

1. Néstor Kohan, *Pensamiento crítico y el debate por las Ciencias sociales en el seno de la revolución cubana* (to be published by CLACSO, Latin American Council on the Social Sciences). With CLACSO's permission, Kohan made this essay available online before its appearance in book form.

CHAPTER 9 — CHANGING HEARTS, MINDS, AND LAW

1. Having had several fathers, when he arrived in Cuba Gregory used Sergio's last name, Mondragón, and then Robert's, which was Cohen. Eventually he went back to using Randall.

2. *Gusano* means worm, and is the word revolutionary Cubans have used for those they accuse of being counterrevolutionary, particularly those leaving the country for good.

3. The only payment required for an operation of any kind was a single blood donation. A medical condition prevented Robert from making the donation, so our CDR got someone else to give in his stead.

4. Carretero, known by the alias "Ariel," was Cuba's liaison with Che's guerrilla.

5. Antonio Castro, my partner after Robert Cohen and I separated.

CHAPTER 10 — "POETRY, LIKE BREAD, IS FOR EVERYONE"

1. "Donde estás, espíritu del hombre de mi tiempo / que te conviertes cada tarde, al regreso de la diaria faena, / en la justa cantera de las miradas hoscas que me reprochan . . . ," *Estos cantos habitados / These Living Songs: Fifteen New Cuban Poets*, translated and with an introduction by Margaret Randall, (Ft. Collins: Colorado State Review Press, 1978).

2. Décimas are ten-line octosyllabic verses with an ABBAACCDDC rhyme scheme, most often created on the spot and sung by one or another of two participants in a competition of voices. Their content is often political, sometimes in celebration of a birthday or other event, and frequently humorous. Decimistas generally accompany themselves on the guitar.

3. People of the Cuban countryside are known as *guajiros*. *Cantor* refers to the act of singing. Carballo invented this name for himself. Margaret Randall and Angel Antonio Moreno, *Sueños y realidades de un guajiricantor* (Mexico, DF: Siglo XXI Editores S.A., 1979).

4. The Cubans who defended the island against the Spanish were called *mambises*.

5. Roque Dalton, "Sobre dolores de cabeza," *Taberna y otros lugares* (Havana, Cuba: Casa de las Américas, 1969), 115. Author's translation.

6. Agostino Neto was then president of Angola and also a fine poet.

7. Line from a poem by Roque Dalton.

CHAPTER 11 — EL QUINQUENIO GRIS

1. *Alma mater*, La Habana, Cuba, #410, 2004.

2. This was a problem because those of us fighting for justice expected inequality from colonialist or imperialist governments but more from the revolution.

3. The three Cuban judges were poets José Lezama Lima, José Z. Tallet, and Manuel Díaz Martínez. The two foreigners were the Peruvian poet César Calvo and the English literary critic J. M. Cohen.

4. Unless otherwise noted, the following fragments of letters and passages from public lectures can be found at http://laventana.casa.cult.cu or http://www.criterio/cubarte.cult.cu.

5. "Real socialism" was a term used by those who looked to the Soviet Union and its allies as the single correct model, thereby relegating Chinese, Vietnamese, and other brands of socialism to a lesser status.

6. "Cuba desde dentro," interview with Eliades Acosta by Isachi Fernández, Cubarte, criterio@cubarte.cult.cu, December 2007.

7. The Klu Klux Klan has long been active and vociferous in the Chicago suburb of Skokie, Illinois, a community with a large number of Holocaust survivors and African Americans. In 1978 the KKK got a permit to march through that city, to loud opposition from those offended by its position of white supremacy. That same year, in *Collens v. Skokie*, the Supreme Court set a precedent for the free speech rights of hate groups.

8. There are many sources for this quote. Some record the words slightly differently, but all attribute them to Martin Niemoller. *Time* magazine, in its August 28, 1989 issue commemorating the fiftieth anniversary of the beginning of World War II, prints the version I transcribe. Other versions, and more information about Niemoller, can be found in *Newsweek*, July 10, 1937, p. 32, and in *Kingdoms in Conflict* by Charles Colson, Vaughn Books, 1987.

CHAPTER 12 —— THE SANDINISTAS

1. I refer to Guevara's brief foray in the Congo followed by his Bolivian campaign. Both these experiences are well documented in a number of books, among them two campaign diaries by the guerrilla leader himself. I especially recommend *Episodes of the Cuban Revolutionary War: 1956-1958, Complete Bolivian Diaries of Che Guevara and Other Captured Documents*, and *The African Dream: The Diaries of the Revolutionary War in the Congo.*

2. The title of the poet Simon Ortíz's book, *Out There Somewhere*, and a line from one of its poems (Tucson: University of Arizona Press, 2002). In his preface Ortíz writes: "I've imagined the outdoors to be out there somewhere in everyday experience . . ."

3. Leonel Rugama died on January 15, 1970, at the age of twenty. His poetry was collected posthumously. "La tierra es un satélite de la luna" (*La tierra es un satélite de la luna*, Managua, Nicaragua: Editorial Nueva Nicaragua, 1987). Author's translation.

4. *Sandino's Daughters* (Vancouver: New Star Books, 1981). This book was eventually reissued by Rutgers University Press. Editions have appeared in Mexico, Brazil, and Holland. It is still in print.

5. New York: New Directions, 1974.

6. The Sandinista Ideological Office.

7. Originally published as *El país bajo mi piel* (Managua, Nicaragua: Plaza Janés / Anamá, 2001). English edition by Knopf, New York, 2002.

8. *Somos millones* (Mexico, DF: Editorial Extemporáneos, 1976). English translation by Elinor Randall published as *Doris Tijerino: Inside the Nicaraguan Revolution* (Vancouver: New Star Books, 1978).

9. For an excellent analysis of the current Oretega administration see Carlos Fernando Chamorro's address, "El 'poder ciudadano' de Ortega en Nicaragua: ¿participación democrática o populismo autoritario?," at the Woodrow Wilson Center's March 10, 2008 Washington DC conference "Understanding Populism and Popular Participation: A New Look at the 'New Left' in Latin America."

10. From the text of a lecture delivered on May 15, 2007 at the Instituto Superior de Arte, in Havana, as part of the cycle "Cultural Policy of the Revolutionary Period: Memory and Reflection," organized by the Theoretical-Cultural Center, Criteria.

11. The Ochoa case is described more fully in Chapter 13, A Question of Power.

CHAPTER 13 — A QUESTION OF POWER

1. Soledad Cruz, "La pelea cubana contra los demonios," *Kaos en la Red*, www.kaosenlared.net, August 21, 2007.

2. Pedro Campos, "Cuba, Dilema y Esperanza II," www.analitica.com. Author's translation.

3. Arnaldo Ochoa (1930–July 12, 1989) was a Cuban general beloved by his troops and by Cubans overall. He had been with Fidel almost from the beginning, led the Cuban fighting contingent in Angola, and worked with the Sandinistas in Nicaragua. In 1989 he and several colleagues were arrested by the Cuban authorities, accused of involvement in the international drug trade, subjected to what can only be described as a mock trial, and summarily executed. It is still unclear to me whether he was guilty as charged (in which case it is hard to believe that Fidel and other high-ranking members of the Cuban leadership wouldn't have known about and turned a blind eye to his activities), dispatched because he represented a threat to the group in power, or if there is another story we cannot know.

CHAPTER 14 — EPILOGUE

1. In 1984 I would marry U.S. American poet Floyce Alexander, a last attempt at living with a man. Our marriage lasted a bit more than a year.

2. *Albuquerque: Coming Back to the U.S.A* (Vancouver: New Star Books, 1986).

3. *This is About Incest* (Ithaca, NY: Firebrand Books, 1987).

4. *Coming Home, Peace Without Complacency* (Albuquerque, NM: West End Press, 1990), and an expanded version of the same essay in *Walking to the Edge: Essays of Resistance* (Boston: South End Press, 1991).

5. *The Unapologetic Life of Margaret Randall*, by Lu Lippold and Pam Colby, available from The Cinema Guild, 130 Madison Avenue, New York 10016 (www.cinemaguild.com).

6. *Sandino's Daughters Revisited: Feminism in Nicaragua* (New Brunswick, NJ: Rutgers University Press, 1994).

INDEX

ABOUT THE AUTHOR

Margaret Randall is an award-winning feminist poet, photographer, and social activist with more than eighty published books, such as *Stones Witness* and *When I Look into the Mirror and See You* (Rutgers University Press). She and her family lived in Cuba from 1969 to 1980, and Randall has several earlier titles about that country, including *Cuban Women Now, Cuban Women Twenty Years Later,* and *Breaking the Silences: 20th Century Poetry by Cuban Women.*